TEAPOT DOME: Oil and Politics in the 1920's

TEAPOT

Oil and Politics

LOUISIANA STATE

Burl Noggle

DOME:

in the 1920's

UNIVERSITY PRESS

q

For Susan

Preface

About fifty miles north of Casper, Wyoming, a formation of eroded Parkman sandstone looms up out of the bare sagebrush flats. Although it resembles a disfigured human hand, this geologic fault is called Teapot Rock. It overlooks a nine-thousand acre portion of Natrona County containing an oil deposit set aside in 1915 as United States Naval Oil Reserve Number Three. With more informality, men in the oil business associate the pool with the landmark and call the reserve Teapot Dome.

In the 1920's, this oil reserve supplied a name for perhaps the most sensational scandal in American politics. Will Rogers once spoke of the "great morality panic of 1924." Panic of a sort there was, as Republicans and Democrats scrambled to get into the headlines or to keep out of them. Morality may have been involved, if we are to believe contemporary as well as subsequent critics of politics in the 1920's. The difficulty, however, lies in determining who was guilty of what crime and in what degree; in deciding which party, Republican or Democrat, was smeared the most. The scandal seems to have blackened some reputations once and for all. Albert B. Fall, for example, has perennially been viewed as a reprehensible figure and as a symbol of an irresponsible Republican administration. Warren G. Harding has been ridiculed for his ineptness and his shallow standards. His successor Calvin Coolidge, although a man of higher standards in his personal life, has been condemned for a seeming passivity in the face of flagrant wrong-doing. On the other hand, the scandal has earned for some men enduring praise in American political annals. Senator Thomas J. Walsh, Democrat of Montana, has usually been regarded as the most heroic figure in the entire Teapot Dome affair, because of his magnificent prosecution as a member of the Senate investigating committee.

There is much truth but not the whole truth in these views—and there is some error. Some participants in the story, Republican and Democrat, deserve more consideration then they have usually received, and some deserve more criticism. Some individuals hitherto not linked with the story need to be associated with it. Most needed, however, is a shift of attention away from the question of guilt, as such, and toward concentration upon the scandal's effects in party politics. Probably the most notable event in Teapot Dome's history was the Republican party's ability to overcome what appeared to be, in the spring of 1924, an insurmountable handicap. The crux of Teapot Dome's history lay in the 1924 election. Preceding that election came months of partisan maneuverings, insinuations, and an ardent grasp for party advantage. This book is, among other things, an attempt to show how the Teapot Dome scandal in 1924 was as embarrassing to some Democrats as it was to some Republicans, to show how a "Republican scandal" was a far greater disadvantage to William Gibbs McAdoo, Democratic presidential hopeful, than it was to Calvin Coolidge, Republican incumbent.

In addition to examining these and other political questions, I have ventured to show the scandal's relationship to the American conservation movement. There was much fortuity in the history of Teapot Dome, and especially in the very uncovering of the scandal. The Teapot Dome investigation grew in an unforeseen fash-

ion out of a conservation feud over forests, principally, and oil
reserves, secondarily. Its effective beginning was in the early
spring of 1921. During his 1920 presidential campaign, Warren
G. Harding received the support of old conservationists such as
Gifford Pinchot and his followers. Harding's appointment of
Albert B. Fall as Secretary of the Interior, however, aroused their
suspicions—of Fall, if not of Harding. It seems clear that Pinchot
and other conservationists then planned a campaign to drive Fall
from office. It is unlikely that at the beginning of Harding's administration they had more than a general suspicion of Fall. Their
original objective was to halt Fall's anticonservation program and
to see him removed from office. The Teapot Dome investigation
was a windfall. It accomplished this original purpose, uncovered
the scandal, and at the same time preserved the United States
naval oil reserves and helped to produce a stronger conservation
program.

Much of the historic debate over conservation in the United
States was summed up in the Teapot Dome affair, with two of
the protagonists, Pinchot and Fall, personifying the forces for and
against conservation. Yet conventional summaries of Teapot
Dome overlook the conservation background and parallels to the
more glittering political headlines that the scandal produced. And
the prominent role in the story of one veteran conservationist,
Harry A. Slattery, has been almost entirely obscured. He, more
than any one individual, needs historical recognition.

With these facts and impressions in mind, then, I have tried to
write a political history of the Teapot Dome scandal, showing its
origins, the bitter partisanship that Teapot Dome aroused within
and between the two major political parties, the tactics that each
party used to exploit or to minimize the scandal, the blights that
Teapot Dome inflicted upon certain political careers, and the
prestige and the opportunities that it supplied to others. I have
suggested the considerable relevance the political scandal had to
conservation before, during, and after the scandal. I have not
tried to write a moral brief for or against Albert Fall and other
leading figures in the story, but I have tried to suggest the need
for a re-examination, and possibly a reappraisal, of politics and
personalities in the 1920's. It is quite posible that our stereotypes
of right and wrong, of hero and villian during the decade, have
been with us too long.

Acknowledgments

During the time this book was taking shape, Richard L. Watson, Jr., of Duke University, and Ira G. Clark, Jr., and Simon F. Kropp, both of New Mexico State University—each in an individual way— made numerous contributions to my work and outlook. Elmo R. Richardson of Washington State University gave me some invaluable appraisals and helped me to clarify my thinking. I am grateful to Jo R. Porter, Alice Winston, and especially Ellen Harrell of the Graduate School Office, Louisiana State University, for typing the manuscript. The dedication is for the one who at all times has mattered most.

B.N.

Baton Rouge, Louisiana

Table of Contents

		PAGE
	Preface	vii
	Acknowledgments	xi
1	The Prelude to Scandal	1
2	The Ambitions of Secretary Fall	15
3	The Suspicions of Senator La Follette	32
4	Harding and Fall Depart	43
5	The Eruption of Scandal	64
6	The Onrush of Scandal	96
7	Teapot Dome and the Presidency	130
8	Teapot Dome and the Election of 1924	152
9	Interlude	177
10	The Residue of Teapot Dome	200
	Bibliographical Note	216
	Index	227

Illustrations

1 Albert B. Fall   FOLLOWING PAGE 142
2 Harry A. Slattery
3 Gifford Pinchot
4 Robert M. La Follette
5 Thomas J. Walsh
6 Mr. and Mrs. Edward L. Doheny
7 Henry F. Sinclair with H. F. Stanford
8 William G. McAdoo

Cartoons

	PAGE
The First Good Laugh They've Had in Years	77
Weather-Vane, Washington	82
"You Splash Me—I Splash You"	102
The Anxious Waiter	113
The Gormand	121
"What a Relief!"	129
Poor Picking	133
"Willie, You Can't Go With That Patch On!"	139
"O We Ain' Gwine Steal No Mo"	157
Samson?	184
"Whiter Than Snow"	188
The Long, Long Trail	212

1

The Prelude to Scandal

The Teapot Dome scandal was kaleidoscopic. Garish, at times weird, it was a tragicomedy of American politics without precise beginning or end. It is appropriate, however, to look first at an event which set in motion certain strategic actions leading directly into scandal and revelation. On the sweltering Saturday afternoon of July 12, 1920, in Chicago, Illinois, members of the seventeenth Republican national convention nominated Warren Gamaliel Harding for President of the United States. For the past three days, supporters of Frank O. Lowden and General Leonard Wood had sweated and balloted to an impasse, with neither able to muster enough votes to win. On the first ballot taken Saturday morning, Harding received seventy-eight votes. His support increased steadily throughout the day, and on the final ballot, the tenth of the four-day convention, he received almost seven hundred votes. A delegate from New Jersey moved that the nomination be made unanimous; he promptly was seconded, and the convention roared assent through the sultry air.[1]

The perfunctory job of naming a vice-presidential candidate still remained. Senator Irvine Lenroot of Wisconsin appears to have been the choice of the senatorial bloc dominating the convention. His name had dutifully been placed in nomination and seconded, when suddenly the great mob revolted. Out of the Oregon delegation arose the foghorn voice of one Wallace McCamant of Portland, crying hoarsely for recognition. Granted it, he forthwith nominated for vice-president the governor of Massachusetts, Calvin Coolidge. Two other hasty nominations were sounded out over the clamor, the voting began, and Coolidge won on the first ballot. His nomination also was made unanimous. The Coolidge choice was a defiance of the convention leaders. Having followed their lead for four days, the delegates finally in the closing minutes displayed a rash of independence and rallied spontaneously behind a man of their own choosing.[2]

Because of Harding's shoddy administration and because of his own obvious incompetence even before it began, historians and political journalists have perennially voiced suspicions about the 1920 Republican convention. As Richard Hofstadter suggests, "corruption itself has the character of conspiracy,"[3] and the corruption of the Harding administration has led analysts backward

---

[1] *Official Report of the Proceedings of the Seventeenth Republican National Convention* (New York, 1920), 196 ff.; hereinafter cited as *Proceedings of the Convention;* William T. Hutchinson, *Lowden of Illinois* (2 vols.; Chicago, 1957), II, 383-469, and especially 458-69.

[2] *Proceedings of the Convention,* 226-32. Claude M. Fuess, *Calvin Coolidge: The Man from Vermont* (Boston, 1940), 261-63; William Allen White, *A Puritan in Babylon* (New York, 1938), 213-14; Charles W. Thompson, *Presidents I've Known and Two Near Presidents* (Indianapolis, 1929), 361 ff.; and George W. Pepper, *Philadelphia Lawyer: An Autobiography* (Philadelphia, 1944), 136, describe Coolidge's nomination as a revolt. Coolidge himself claimed that the convention broke away from the "coterie of . . . Senators" and "literally stampeded to me." Calvin Coolidge, *The Autobiography of Calvin Coolidge* (New York, 1929), 148. Hutchinson, *Lowden of Illinois,* II, 469, suggests that the delegates, having nominated Harding, "evidenced more pleasure when—almost by accident it would seem—they spurned the will of the Old Guard voiced in Medill McCormick's nomination of Senator Lenroot . . . and conferred that prize of doubtful value upon . . . Coolidge."

[3] Richard Hofstadter, *The Age of Reform* (New York, 1955), 71.

to 1920 in search of a "conspiracy" in Chicago. The story of the senatorial cabal in the "smoke-filled room" has become legend; and in 1924, charges were to arise that oil company money was improperly at work during the convention.[4]

It seems clear, however, that the only direct connection between the convention and the subsequent Teapot Dome scandal was the fact that Harding won the nomination, then the election, and chose a Secretary of the Interior whose actions led to scandal. A small group of Republican senators did dominate the convention, but they did not absolutely control it. Harding won the nomination not because of a plot by the senators, but rather as a logical outgrowth of the four-day ordeal. Harry M. Daugherty, his campaign manager, had planned Harding's campaign shrewdly and minutely and was partly responsible for Harding's appeal as a solution of an impasse. A group of politicos in the Blackstone Hotel did agree in the stale hours of a Friday night conference to contrive for Harding's nomination, but he was their choice because of the deadlock between Wood and Lowden and not because of shady backstairs maneuvers tainted with oil. Harding was available, pliable, and—as the popular phrase had it— "looked like a President." He had few enemies and many friends. The senators, anxious to regain legislative leadership after years of frustration under strong executives Theodore Roosevelt and Woodrow Wilson, considered Harding an ideal selection.[5]

[4] See, for example, Oswald Garrison Villard, "The 'Unbossed' Republican Convention," *The Nation*, CX (June 19, 1920), 820-21; Thompson, *Presidents I've Known and Two Near Presidents*, 325 ff.; and especially William Allen White, *The Autobiography of William Allen White* (New York, 1946), 582 ff. White, from his coverage of the convention in 1920 to his autobiography of 1946, persisted in seeing the dictatorial hand of the Old Guard throughout the convention. In 1936, in a private letter, he wrote of having "a hunch that . . . the Senators were merely fulfilling orders from a money-raising group, probably largely oil." White to Harry A. Slattery, March 18, 1936, in Harry A. Slattery Papers, Duke University Library. For further comments on oil interests and the 1920 convention, see pp. 141-43.

[5] Henry S. New, "The Senatorial Oligarchy," *Saturday Evening Post*, XXIV (May 28, 1932), 21 and 84, is an early attempt to refute the charge of senatorial control. Wesley M. Bagby, "The 'Smoke-Filled Room' and the Nomination of Warren G. Harding," *Mississippi Valley Historical Review*, XLI (March, 1955), 657-74, is an intense and scholarly study of the nomination, giving no credit to the traditional smoke-filled room plot, or to a "senatorial cabal" bossing the convention. See also Hutchinson, *Lowden of Illinois*, II, 462 ff. Mark Sullivan, *Our Times: The United States 1900-1925*

In his acceptance speech Harding, with characteristic opacity, made a brief allusion to conservation. The Republican party, he said, held to "that harmony of relationship between conservation and development which fittingly appraises our natural resources and makes them available to developing America of today, and still holds to the conserving thought for the America of tomorrow." Coolidge, too, mentioned conservation. He defined it, in part, as "a desire honestly to administer the public domain" and said the time had passed when "public franchises and public grants" could be used "for private speculation."[6] The future would give to both men's remarks an irony that neither of them had intended.

To Gifford Pinchot, a great and luminous name in the American conservation movement, as well as to many other friends of conservation, the Republican ticket seemed entirely acceptable.[7] One of these conservationists, a key figure in the Teapot Dome story, was a Washington lawyer named Harry A. Slattery. Born in Greenville, South Carolina, in 1887, and reared there, he attended George Washington University for awhile and later the law school at nearby Georgetown University. From school he went to work for the Theodore Roosevelt administration, as a clerk-stenographer with the Inland Waterways Commission. There he met the men who, he wrote, "were afterwards to become lasting influences in my life"—pioneers in the conservation movement, such as W J McGee, Francis Newlands, and Gifford Pinchot.[8] Almost immediately, Slattery became a devoted and energetic

---

(6 vols.; New York, 1927-35), VI (*The Twenties*), 16-77, contains detailed treatment of Daughtery's relationship with Harding. Valuable letters revealing Daughtery's role in Harding's nomination are in Randolph C. Downes, ed., "President Making: The Influence of Newton H. Fairbanks and Harry M. Daugherty on the Nomination of Warren G. Harding for the Presidency," *Northwest Ohio Quarterly*, XXI (Fall, 1959), 170-78. See also Charles Elsworth Hard, "The Man Who Did Not Want To Become President," *Northwest Ohio Quarterly*, XXXI (Summer, 1959), 120-25.

[6] *Proceedings of the Convention*, 268-69, 279-80.

[7] Before the Republican convention met, Pinchot declared his opposition to "a reactionary" like Harding and even wrote publicly that "Harding is utterly unfit to be President." But after the convention, Pinchot fell into line. See M. Nelson McGeary, *Gifford Pinchot* (Princeton, 1960), 270-71.

[8] Harry A. Slattery, "From Roosevelt to Roosevelt," MS in Slattery Papers, Duke University Library, 21-32. For biographical information on Slattery, see his autobiography and his voluminous personal papers, Duke University Library.

disciple of conservation and remained one until the very day he died. A rather prosaic if likeable personality, he sought and found happiness and satisfaction in his work. Shunning publicity, although sometimes deserving it, he chose to lead a quiet bachelor's life in Washington, a city that he loved. There, from 1909 to 1912, Slattery was secretary to Gifford Pinchot. From 1912 to 1917, he was secretary of the National Conservation Association, "the organized voice of the Conservation Movement in America."[9] For two years during World War I, he was special assistant to Secretary of the Interior Franklin K. Lane. In 1933, Secretary of the Interior Harold L. Ickes named him personal assistant. In 1938, he became Undersecretary of the Interior, and from 1939 to 1944 he was administrator of the Rural Electrification Administration. Throughout his career, Slattery was investigator, counsel, legislative draftsman, and confidant for numerous friends of conservation in Congress, as well as for others in private life. His shrewdness and his industrious nature were rich assets to the friends of conservation.

In 1920, Slattery was practicing law in Washington, but still burrowing, as had long been his habit, through the *Congressional Record* and other government publications, and through stacks of metropolitan daily newspapers. He was corresponding regularly with Pinchot, with numerous friends of conservation, and with a selected circle of newspaper reporters and columnists. Occasionally, he submitted an expense account to Pinchot for labors in conservation that the latter had requested, although to him and the conservation movement Slattery gave more than even the wealthy Pinchot could buy.

As the 1920 presidential campaign opened, Slattery believed the Republicans were firm supporters of conservation. Harding's platform had "emphasized the Republican devotion to . . . conservation." It was, said Slattery, "no secret that this plank in the platform was written by the conservationists."[10] Late in the

---

[9] Slattery's description of the association, in a statement to Consolidated Publishing Company of Washington, D.C., June 12, 1921, Slattery Papers.

[10] Harry A. Slattery, "The Story of the Teapot Dome Scandal," MS in Slattery Papers, 19-20. The Republican platform stated, in part: "Conservation is a Republican policy. It began with the passage of the Reclamation Act signed by President Roosevelt." See Republican National Committee, *Republican Campaign Text-Book, 1920* (n.p., n.d.), 95.

summer, Harding's publicity man Judson Welliver, a close acquaintance of Slattery, invited him to come to Marion, Ohio, where Harding was conducting a front-porch campaign. There Slattery helped to prepare an address for Harding to make on conservation, one that Slattery later described as "a direct commitment for the conservation policies—strong and clear-cut."[11]

At about this same time Slattery arranged a meeting with Pinchot and Harding. To Harding's campaign secretary, Slattery wrote: "Just before he left Washington Senator Harding was anxious to have Pinchot come [to Marion] and go over with him the conservation, agricultural, and other progressive matters in which GP has worked." Pinchot had agreed to make the trip at Harding's convenience. Slattery, now pressing the issue, pointed out that "the Senator will be anxious to have all the facts and the soundest and most constructive advice possible on conservation. It is a question that will deeply affect the West, and likewise it is a Progressive policy . . . with a special appeal." Slattery suggested that Harding "go over the whole matter with Mr. Pinchot before committing himself on conservation." The Marion headquarters accepted Slattery's suggestion. Late in August, following his visit to Marion, Pinchot publicly endorsed Harding's candidacy. As one newspaper phrased it, Pinchot was "much pleased" with Harding's views on conservation. Later, in October, the Republican national committee released to the press a letter from Pinchot explaining his support for Harding: what Harding had said "about forestry, conservation, and agriculture at Marion is sound and right."[12]

Gifford Pinchot in 1920 was a private citizen of Milford, Pennsylvania. Perennially ambitious for high political office, he thought of himself as a Roosevelt Republican, with a mission to promote conservation, as well as other policies that Theodore Roosevelt had supported. In 1920, he had made the first of several annual pilgrimages to the Rough Rider's grave, perhaps

[11] Slattery, "From Roosevelt to Roosevelt," 74-75.

[12] Slattery to Elijah Hanson, July 13, 1920; Slattery to John C. McCarl, July 17, 1920; Slattery to John Snure, July 17, 1920; Hanson to Slattery, July 23, 1920; McCarl to Slattery, June 26, 1920; Snure to Slattery, June 28, 1920, Slattery Papers. Charlotte (N.C.) *Observer*, August 31, 1920; Philadelphia *Public Ledger*, August 31, 1920; and New York *Times*, October 4, 1920, p. 5.

there to live again those heady days of the Roosevelt administration when the conservation movement reached its first fruition
and Pinchot enjoyed a political power he had never held since.
In 1910, during the heated clashes of the Ballinger-Pinchot controversy, President William H. Taft had demanded and received
Pinchot's resignation as chief forester of the United States. To
many of the public, and certainly to his numerous close followers,
Pinchot was a martyr to conservation. And in private life he
continued to dominate the conservation movement, providing it
with an inspirational leadership.[13] In a lifetime of devoted labor,
he, as much as any single man, made conservation a crusader's
program and over the years revealed consummate skill in protecting and promoting the movement that he considered, in
large measure, his peculiar creation. In 1920, one of his great
fights lay immediately ahead.[14]

When Harding swept into office with ease in November, receiving over sixteen million votes out of the twenty-five million
votes cast, the friends of conservation felt secure. The campaign

[13] A former chief of the Forest Service, William B. Greeley, who worked
with Pinchot for many years, has written that Pinchot made his associates
"feel like soldiers in a patriotic cause" and that he brought to this cause "a
fervor of religious intensity and a magnetic personal leadership . . . rarely
equaled in the American drama." William B. Greeley, *Forests and Men*
(Garden City, 1951), 58, 82. For contemporary reactions to Pinchot's dismissal by Taft, see McGeary, *Gifford Pinchot*, 161-62.

[14] For my estimates of Pinchot in this study, I have relied upon portions
of the Gifford Pinchot Papers, Division of Manuscripts, Library of Congress,
numerous items in the Slattery Papers, and, among other published sources,
the following: Gifford Pinchot, *Breaking New Ground* (New York, 1947);
Gifford Pinchot, *The Fight for Conservation* (New York, 1910); John T.
Ganoe, "Some Constitutional and Political Aspects of the Ballinger-Pinchot
Controversy," *Pacific Historical Review*, III (September, 1934), 32-33; Alpheus T. Mason, *Bureaucracy Convicts Itself: The Ballinger-Pinchot Con-
troversy of 1910* (New York, 1941); Harold L. Ickes, *Not Guilty: An Official
Inquiry into the Charges Made by Glavis and Pinchot against Richard A.
Ballinger, Secretary of Interior, 1909-11* (Washington, 1940); Whitney R.
Cross, "W J McGee and the Idea of Conservation," *Historian*, XV (Spring,
1953), 148-62; Elmo R. Richardson, "The Struggle for the Valley: Cali-
fornia's Hetch Hetchy Controversy, 1905-1913," *California Historical Society
Quarterly*, XXXVIII (September, 1959), 249-58; J. Leonard Bates, "Ful-
filling American Democracy: The Conservation Movement, 1907 to 1921,"
Mississippi Valley Historical Review, XLIV (June, 1957), 29-57; Harold T.
Pinckett, "Gifford Pinchot and the Early Conservation Movement in the
United States" (Ph.D. dissertation, American University, 1953); and Mc-
Geary, *Gifford Pinchot*.

had assured them that the new President would support their
policies. Furthermore, soon after the victory, Pinchot was called
to Marion again. There he talked about forestry with Harding,
who also had him submit a list of five men as possible candidates for the post of Secretary of the Interior. Harding said that
he was anxious to support a conservation program and wanted
a man for the office who would promote conservation as an
administration policy. Pinchot wrote down five names, including
that of his old friend, James R. Garfield, a charter member in
the Pinchot-Roosevelt conservation crusade and Secretary of
the Interior under Roosevelt. To R. C. Bryant at Yale's forestry
school, Pinchot wrote that his talk with Harding was "most
satisfactory" and added: "Altogether I am much better pleased
with the situation than I expected to be a month ago."[15] But
even as Pinchot was writing to Bryant, the political situation
was changing with the appearance of another personality.

Late in the afternoon of November 15, 1920, Senator Albert
B. Fall of New Mexico arrived at Brownsville, Texas. That night
he dined and talked with his old Senate companion, President-
elect Harding, who was spending a brief vacation with friends
near Brownsville.[16] Fall was chairman of the Senate subcommittee on Mexican Affairs and had been an acidulous critic of
President Woodrow Wilson's policy toward Mexico. In turn,
from Mexico City had come attacks upon Fall because of his
outspoken partisanship for sundry Mexican generals and politicians in the epic Revolution, and there were rumors that Fall,
with a financial stake in Mexico, had invested in the counter-
revolution. At the 1920 Republican convention Fall had written
the party plank on Mexican policy.[17]

    [15] John Lathrop to Pinchot, March 11, 1924; Pinchot to R. C. Bryant,
January 4, 1921, Box 236, Pinchot Papers.
    [16] New York *Times*, November 16, 1920, p. 1.
    [17] See Arthur S. Link, *Woodrow Wilson and the Progressive Era, 1910-
1917* (New York, 1953), 124-25, n. 40; New York *Times*, February 22,
1913, p. 3; June 28, 1913, p. 3; June 30, 1913, p. 1; July 2, 1913, p. 1; August 28, 1913, p. 2; February 25, 1914, p. 3; March 10, 1914, p. 2; April
22, 1914, p. 4; February 23, 1915, p. 5; February 18, 1916, p. 1; April 11,
1916, p. 24; May 18, 1916, p. 4; October 2, 1916, p. 6; March 26, 1917,
p. 9; July 24, 1919, p. 4; January 12, 1920, p. 3; January 18, 1920, p. 5;
and June 5, 1920, p. 3. See also Senate Foreign Relations Committee, *Investigation of Mexican Affairs* (Hearings of Senate Foreign Relations Subcommittee, 66 Cong., 2 Sess., Doc. No. 285, [2 vols.; Washington, 1920]),
II, 2788 ff., 2953 ff., for a clear index to Fall's position on Mexican affairs.

Fall's background helped explain his interest in Mexico and his political outlook. When Fall settled in New Mexico Territory in 1886, behind him lay a Kentucky childhood, a minimum of formal education, and several years of rough toil and gold and silver prospecting in the American Southwest and northern Mexico. In New Mexico, he acquired much land and power, many friends and enemies. From mine holdings in Mexico and New Mexico, from bank holdings, and from his law practice, he began to build a fortune. His appointment as general counsel to Colonel William C. Greene, owner of huge holdings in mining, timber, and railroads in northern Mexico, gave Fall an unusual chance to exercise his ample talents in investments. In 1904, he moved his home to Three Rivers, a sprawling ranch near Tularosa, New Mexico. Here he invested much money and time; here he thrived as a great southwestern rancher; and to Three Rivers, in time, he returned for solitude and recuperation from Washington politics in the 1920's.[18]

Soon after settling in New Mexico, Fall opened a law office in Las Cruces, a political hotbed in the southern part of the state. For several years he applied his capable mind to legal studies, and especially to Mexican law. In 1891, he was formally admitted to practice in the New Mexico territorial courts. Meanwhile, with alacrity and aggressiveness, he moved into territorial politics, a Democrat in a Republican stronghold. Soon this "master of sulphurous phrases and political vitriol" became political boss of southern New Mexico,[19] Fall, who according to one contemporary opponent was the "most rabid and intense Democrat in the whole Southwest,"[20] in 1906 switched to the Re-

[18] David H. Stratton, "New Mexican Machiavellian?" *Montana, the Magazine of Western History*, VII (Autumn, 1957), 2-5, 10-11; Santa Fe *New Mexican*, February 13, 1924, p. 7; George Curry, *George Curry, 1861-1947, An Autobiography*, ed. H. B. Hening (Albuquerque, 1958), 39; W. H. Hutchinson, *A Bar-Cross Man, The Life and Personal Writings of Eugene Manlove Rhodes* (Norman, 1956), 235-36; William C. Keleher, *The Fabulous Frontier* (Santa Fe, 1945), 190; and Fall to Mrs. (Emma) Fall, August 1, 1922, Box 1, Albert B. Fall Papers, University of New Mexico Library. C. L. Sonnichsen, *Tularosa: Last of the Frontier West* (New York, 1960), contains much information, vividly presented, about Fall's early years in New Mexico; see especially pp. 68-78, 259-65.

[19] Stratton, "New Mexican Machiavellian?" *loc. cit.*, 9.

[20] Miguel A. Otero, *My Nine Years as Governor of the Territory of New Mexico, 1897-1906* (Albuquerque, 1940), 153. This description of Fall is from a broadside criticizing New Mexico Governor Otero for bringing Fall, a former Democrat, into the territory's Republican administration.

publican party. New Mexico was predominantly Republican, and
he probably anticipated statehood for the territory and the possibility of his serving the state in the United States Senate.[21]
Fall quickly became a power in Republican circles in New Mexico. He held several political offices in the territory, and when
New Mexico became a state in 1912, the legislature elected him
to the United States Senate. He faced accusations of bribery
and other illegalities in connection with this election. The
charges, although prevalent, were unsubstantiated. Even his bitter political rival Thomas Catron, who became the state's other
Republican senator in 1912, thought that Fall had gained the
office legally. Moreover, he took office without dissent from the
Senate.[22]

In Washington, this frontier baron with his erect, confident
bearing, and his wide-brimmed black Stetson shading his narrow face, became a conspicuous figure. His personality reflected
his hard but lucrative struggle for wealth and his strong political ambition, nurtured by the individualism of the southwestern
frontier. His reckless courage and his encounters with western
gunmen and hard-fisted poker players were only part of a prevalent legend about Fall during his senatorial days. One old
acquaintance, recalling how Fall once disarmed gunman John
Wesley Hardin in an El Paso saloon, wrote: "I have known
many brave men. Fall was one of the most courageous of them
all."[23] Fall's very arrogance and frontier confidence worked to
his advantage. In 1923, a critic of Fall's conservation policy admitted that Fall could be "very winning when he chooses [to be].

[21] This is the conclusion of David Stratton, "New Mexican Machiavellian?" loc. cit., 11-12, who quotes Fall as saying in reference to the switch,
"I know when to change horses." But Fall also once said that he was a
Democrat "until William Jennings Bryan muddied the pond." New York
Times, December 24, 1922, Sec. 8, p. 2. Fall, while still a Democrat, opposed Bryan and the free silver program in the 1896 territorial convention
at Las Vegas, New Mexico. See Curry, An Autobiography, 93.
[22] Curry, An Autobiography, 121, 266; Fall to Thomas B. Catron, November 16, 1912, Box 1, Fall Papers.
[23] Curry, An Autobiography, 91. See also "A Cabinet Member Whose
Life Story Reads Like a Dime Novel," Current Opinion, LXXI (July, 1921),
34-36; New York Times, Dec. 24, 1922, Sec. 8, p. 2; Stratton, "New Mexican Machiavellian?" loc. cit., 8-9, 12-13; O. P. White, "Five El Paso Worth-
ies," American Mercury, XVIII (December, 1929), 433-40; and W. H.
Hutchinson, A Bar-Cross Man, 124, 101, 110.

His forceful, picturesque personality carries far, and he uses it to the limit in gaining his objectives. His speech is fast, his manner is impetuous, and he becomes instantly aggressive at opposition. At these times his powerful face clouds to sternness, he sits forward in his chair, and pounds his statements home with gesticulation; or throws his head back till he faces the ceiling while roaring with laughter at his opponents' replies. He does not argue, because he does not listen. He controls absolutely the attention of all hearers and deeply impresses many with his impetuous advocacy and assertion."[24] As a senator, Fall created close friendships as well as bitter enmities. One of his more intimate cronies was the colleague who sat next to him in the Senate, Warren G. Harding of Ohio. Perhaps this friendship had brought Fall to Brownsville during Harding's winter of indecision, when the President-elect struggled to select a cabinet that would include friends as well as statesmen.

Perhaps, too, it was friendship, mixed with ambition, that took Fall to Washington early in December and then to Marion later in the month for conferences with Harding. By mid-December, press reports had Fall clearly in line for a cabinet post, either as Secretary of State or of Interior.[25] These were not the first of such reports. At the 1920 Republican convention, New Mexico's delegation, instructed for General Leonard Wood, had stood by him to the final ballot; meanwhile, Fall, showing little interest in the campaign, refused even to be a delegate to the convention. Evidently he stayed away since he had wanted the New Mexicans to go to Chicago uninstructed, although the Santa Fe *New Mexican*, a perennial critic of Fall, claimed that he did so because the delegation did not go instructed for Harding.[26] Whatever his preconvention views were, in August, after the convention, Fall went to Marion at Harding's request to aid him in the campaign; and at about the same time, according to the

[24] National Park Bulletin, reprinted in Santa Fe *New Mexican*, Feb. 22, 1923, p. 2.

[25] Santa Fe *New Mexican*, Dec. 7, 1920, p. 1; Dec. 12, 1920, p. 1; and New York *Times*, Dec. 16, 1920, p. 9, and Dec. 24, 1920, p. 1.

[26] David H. Statton, "Albert B. Fall and the Teapot Dome Affair" (Ph.D. dissertation, University of Colorado, 1955), University Microfilms (Ann Arbor, Michigan), Publication 16,944, pp. 58-59; Santa Fe *New Mexican*, March 27, 1920, p. 1; Curry, *An Autobiography*, 287-88.

New Mexican, the story "leaked out . . . that . . . Fall expects to get a snug berth in the Harding Cabinet-to-be."[27]

Late in December, the Chicago *Tribune* reported that Harding had decided upon at least three cabinet appointments, and with these as a basis for his official family, the President-elect would "shift his other Cabinet cards to suit the changing conditions."[28] But Harding continued to reshuffle the deck. Through December and January, he worried over his selections and over friends and associates beseeching him from all sides. Late in January, 1921, Harding, perhaps fleeing from decision as well as from the cold, went to Florida as a guest of Senator Joseph S. Frelinghuysen of New Jersey, and with him was Fall. As the Harding party left Miami harbor on January 30 for a fishing cruise, the press wires reported that Fall had been chosen for the Interior post. Certainty of Fall's nomination increased through February, and on March 1, Harding announced from Marion that he was choosing Fall as the Secretary of the Interior.[29] Meanwhile, Harding had been filling in the other cabinet names, and when he appeared before the Senate on Inauguration Day to present the nominations, his old chums and former colleagues cheered him tumultuously. The burst of

[27] Stratton, "Albert B. Fall and the Teapot Dome Affair," 60; Santa Fe *New Mexican,* Aug. 22, 1920, p. 1; Rio Grande *Republic* (Las Cruces, N.M.), July 15, 1920, p. 6.

[28] Chicago *Tribune,* Dec. 23, 1920, as reported in New York *Times,* Dec. 24, 1920, p. 1.

[29] New York *Times,* Jan. 22, 1921, p. 1; Jan. 28, 1921, p. 1; Jan. 31, 1921, p. 1; Feb. 4, 1921, p. 15; and March 2, 1921, p. 1; Santa Fe *New Mexican,* Feb. 16, 1921, p. 1; Feb. 22, 1921, p. 1; and March 2, 1921, p. 1; and Rio Grande *Republic,* Feb. 17, 1921, p. 4.

Republican Senator Walter Edge of New Jersey, who considered himself "particularly fortunate" in being "the only companion of the President-elect while he was resting at the Hotel Ponce de Leon at St. Augustine, Florida, in February, 1921," states that Harding's appointments of such close personal friends as Harry Daugherty (Attorney-General) and Albert Fall "were, as he often said, personal appointments and obligations." Edge, *A Jerseyman's Journal* (Princeton, 1948), 120-22. George Curry, an old New Mexico friend of Fall, wrote: "Upon Harding's election in 1920, it was a foregone conclusion that Fall could have a place in the Cabinet and that he was likely to be made Secretary of the Interior, the post he desired." Curry, *An Autobiography,* 301. Finley Peter Dunne, "A Look at Harding," *Saturday Evening Post,* CCIX (September 12, 1936), 74-76, discusses briefly Harding's Cabinet selections and reports a revealing conversation with Harding about the Cabinet a few weeks before the inauguration in 1921.

applause which followed the reading of Fall's name suggested that his Senate friends approved his selection.[30]

The friends of conservation, however, were up in arms. While Harding had fished and golfed in Florida, they had consulted each other in growing anxiety. A wire to Gifford Pinchot in late February asked, "How is Fall on Conservation?" Pinchot replied: "Don't quote me yet on Fall. Want to go carefully over his record in Senate and other records not immediately available. He has been with exploitation gang, but not a leader. Has large personal holdings in mining and other resources in this country and Mexico. Trouble ahead." His examination of the record did not reassure him, and two days after the inauguration he wrote: "On the record, it would have been possible to pick a worse man for Secretary of the Interior, but not altogether easy." This judgment would later be expressed more specifically by another conservationist, who, pointing out that the position of Secretary of the Interior "called for a man with a strong appreciation of public rights and interests," said: "Fall was condemned as absolutely unfit for such a post by every detail of his record in the Senate. He had been an exploiter, and a friend of the exploiters. He had always opposed the conservation movement."[31]

To Harry Slattery, thinking back to the Republican campaign and his own contacts with it, "announcement of the Harding Cabinet . . . came as something of a shock." The appointment of Fall "placed in the key conservation post in the Cabinet one who for years had bitterly opposed the conservation program as a Senator." Both Pinchot and Slattery were also fearful over the selection of Edwin Denby as Secretary of the Navy. Pinchot recalled that as a congressman from Michigan during the Taft administration Denby had been a member of the committee which reported in favor of Ballinger. "I went to Detroit afterwards," he said, "and helped beat him for re-election. Why he should have been appointed, nobody seems to know." Further, according to Slattery, the conservationists were also worried over the

[30] *Congressional Record*, 67 Cong., 1 Sess., (March 4, 1921), 7; hereinafter cited as *Cong. Rec.*; New York *Times*, March 5, 1921, pp. 1 and 9.

[31] Walter Darlington to Pinchot, and Pinchot to Darlington, Feb. 24, 1921, Box 237; Pinchot to Samuel McCune Lindsay, March 6, 1921, Box 239, Pinchot Papers; and John Ise, *The United States Oil Policy* (New Haven, 1926), 365-66.

fact that "several assistant secretaries were appointed in the Navy and Interior Departments and the Department of Justice who were not likely to be friends from their past records and affiliations."[32]

Almost the sole comfort to the conservationists was the new Secretary of Agriculture, Henry C. Wallace, veteran farm-belt editor from Iowa and long-time friend of Gifford Pinchot. Pinchot thought Wallace was "the best appointment." An influential conservationist, writing later of the "incongurous team . . . assembled . . . in the first Harding Cabinet," noted that Wallace was "an able and forthright exponent of all that the conservation of natural resources stood for," whereas Fall was "an unreconstructed apostle of the free land, come-and-get it tradition of the young West."[33] Spurred by their fears and suspicions, conservationists went to work almost at once to preserve the cause of conservation from attack by the unreconstructed apostle in the Department of the Interior.

[32] Slattery, "From Roosevelt to Roosevelt," 75; Pinchot to Lindsay, March 6, 1921, Box 239, Pinchot Papers; and Slattery, "Story of Teapot Dome," 20.
[33] Pinchot to Lindsay, March 6, 1921, Box 239, Pinchot Papers; William B. Greeley, *Forests and Men*, 95.

2

The Ambitions
of Secretary Fall

Harry Slattery was a conservation watchdog, quick to take
alarm. Soon after Harding's inauguration, Slattery talked with
an associate editor of *The Survey*, a liberal fortnightly magazine.
He spoke of "prizes" that the Interior Department had to give
away and inferred that Fall was ready to distribute them. When
The Survey asked Slattery to write "a straight 'fact' story" about
the power Fall had, he first procrastinated and two months later
finally declined to contribute the article.[1] By then, he was finding Albert Fall involved in complexities hitherto undreamed of
by the friends of conservation, and for Slattery a brief article
was entirely insufficient for the new purposes taking shape in
his wary mind.

[1] S. Adele Shaw to Slattery, March 31, 1921, and April 14, 1921; Slattery
to Shaw, April 4, 1921, April 5, 1921, and June 2, 1921, Slattery Papers.

Soon after Fall took over the Interior Department, Slattery
heard that he was moving out "many trained and zealous public
servants" and surrounding himself with his personal friends and
that as a result a "lowering of tone was going down through the
whole Department." Then he picked up the "unbelievable rumor" that Fall had, by executive order, secured the transfer of
the naval oil reserves from the Navy Department into his own
ambitious hands. "This was so bold a move," said Slattery, "that
it at first did not sound true." If true, this might mean that Fall
was preparing the way for a direct assault on one of the most
important conservationist gains of the two preceding presidential
administrations.[2]

During the Taft administration, a concerted drive by the
friends of conservation had led to creation of two great naval
oil reserves on government lands in California oil country. Then
in 1915, President Wilson had set aside the Teapot Dome tract
in Wyoming as Naval Oil Reserve Number Three.[3] Taft and
Wilson had specifically designated these three areas as oil reserves for the exclusive use or benefit of the United States Navy,
but oil men now and then gazed upon them with envy. Throughout the Wilson administration, conservationists, determined to
reserve the navy's oil at its source below the surface, contested
with vociferous oil interests wanting to lease portions of the
government oil lands. Harry Slattery voiced the conservationist
viewpoint when he referred to the oil in these reserves as "a
supply laid up for some unexpected emergency" and insisted

[2] Slattery, "From Roosevelt to Roosevelt," 81-82.
[3] Max W. Ball, *Petroleum Withdrawals and Restorations Affecting the
Public Domain* (U.S. Geological Survey, Bulletin 623 [Washington, 1916]),
283-84, 291, 333. For recent studies that place these withdrawals in historical perspective, see John A. DeNovo, "Petroleum and the United States
Navy before World War I," *Mississippi Valley Historical Review*, XLI
(March, 1955), 641-56; and J. Leonard Bates, "Fulfilling American Democracy: The Conservation Movement, 1907 to 1921," *Mississippi Valley
Historical Review*, XLI (June, 1955), 46-54. See also J. Leonard Bates,
"The Midwest Decision, 1915: A Landmark in Conservation History," *Pacific Northwest Quarterly*, LI (January, 1960), 26-34, for an informative
discussion of the pressures for and against the Taft and Wilson withdrawals.
Ise, *United States Oil Policy*, is basic for any study of oil conservation; see
especially pp. 274-356, for discussion of the oil withdrawals. See also Samuel P. Hays, *Conservation and the Gospel of Efficiency* (Cambridge, 1959),
88-90.

that it should be left underground, intact and safe, serving as "an insurance policy for national defense."[4]

During the Wilson years, Secretary of the Interior Franklin K. Lane raised the hackles of Pinchot and his friends over the leasing issue. In the Wilson Cabinet a running fight developed between Lane and the Secretary of the Navy Josephus Daniels, who was backed by Pinchot, Senator Robert M. La Follette of Wisconsin, and a number of naval officers. Daniels wanted the naval oil reserves entirely closed to leasing. Lane felt that individuals with claims filed upon the oil lands before they were withdrawn had a legitimate complaint. Wilson usually sided with Daniels, but there was bickering within the administration and at least one interdepartmental feud.[5]

At one stage in the weary hassle, Lane gave support to legislative proposals that, in Pinchot's view, would break down existing oil conservation policy. Pinchot thereupon published a long and harsh "Open Letter" to Lane. It was little more than a public protest, but it illustrated Pinchot's customary readiness to slash out at the enemy, especially if his foe had sallied forth from the Department of the Interior. Albert Fall's turn to meet this patterned attack would soon come.[6]

Finally, in 1920, Daniels managed to acquire control of the reserves. Working through the House Naval Affairs Committee, he pushed through a special amendment to the 1920 naval appropriations bill. The amendment directed the Secretary of the Navy to take possession of the naval oil reserves and "to conserve, develop, use and operate the same in his discretion, directly

[4] Slattery, "Conservation of Public Oil Lands," Unpublished memorandum, March, 1924, Slattery Papers, 10.

[5] E. Louise Peffer, Closing of the Public Domain (Stanford, 1951), 127-28; Ise, United States Oil Policy, 335 ff.; J. Leonard Bates, "Josephus Daniels and the Naval Oil Reserves," Proceedings of the United States Naval Institute, LXXXIX (February, 1953), 171-79; Slattery "Story of the Teapot Dome Scandal," 19. See Daniels to William C. Redfield, Feb. 2, 1924, Josephus Daniels Papers, Division of Manuscripts, Library of Congress, Box 578, for Daniels' statement that "Wilson stood with me throughout the whole controversy when Lane and I disagreed." See also J. Leonard Bates, "The Midwest Decision," loc. cit., 31-33.

[6] Slattery, "Conservation of Oil Lands," Slattery Papers. A copy of Pinchot's "Open Letter" to Lane, dated August 12, 1916, and printed in pamphlet form, is in the Slattery Papers.

or by contract, lease or otherwise."[7] The bill was more of a compromise than a clear victory for conservation, although Pinchot
called it "the best leasing measure that has passed either House."
A number of congressmen believed the bill was reasonably fair
both to oil men and the government. Most significant to the
friends of conservation, however, was the fact that Daniels, a
stubborn conservationist, now controlled the reserves.[8] But then
Harding replaced Wilson, Josephus Daniels went home to North
Carolina, and Edwin Denby moved in as head of the Navy
Department. About a month after Fall took office, Slattery
heard the rumor that he, through Harding's executive order, had
acquired control of the reserves from Denby.

About the same time Slattery first picked up this rumor, he
also read a *Navy News* release of April 16, in which Secretary
Denby made an announcement that bothered him still more.
Denby, according to the press story, had decided to lease drilling
rights in one of the California naval oil reserves to private oil
companies, and he soon would begin accepting bids. Denby,
admitting this was the first time such rights were being granted,
justified his decision by claiming that government oil was draining into the wells of private companies operating on the rim of
the naval oil reserve. Slattery, believing the reserves to be in
danger, dashed off a message to Pinchot: "Some good might
come out of it if you would give me a note of introduction to
TR, Jr. [Theodore Roosevelt, Jr., Assistant Secretary of the Navy
under Denby], and I could discuss this briefly with him." Pinchot at once addressed a note to "Dear Ted," introducing Slattery
as "a man in whom you may have complete dependence from
every point of view. Not only will whatever he tells you be true,

---

[7] For the text of the amendment, see *Cong. Rec.*, 66 Cong., 2 Sess. (April
28, 1920), 6214-15. Ise, *United States Oil Policy*, 351, contains a detailed
discussion of the law.

[8] See Pinchot to Nicholas J. Sinnott, Chairman, House Public Lands Committee, and Daniels to Sinnott, *Cong. Rec.*, 66 Cong., 2 Sess. (Feb. 10,
1920), 2709; for views of Congressmen, see *Cong. Rec.*, 66 Cong., 1 Sess.
(Oct. 25, 1919), 7510-11, 7526. Bates, "The Midwest Decision," *loc. cit.*,
33, suggests that the leasing law of 1920 "represented a compromise of interests. Many claimants, with rights acquired after the executive withdrawal of 1909, but previous to the second withdrawal of 1910, were permitted to take out leases. They did not, however, receive the patents, or
leases on extremely generous terms, such as they originally had sought."

but you will find him thoroughly posted on whatever . . . he
desires to take up with you. . . . He is especially interested, as
I am, in the oil policy of the Navy Department."[9]

Slattery at this point was perturbed, not alarmed. Perhaps
for this reason, he let the letter to Roosevelt lie idle for a few
weeks. Then, on June 1, came confirmation of Slattery's earlier
rumor, when the White House announced that the President
had signed an executive order transferring the naval oil reserves
from the Navy Department to the Department of the Interior.
The action, said the White House, had been recommended jointly by Secretaries Denby and Fall, and the Secretary of the
Interior now possessed authority to grant drilling rights in
Reserve Number One in California, the only reserve thus far
opened to drilling.[10]

Although this transfer gave Fall the reserves, Slattery still had
confidence in the Roosevelt name. He went to the Navy Department, carrying Pinchot's letter with him. He told Roosevelt
of the old "naval oil fights and of my knowledge of them, and
the vital necessity of oil for the Navy." Roosevelt, according to
Slattery, began showing irritation. When Slattery spoke of Fall's
poor conservation record, Roosevelt "hit the ceiling." He told
Slattery that Fall had been in his father's Rough Riders and that
Slattery must not "say anything derogatory of this great, good
friend." Slattery recalled that he and Roosevelt "sparred back
and forth" for awhile, until Roosevelt "finally admitted he himself had carried the Executive Order, written by Fall and with
Denby's approval, to President Harding . . . [who] then signed
it." Slattery, although "shocked," felt that this information was
worth the visit. He predicted to Roosevelt that Fall "would
turn over the Naval reserves to private interests in the oil industry." Roosevelt, in anger, showed Slattery the door.[11]

[9] Slattery to Pinchot, April 25, 1921, and Pinchot to Theodore Roosevelt,
Jr., April 28, 1921, Slattery Papers. A copy of the *Navy News* release of
April 16, 1921, is also in the Slattery Papers.

[10] The executive order is reprinted in Senate Committee on Public Lands
and Surveys (68 Cong., 1 Sess.), *Leases upon Naval Oil Reserves* (3 vols.;
Washington, 1924), I, 177-78; hereafter cited as *Leases upon Reserves*
(1924).

[11] See Slattery's account of this visit, "From Roosevelt to Roosevelt," 82-
83. In the early 1930's, Slattery told Ralph Sucher, a former secretary of

The New York *Times* had buried the oil transfer story on page twelve. Slattery thought it deserved much more attention. He went to see Senator La Follette, the old crusader who had a deserved reputation as a friend of conservation and who had backed Daniels in his maneuver to gain control of the reserves. La Follette and Slattery had worked together on conservation problems in the past; they now resumed co-operative operations. La Follette, first informed of the oil transfer by Slattery, was disturbed at the news and encouraged the latter to investigate the transfer.[12]

Urged on partly by La Follette and partly by his own concern, Slattery began to study Fall's conservation record. For ten months, quietly and exhaustively, he probed. Gradually, he came to the conclusion that the oil transfer was only one part of a series of policies, planned and inaugurated "under a veil of secrecy" by Fall and that these policies comprised a major anticonservation campaign. The oil transfer began to shrink in importance when he learned of plans in the Interior Department to enlarge private exploitation of resources in Alaska and to bring all or part of the Forest Service—then in the Department of Agriculture—under control of the Department of the Interior.[13] As Slattery probed Fall's maneuverings, he began reporting periodically not only to La Follette but also to Gifford Pinchot, who eagerly spurred on the search. For when Fall reached for the forest reserves, he touched Pinchot's vital nerve.

Pinchot had long viewed the United States Forest Service as the seedbed of the conservation movement. He believed it "a self-evident fact that forestry is the key-stone of the arch of the conservation of natural resources." Holding this view, he had labored for half a century to keep the Service out of the hands of what he considered to be a predatory Interior Department. Early in his government career Pinchot formed a dispar-

La Follette's, of his visit with Roosevelt. See Sucher memorandum, February 24, 1932, Slattery Papers, and Sucher to Slattery, February 24, 1932, Slattery Papers.

[12] New York *Times*, June 2, 1921, p. 12; and statements by Robert M. La Follette, Jr., at a dinner in honor of Slattery, Cosmos Club, Washington, D.C., June 25, 1932, quoted in *Cong. Rec.*, 72 Cong., 1 Sess. (July 15, 1932), 15457-58.

[13] Sucher memorandum, Feb. 24, 1932; Slattery to Gifford Pinchot, June 21, 1921, and June 23, 1921, Slattery Papers.

aging opinion of the department, and in particular of its General Land Office, which to him was filled with "political stupidity, . . . crookedness and incompetence."[14] The Ballinger controversy in 1910, leading to Pinchot's dismissal, merely added dimensions to his scorn. One responsible scholar believes that this great controversy "left scar tissue which distorted the conservation picture for thirty years." After the Pinchot-Ballinger affair, Pinchot and his adherents began "pressing the charges . . . that the Department of the Interior had no proper conception of conservation, and that the Department of Agriculture, meaning the Forest Service, was the sole governmental agency sufficiently experienced and high-minded to have the country's interest at heart [in conserving and administering natural resources]."[15]

Conservationists themselves were not unanimous in supporting Pinchot's version of the Ballinger episode. Late in his life, Harold L. Ickes, who no doubt had picked up an undue prejudice toward him, wrote Pinchot a remarkable letter. Brutally and with eloquent candor he told Pinchot what he thought of of him. At one point, he flicked Pinchot with an accusing analysis: "Throughout the years, it has apparently been your deliberate effort to tie up Ballinger with some definite 'forest scandal' in Interior, [and] in private conversations with me you have used the argument 'Ballinger' as a reason against the retransferring of Forestry to Interior. You have done this cunningly and persistently." To Ickes, Pinchot viewed himself "not only as having conceived but as having given birth, quite immaculately of course, to the Forest Service." Not only had Pinchot protected the Service with "maniacal protestations," but he had also made "persistent and scurrilous efforts . . . to induce people to believe as badly as possible of . . . Interior."[16]

[14] Pinchot to Henry S. Graves [December, 1923?], Personal Correspondence, 1923-24, G, Box 247, Pinchot Papers; Pinchot, *Breaking New Ground*, 196-97, and 243 ff.; McGeary, *Gifford Pinchot*, 58; and Marion Clawson, *Uncle Sam's Acres* (Toronto, 1951), 108-11.

[15] Peffer, *Closing of the Public Domain*, 327 and 233 ff.

[16] A copy of this letter, dated May 18, 1940, is in the Slattery Papers. It is nineteen typewritten pages long, and Ickes did not repeat himself, nor use two words where one blistering adjective would do. At the time, Ickes was Secretary of the Interior, and he and Pinchot were wrangling over Ickes's proposal to bring the Forest Service into the Department; Ickes was about to publish an article, "Not Guilty! Richard A. Ballinger—An American Dreyfus," in the *Saturday Evening Post*, CCXII (May 25, 1940), 9-11;

Ickes was defending Ballinger, not Fall, but his analysis of Pinchot was relevant to the campaign against Fall. For in the summer of 1921, "Sir Galahad of the Woodlands" (as Ickes so brilliantly dubbed him) galloped forth to do battle over the forest reserves with Secretary Fall. To Pinchot, Albert B. Fall, as Secretary of the Interior, was an enemy. Already Pinchot had tried to stop the oil transfer by Harding. Immediately after learning that "powerful oil interests" were trying to get through executive action what they had failed to get through congressional action, he made an urgent personal appeal to Harding not to sign the executive order.[17] And now, goaded to furious activity by Fall's apparent threat to forest conservation, as well, Pinchot in mid-1921 became an active and powerful force behind a growing conservationist opposition to the new policies forming in the Department of the Interior.

Secretary Fall was clearly showing interest in more than oil reserves in California and Wyoming. Soon after taking office he began talking about the resources of Alaska. He culled through old reports and data, and had several conferences with President Harding, who finally, according to the New York *Times*, "told the Secretary . . . to go ahead and carry out the program which both are convinced will mean a greater Alaska." Fall reportedly was impressed by the vast coal fields, the high quality oil, and "the wonderful forests of Alaska, with, we hope, a future that is bright for the wood pulp and paper industries." To him, Alaska's greatest handicap was its decentralized administration. Division of authority led to conflict of authority. There was, he said, "just one way to develop Alaska, and that is to vest absolute authority in a single head . . . the President himself."[18]

123-29, which was based on the study he had ordered made in his department, *Not Guilty: An Official Inquiry* (Washington, 1940). In each of these publications, Ickes continued to sear the pages with Pinchot's name. For an account of the Ickes-Pinchot episode, see McGeary, *Gifford Pinchot*, 408-13.

[17] Philadelphia *Ledger*, March 5, 1924; New York *Times*, March 5, 1924, p. 2.

[18] New York *Times*, July 17, 1921, Sec. 7, p. 2. Scott Bone, appointed by Harding as governor of Alaska (to the displeasure of Pinchot, who complained that Harding had promised to consult with him about an appointment), agreed with Fall: "A simplified and centralized system brought closer home to Alaska is urgently and obviously needed to speed the progress of

But Fall also had other solutions for the Alaskan bureaucracy. In particular, he had ideas about the forests in the territory, as well as about those in the states. He wanted to transfer the Forest Service to the Interior Department or else to have the functions of Interior moved over to Agriculture. Naturally, he preferred to preserve his own domain, and two months after he took office he had drawn up for Harding's signature an executive order to transfer the Forest Service to the Interior Department. Later, in July, he supported an alternative move that would bring about the transfer by congressional action.[19]

Fall may have been planning a genuine program of efficiency and useful development for Alaska and for the Forest Service, but his past behavior raised doubts in the minds of the old conservationists. In 1910, when Pinchot's judgement had been irrevocably affected, Fall also had experienced a defeat that may have left an enduring impression. Forest Service rangers discovered that Rancher Fall was running too many sheep on the Alamo National Forest range near his home in New Mexico. He was authorized to graze a maximum of two thousand, but by entering two thousand sheep under his son's name and two thousand under an employee's name, he intended to graze four thousand sheep above his legal share on the public domain. The Forest Service reacted promptly. In a letter to Fall, it served notice that this practice would not be tolerated. In reply, Fall wrote that the Forest Service would "rue the day" and promised "punishment." Subsequently, he had a disagreement with national forest officials near the White Mountains, this time over fencing for his cattle. He

the Territory." Department of the Interior, *Report of the Governor of Alaska to the Secretary of the Interior, 1923* (Washington, 1923), 2-3; Pinchot to John N. Cobb, Aug. 1, 1921, Box 237, Pinchot Papers.

[19] Secretary of the Interior, *Annual Report, 1921* (Washington, 1921), 7; Slattery, "Conservation of Public Oil Lands," and New York *Times*, Nov. 10, 1921, p. 23. For the suggested executive order, see Russell Lord, *The Wallaces of Iowa* (Boston, 1947), 227. In the summer of 1922, Fall would explain his reasoning to a friend: ". . . in administration of the Forest Reserves upon the one hand, and of mining and homestead entries, etc. upon the other, there was inevitable conflict and would continue to be, and I gave as my conclusion that either the Agricultural Department should be vested with authority over all these matters, which would . . . mean the taking over of land office administration and possibly the Mining Bureau; or else that the Forestry Bureau should be transferred to this Department." Fall to W. A. Hawkins, Aug. 11, 1922, Box 1, Fall Papers.

chose to pull his cattle out of the area and pay three dollars
per head on the Indian reservations in preference to running
his stock on land in the national forests.[20]

Whether or not Fall was now seeking to impose his promised
"punishment" of 1910, the conservationists were hurt at the very
thought of a transfer of the forests to Interior. At Slattery's suggestion, Pinchot sought a conference with the Secretary of the
Interior, who agreed to a meeting on July 29. Pinchot afterwards
reported that at the meeting Fall was "most gratified that I had
asked to see him, and expressed himself generally in a most
friendly manner." According to Pinchot, Fall "specifically and
definitely" did not want the administration of Alaskan forests
transferred to his department. He merely wanted "control of
the business end of the timber sales," leaving with the Forest
Service in Agriculture "the marking of timber, and other details
of the management on the ground." During the conversation,
Pinchot received a confidential copy of a congressional bill which
included Fall's views on Alaskan development.[21]

Pinchot had mixed reactions to his talk with Fall. To Frederick H. Newell, a conservation pioneer, he wrote immediately
about "a long and very satisfactory conference." But to an old
Bureau of Fisheries expert, John N. Cobb of Juneau, Alaska,
Pinchot dispatched a less optimistic note. He related to Cobb
the gist of his conversation, pointing out that Fall did not want
the forests transferred to Interior, but did want "to take control
of the business end of timber sales." Pinchot thought that
"such a separation would not work well for fairly obvious reasons" and asked Cobb to do what he could "to promote the

[20] Lord, *The Wallaces of Iowa*, 227, 591; "Notes of G. P.'s talk with Sec-
retary Fall, on Friday afternoon, July 29, 1921," Slattery Papers. (Alamo
National Forest, in southern New Mexico, later became Lincoln National
Forest.)

[21] Slattery to Pinchot, July 20 and July 23, 1921; Pinchot to Slattery,
July 22 and July 25, 1921, Slattery Papers. A copy of "Confidential Committee Print, 67 Cong., 1 Sess., House Bill," given to Pinchot on July 29,
1921, by Fall, is in the Slattery Papers, along with "Notes of G.P.'s talks.
. . ." Pinchot sent these to Slattery "for the files of the Conservation Association," with an explanation that "These notes were made immediately after
the talk, and accurately represent the position taken by the Secretary."
Pinchot to Slattery, September 26, 1921, Slattery Papers.

keeping of the whole forest problem in the hands of the men who are best able to handle it—very obviously, the Forest Service men themselves." To Frederick E. Olmsted, consulting forester at Stanford University, Pinchot sent notes on his interview with Fall, as well as those from a subsequent conversation with Harding. Olmsted found them "most instructive" and predicted: "Off hand, I should say it looks like a fight, for I doubt if anything else will knock sense into their big business heads. I haven't the slightest doubt . . . that the lumber interests are behind Fall and coaxing him along." Olmsted thought that "an open fight on the whole conservation business would be an excellent thing. With the . . . present administration . . . out and out for big business, there is bound to be a lot of damage done secretly, anyway; why not have a show-down?"[22]

Pinchot already had decided to look for a showdown. After trailing the Secretary of the Interior through the spring and summer of 1921, he became convinced, despite his recent talk with him, that Fall was attacking the government's entire conservation program. He decided that Fall and his friends were after "billions of dollars worth of . . . natural resources held by the Government . . . " and that Fall was trying to transfer the Forest Service to Interior just to get even for his own disagreeable experience with the Service in the past.[23] When Pinchot reached this stage in his thinking, he set in motion a favorite maneuver of the conservationists—enlisting the aid of the press, this time in a publicity war against Fall. Slattery was a key figure in the propaganda campaign, and by September he had managed to place in the Christian Science Monitor the first of four stories on forestry, written by E. A. Sherman, Associate Forester of the United States. Essentially, the articles defended the status quo in Alaska. Slattery thought they had "a good slant." Ten days later, he reported to Pinchot: "In addition to . . . the Monitor . . . I have got NEA, Chicago Tribune, New

[22] Pinchot to Frederick H. Newell, Aug. 1, 1921, Box 240; Pinchot to John N. Cobb, Aug. 1, 1921, Box 237; Frederick E. Olmsted to Pinchot, Dec. 5, 1921, Box 240, Pinchot Papers.

[23] Speech by Pinchot at Atlantic City meeting of American Society of Newspaper Editors, April 25, 1924, reported in New York Times, April 25, 1924, p. 4.

York Tribune, Federated Press, and Consolidated folks to use
a part or all of it. It is good stuff."[24]

In early December, 1921, as Fall persisted in his plans, Pinchot
began calling out new reserves and adopting new tactics. On
August 10, Senator Harry S. New of Indiana had introduced a
bill to implement some of Fall's Alaskan proposals, and on
November 16, Senator William H. King of Utah had proposed a
bill to transfer the national forests to Interior. Pinchot mustered
the state forestry associations against both bills. He wired a friend
in Massachusetts that "efforts to transfer Forest Service . . . is
[sic] serious and threatening. Suggest Massachusetts Forestry
Association take strong action [against the proposed forestry
bill], and communicate with all Massachusetts Senators and Representatives, also with President." He informed R. C. Bryant at
Yale's forestry school that he was going to write to all the forestry associations: "Generally, I am starting to stir things up.
The situation is thoroughly serious, and while we are going to
beat them in the end, it is going to take some fighting." Pinchot
hoped that the executive committee of the Society of American
Foresters could take action. "If so, what they say ought to be
sent to every Senator and Congressman, and to all members of
the Cabinet." Bryant replied: "As President of the Society . . .
I have been trying to stir up opposition to the King Bill. . . .
You will be the leader in the fight . . . as you have always been
and . . . you may rely upon our support in any way that you
need it."[25]

From the state forestry associations, as well as from any other
source, Pinchot wanted pressure put upon the administration to
prevent the Forest Service transfer. As he told a close friend,
"Fall has made up his mind to get the Service, and Harding is
on the fence." As a result, Pinchot himself was "seriously dis-

[24] Slattery to Pinchot, Sept. 22, Sept. 29, and Oct. 2, 1921; Slattery to
E. A. Sherman, Sept. 29, 1921, Slattery Papers. For discussion of Pinchot's
press campaigns, see McGeary, *Gifford Pinchot*, 50-51, 200-205. See also
Pinchot's annual report as Forester in 1907, in Secretary of Agriculture, *Annual Report . . . 1907* (Washington, 1907), 347-49.

[25] *Cong. Rec.,* 67 Cong., 1 Sess. (Aug. 10, 1921), 4805, and (Nov. 16,
1921), 7746; Pinchot to Bryant, Dec., 1921; Bryant to Pinchot, Dec. 6, 1921,
Box 236, Pinchot Papers.

quieted by the situation." In his opinion, of course, Fall had no justification for the transfer: "The argument our way is . . . overwhelming, but argument as compared with letters from the folks back home is a mighty ineffective means of persuasion."[26]

By mid-December, 1921, Pinchot could write that the fight was "going merrily on." To maintain its impetus, he drew up a letter, which went out to "all newspapers." Another, he advised, would go to "every Association I can lay my claws on which is likely to be useful." If, he said, Chief Forester William B. Greeley had been "letting the whole thing go by default," Secretary of Agriculture Henry C. Wallace had "at last got his fighting clothes on," and Pinchot was confident of success. By Christmas, he was even more optimistic. To his brother Amos he wrote: "I think we have won our fight on the transfer." Certainly his press campaign was booming. The American Forestry Association was able to publish a news sheet, made up largely of excerpts from newspapers throughout the country, all of them attacking Fall, the proposed forest transfer, or both.[27]

On March 8, 1922, the association sent directly to President Harding, to Congress, and to newspapers throughout the country a special sheet, captioned "The Case of the People vs. the Proposal to Transfer the U. S. Forest Service to the Department of the Interior," in which it presented "a resume of the editorial opinion of the country denouncing the proposed plan to take the Forest Service out of the Department of Agriculture." In April, *American Forestry* magazine claimed that "as a result of widespread information, the opposition [to the transfer] has become most pronounced. The newspapers are practically a unit in pro-

[26] Pinchot to Philip Wells, Dec. 8, 1921, Box 243, Pinchot Papers (Wells was a counsel of the National Conservation Association, and a long-time legal adviser and friend of Pinchot's).

[27] Pinchot to Frederick Olmsted, Dec. 12, 1921, Box 240; Pinchot to Amos Pinchot, Dec. 23, 1921, Box 240; Pinchot to S. T. Dana, Forest Commissioner, Augusta, Maine (no date), Box 237, Pinchot Papers; copy of News Sheet, American Forestry Association, Washington, D.C., undated, in Slattery Papers. Wallace evidently had been slow to join Pinchot's campaign because of a reluctance to openly reveal what was rapidly becoming an interdepartmental dispute between Interior and Agriculture. See Barrington Moore to Pinchot, Dec. 15, 1921; Pinchot to Moore, Dec. 20, 1921, Box 240, Pinchot Papers.

testing against the proposal and scores of influential organizations have condemned it."[28]

Pinchot later claimed that during his campaign "direct personal communication was established with the editors of five or six thousand of the most influential journals in America. A stream of editorials came pouring into Washington so definite, so forceful, so influential, that . . . Harding said to me in the White House, 'You are absolutely wrong in opposing the transfer of the national forests, but I pay you the compliment of saying that he [Fall] cannot put it over against your opposition.' "[29]

Whatever their effects upon Congress and the President, the conservation crusaders began to pierce Fall's crusty but sensitive armor. Vociferously, he struck back. He complained to Harding about the "impropriety" of the "vicious and unwarranted attack" by Pinchot and by the Forest Service itself upon "the head of a coordinate department of the Government," and he accused the Department of Agriculture and Secretary Wallace of fathering "vicious propaganda" against him and his policies.[30] In a "Memorandum to the Press," a twelve-page document which he had drawn up, Fall strongly defended his forest and general conservation policies and scathingly denounced "Pinchotism." Toward Alaska he remained obdurate; the country must be opened up, and its natural resources exploited. Privately, he was less belligerent. He admitted to a friend: "The reorganization plan [for Alaska] seems to have gotten nowhere. I have been told that . . . the President's representative reported in favor of the transfer of the Forestry Bureau to this Department. I . . . have also been told in other high quarters that such plan was favored. Whether it will ever be carried out or not I don't know, and insofar as I am personally concerned don't care." Fall felt it was his duty to state his convictions "as to what is best for the public

[28] *American Forestry*, XXVIII (April, 1922), 200, with a photographic reproduction of the special sheet, which included comments from *Country Gentleman*, the *Christian Science Monitor*, the Pittsburgh *Post*, the Pueblo *Journal*, and various other papers and magazines.

[29] New York *Times*, April 26, 1924, p. 4.

[30] *Wallace's Farmer*, March 24, 1922, p. 8; New York *Times*, March 7, 1922, p. 2, quoting a letter from Fall to "Chairman of one of the principal committees of the House." The latter was Congressmen N. J. Sinnott, chairman of the Committee on Public Lands. See Fall to Sinnott, March 3, 1922, Box 7, Fall Papers.

service." If, he concluded, "those who have the authority or power to carry out suggestions do not see fit to do so . . . the responsibility is not mine and therefore I am not personally intending to
inaugurate any campaign whatsoever."[31]

When portions of Fall's memorandum appeared in the press,
Slattery joyfully clipped them and sent them to Pinchot, saying:
"You will note by these . . . that Mr. Fall has been having a
nice time digging himself in a hole that he won't be able to
get out of so easy. You will get some laughs out of some of it."
Slattery thought that Pinchot now should "sit tight . . . and let
the heathen rage."[32]

President Harding apparently was bewildered by all the noise
over conservation, and wondered which side to support. Loyal
to Fall as a friend, the President, having earlier supported him
in the Alaska proposals, now became silent about forestry. As
Fall began lashing back at the conservationists, newspapers reported "a widening in the gulf" between the President and his
Secretary of the Interior. There were "surface indications" that
Fall might soon resign. The New York *Times,* summarizing part
of the conservation dispute, observed that during the first year
of the Harding administration the President had "become attached to the point of view and the counsel of Secretary Hughes
and Secretary Hoover." Fall, meantime, had become "a mere
member of the Cabinet."[33]

As spring neared, the conservationists' relentless pressure upon
Fall continued to tighten, but they soon began to focus more on
oil than on forests. On March 10, Slattery made a prepared
speech at a luncheon at the Ebbitt House in Washington, where
he spoke before a forum of the National Popular Government
League. Judson King, the executive secretary and driving force
of the league, had asked Slattery to present the "facts" on the
current controversy over the Forest Service. Slattery made a

[31] Copy of Fall's memorandum, dated March 4, 1922, Slattery Papers (see
also Box 7, Fall Papers); Fall to W. A. Hawkins, Aug. 11, 1922, Box 1, Fall
Papers.
[32] Slattery to Pinchot, March 7, 1922, Slattery Papers.
[33] New York *Times,* March 12, 1922, Sec. 7, p. 1. See also Santa Fe *New
Mexican,* Feb. 19, 1922, and March 11, 1922; *Wallace's Farmer,* March 24,
1922, p. 8; and the intimate portrait of Harding in White, *Autobiography,*
615 ff.

robust speech, striking hard at Fall and arguing strongly for leaving the Service in Agriculture. Having covered his subject, he spoke further, almost parenthetically, about the naval oil reserves: "I think Mr. Fall will be asked a few questions about his stewardship . . . and one of these . . . will be about the leasing of the oil lands in Naval Reserve Number One [to] a Doheny interest." Slattery's evident reference was to a lease granted by Fall on July 12, 1921, shortly after he acquired control of the reserves from the Navy Department, in which he awarded to Edward L. Doheny the right to drill offset wells in Reserve Number One. There had been little criticism of this lease, since the drainage by adjoining wells was evident and the bidding for the lease had been open and competitive. Nevertheless, Slattery believed that Congress would be inquiring about Fall's private leases of the reserves, because "we have heard stories about Mr. Fall being quite friendly with large interests of an oleaginous nature."[34]

Immediately after the forum, a slow fuse began to burn under Harding's Cabinet. Secretary Wallace had sent a stenographer to the luncheon to take notes on Slattery's remarks, and Wallace himself carried these notes to the President. But Harding evidently was not going to give full support to one cabinet member against another. He would not alter the action taken some nine months earlier which transferred control of the naval oil reserves to Fall, but he did postpone decision on the proposed transfer of the Forest Service. Wallace then stirred up a row in a cabinet meeting by broaching the question of Fall's conservation policies; he was reported to have told the cabinet that if the Forest Service were transferred, he would resign, call public meetings in large cities of the Midwest, and put before the country "the case against Fall and his colleagues—forests, oil, and everything."[35]

The month of March, 1922, which saw Wallace joining the conservation campaign against Fall, marked also a change of di-

---

[34] Quotations from the speech appear in a copy of a National Popular Government League Bulletin, March 10, 1922, Slattery Papers. For the Doheny lease, see Ise, *United States Oil Policy*, 372. The Fall Papers (Box 7) contain a very extensive and seemingly verbatim report of Slattery's speech and of the question and answer period following it.

[35] Lord, *The Wallaces of Iowa*, 227-28. The quotation is Lord's version of Wallace's sentiment. See also Slattery, "From Roosevelt to Roosevelt," 88.

rection in that attack. Since the summer of 1921, Slattery's major concern had been Fall's proposed transfer of the Forest Service; the oil conservation issue he had temporarily shelved. After March, the relative importance of forests and oil began to shift, and oil conservation policies soon made the forestry issue a secondary question. The change was marked, too, by Pinchot's announcement, two days after Slattery's March speech, of his candidacy for the governorship of Pennsylvania; thereafter, Pinchot began to turn his driving energies to state politics, seemingly content in the belief that the Forest Service was safe from Fall. Slattery and other conservationists, however, did not slacken their drive. Four days after his Ebbitt House speech, Slattery wrote to H. H. Chapman that "the Fall war still goes on." Near the end of March, he wrote to Philip Wells: "[although] the transfer scrap has died down . . . I am still afraid that Harding is going to side with Fall." It was not encouraging news, he said, "to hear that Fall has been to White House twice lately and had long pow-wows with Harding." To Chapman, he suggested: "Something must be done. . . . Our friends in American Forestry evidently fear to offend the Powers that Be—and GP is all absorbed with his Pa. campaign. You and I could conspire together to throw a few brickbats—certainly the situation is going to need it."[36]

At this point, Slattery was discouraged. For more than a year, the conservationists had been probing for weaknesses in Fall's defenses, yet their latest barrage had merely forced him to cover. Then Slattery stumbled upon an opening, one that led directly to scandal.

---

[36] Slattery to H. H. Chapman, March 15, 1922; Slattery to Philip Wells, March 30, 1922; Slattery to Chapman, March 31, 1922, Slattery Papers. Slattery, if not Pinchot, continued to send material to the newspaper syndicates. See, for example, his letter to the Universal Service, March 15, 1922, Slattery Papers.

3

The Suspicions
of Senator La Follette

Although Slattery had learned in April of 1921 that Fall controlled the naval oil reserves, he discovered little overt activity in the Interior Department that would document his anxieties during the following year. True, Fall had granted Doheny the right to drill offset wells in Reserve Number One, but this was not major exploitation of the reserve. Fall was also opening old hearings on certain oil claims decided against great oil companies during the Wilson administration and was rendering decisions now in their favor. This knowledge, however, only frustrated Slattery. Fall's behavior was highly suspect, still it was legal.

Some time in early March, 1922, Slattery decided to search for fire beneath the oil smoke. His speech at the Ebbitt House luncheon had indicated a growing interest in the oil question, although, as he had stated there, the forest transfer was "the real issue." Perhaps he decided that Fall could be brought to bay on the Forest Service through a flanking attack on oil. Whatever his thoughts, on March 15 he sent Senator La Follette a noteworthy letter.

Slattery discovered, "on reliable authority," that Fall had just leased a large acreage within Reserve Number One to the Doheny oil interests, the same group which had earlier been granted the limited right to drill offset wells. He reminded La Follette that this reserve "was the one the naval experts said was best fitted to store oil underground for naval use." Moreover, Fall had recently reopened another oil claim case, and the naval coal reserve in Alaska, also transferred to his department, was "known to be up for private leasing." Slattery had drawn up a proposed Senate resolution that would direct the Secretary of the Interior to send to the Senate a list of all oil leases made by Interior within Naval Reserves One and Two, with full details on them; all executive orders and other papers in Interior files authorizing or regulating such leases; and "all correspondence, papers, and files showing and concerning the application for such leases and the actions of . . . Interior . . . thereon." Slattery told LaFollette that he would be glad to go over the resolutions with him at any time. La Follette replied soon afterwards: "I am interested in this . . . and hope you will take it up at your earliest convenience."[1]

Actually, Slattery had little more than hunches at this point, and his letter to La Follette was only a new tactic in the "Fall war." As he informed a friend: " . . . there has been a sudden change—and we are fighting old Fall on 'the oil line'—particularly naval oil reserves." To Philip Wells he expressed his hopes: "We still have our scheme to launch a few bolts at Mr. F. under cover—and I hope you will hear it clear to Middletown when it comes through."[2]

Early in April, 1922, Slattery had a long talk with La Follette. They decided "that a Senate resolution would be the only way to get at the facts," and they began to gather data to incorporate in a resolution calling for information from Fall. Slattery later

[1] Slattery to La Follette, March 15, 1922; La Follette to Slattery, March 20, 1922, Slattery Papers.

[2] Slattery to H. H. Chapman, April 19, 1922; Slattery to Wells, March 20, 1922, Slattery Papers.

recalled that La Follette was at first reluctant to bring up the proposed resolution "because of his complete independence of the Republican majority and because of possible opposition among the Democrats engendered by issues of World War I." La Follette suggested that Slattery discuss the problem with Senator Hiram W. Johnson of California and then, when Johnson was unreceptive, with Senator William E. Borah of Idaho. By telephone La Follette arranged the meetings for Slattery with Johnson, then Borah. Slattery saw them, "but it was," he wrote, "a water-haul—they would not introduce it." He came back to La Follette, who said, "Harry, we will go ahead."[3]

On April 6, La Follette, remembering Josephus Daniels' doughty paternalism toward the reserves, wrote him of his intentions to bring the question before the Senate "at the first opportunity." La Follette was surprised that no naval officer connected with the reserves and aware of their significance had made any adverse comment on Fall's oil policy. Would Daniels offer an opinion on the situation?[4] The same day, La Follette began searching for necessary documents. Harding's executive order of May 31, 1921, transferring the reserves, had never been published and was not filed in the customary section at the State Department. He wrote to Secretary of State Charles Evans Hughes asking for "copies of the President's orders relating to naval oil and coal reserves." Without replying, Hughes sent the letter to Fall, who, La Follette claimed, did not reply. The Senator next managed to procure a copy of the executive order and upon reading it decided that it was illegal and that Harding had no authority to issue it.[5]

[3] Slattery, "From Roosevelt to Roosevelt," 87.

[4] La Follette to Daniels, April 6, 1922, quoted in Sucher memorandum, Feb. 24, 1932, Slattery Papers.

[5] La Follette to Hughes, April 6, 1922, cited in Belle C. and Fola La Follette, *Robert M. La Follette* (2 vols.; New York, 1953), II, 1045; Sucher memorandum, Feb. 24, 1932, Slattery Papers. The Sucher memorandum indicates that La Follette never received an answer from Fall and that when Fall produced the supposed reply eighteen months later, La Follette decided that it had been drafted at a later period to avoid any charges of concealment. On the other hand, La Follette, *Robert M. La Follette,* II, 1045, refers to a letter from Fall to La Follette, dated April 12, 1922, without questioning when it may have been written. Fall's letter, whenever written, is printed in *Leases upon Reserves* (1924), I, 265-66. For a legal scholar's opinion that the lease was illegal, see Charles G. Hagland, "The Naval Reserve Leases," *Georgetown Law Journal,* XX (March, 1932), 296.

Gradually, more evidence began to filter in to the Senator. Daniels, replying to his letter of April 6, suggested that La Follette consult Rear Admiral Robert S. Griffin, who had been Chief of the Navy Bureau of Engineering for over eight years and who had opposed the naval oil reserve transfer. La Follette gave Slattery letters of introduction to Admiral Griffin and to several other naval officers, including Captain John Halligan, "one of the Navy's experts on oil," as Slattery called him. He saw them all. The Admiral, although retired, was still a member of the Naval Consulting Board and wrote Slattery that he was "in a delicate position, since . . . Denby was his chief, but he clearly indicated his hope that the Senator would force an investigation." He told Slattery: "If they get into this thing, they will find stranger things in heaven and earth than we have dreamed of." Slattery reported the interview to La Follette, "and the significance of Admiral Griffin's remark was not lost upon him." La Follette was also soliciting viewpoints of other naval officers, "men, who, he knew had stood staunchly against the transfer or leasing of the reserves"; but he learned that they had all been ordered to distant stations. This news, too, aroused his suspicions.[6]

Perhaps the conservationists forced Fall's hand, or, conceivably, he was preparing the way for other announcements to follow later. At any rate, on April 7, he announced the adoption by the Interior Department of a policy for protecting the government against further losses of oil in the California reserves. He estimated that around twenty-two million barrels of oil had been lost through failure of the Wilson administration to drill protective offset wells there. This loss was irrecoverable, and Interior could only inaugurate a drilling campaign to save the oil that still remained in the ground. This campaign already had started. Fall announced leases on Reserve Number Two to companies with preferential rights to drill, based upon claims held prior to

---

[6] Daniels to La Follette, April 15, 1922, cited in La Follette, *Robert M. La Follette*, II, 1048; Slattery, "From Roosevelt to Roosevelt," 87; Sucher memorandum, Feb. 24, 1932, Slattery Papers. On April 8, 1922, Slattery, still in his role as publicist, wrote to John E. Lathrop of the New York *World:* "You have no doubt noticed a war that has begun on Secretary Fall along the Potomac. . . . I want to ask if you can put a few spikes in the schemes of this gent . . . and if I might take the liberty of furnishing you some 'dope' now and then." Lathrop replied that he would be glad to receive news about Fall's conservation plans. Slattery to Lathrop, April 8, 1922; Lathrop to Slattery, April 10, 1922, Slattery Papers.

withdrawal of the land by President Taft. No definite contracts, other than the limited one to Doheny of July 12, 1921, had yet been made for Reserve Number One, but a permanent policy was "being rapidly formulated" whereby the government would receive a portion of the oil produced and would store it in steel tanks for future needs by the navy.[7]

In his statement Fall committed a sin of omission. He failed to announce that on this same day, April 7, he had leased the entire area of Teapot Dome to an oil man named Harry Sinclair. Someone told Slattery of this lease three days later.[8] Slattery's private information became public, on April 14, when the *Wall Street Journal* carried a front-page report that Fall had leased Teapot Dome to Sinclair's Mammoth Oil Company. Interior officials, the paper reported, had indicated that "the arrangement . . . marks one of the greatest petroleum undertakings of the age and signalizes a notable departure on the part of the government in seeking partnership with private capital for the working of government-owned natural resources."[9]

Meanwhile, the investigation of Fall's conservation policy had begun to slip from the hands of the conservationists into those of the United States Senate and the public press. At the same time that La Follette was writing to Daniels and Hughes, Senator John B. Kendrick of Wyoming began receiving telegrams and letters from his constituents, asking him to inquire into rumors that Teapot Dome had been, or was about to be, leased to private inter-

[7] New York *Times*, April 8, 1922, 19; see also mimeographed copy of Fall's "Memo for the Press." dated April 6, 1922, Box 7, Fall Papers.

[8] Slattery would not reveal his informers. On April 10, he typed out a memorandum, labeled "Confidential—Not to be used," in which he noted: "Had conversation with X. He came to office, told me that he knew definitely that Interior Department was leasing Teapot Dome in Naval Reserve No. 3 (Wyo.) to Sinclair . . . and that it was one of the finest oil domes in mid-continental field." Slattery Memo, April 10, 1922, Slattery Papers.

[9] *Wall Street Journal*, April 14, 1922, pp. 1, 8. A Department of the Interior memo, dated April 6, 1922—one day before Fall's lease of Teapot Dome to Sinclair—stated that "the attention of the Secretary [had] been called to a Denver telegram published in the New York Globe April 5 relating to some rumored contract for the development of the oil in what is known as the 'Teapot Dome.'" Although the department, in behalf of the navy, had carried on extensive investigations in Reserves One, Two, and Three, "no definite contracts" had yet been made "for the development, use, storage, or any other purpose, in either . . . Reserve." Memo of April 6, 1922, Box 7, Fall Papers.

ests. Kendrick asked the Interior Department for information, and on April 10 he received a reply that no contract for a lease had been made. The rumors echoed beyond Wyoming, and newspapers tried to get a verification. They, too, learned nothing.[10] But they, as did Kendrick, began to dig. On April 15, the day after the *Wall Street Journal* story appeared, Kendrick rose in the Senate chamber near the end of the day and introduced a brief resolution. He proposed that the secretaries of the Navy and Interior Departments "inform the Senate, if not incompatible with the public interests," about "all proposed operating agreements" upon the Teapot Dome reserve. The Senate agreed to Kendrick's resolution without comment and without a roll call vote.[11]

While Kendrick's call for this information on Teapot Dome was evidently motivated by pressure from his own constituents, he was now joining—consciously or not—the campaign of the conservationists, who had been probing Fall's actions since the day he became Secretary of the Interior. In time, Kendrick alone might have instigated a full-dress investigation of Fall's oil leasing policy. Yet, until April 15, he had not entered the "Fall war," and even then he merely questioned rather than attacked Fall's policy. In late April, however, his position would be greatly reinforced by La Follette, demanding an exhaustive investigation of "this entire subject of leases upon naval oil reserves." La Follette was incited to activity by Slattery, who, with the encouragement and aid of Gifford Pinchot, had kept alive a continuing campaign, already over a year old, against Secretary Fall. The shock of Fall's appointment had stirred the old conservationists to mobilize against him. Memories of Ballinger furnished them example and inspiration. Ballinger, honest or not, was hounded from office by Pinchot and the men who thought like him. In the spring of 1922, Albert Fall was still very much in office, although the sounds of pursuit were loud and clear, and for the conservationists, there were no doubts about his character.

On April 18, while Fall was on an inspection tour of Reclamation Bureau projects in the West, acting Secretary of the Interior

---

10 See *Cong. Rec.*, 67 Cong., 2 Sess. (August 25, 1922), 11785, for Kendrick's account of his activities concerning Teapot Dome in early April, 1922. See also New York *Times*, March 12, 1924, p. 6, and Ise, *United States Oil Policy*, 357.

11 *Cong. Rec.*, 67 Cong., 2 Sess. (April 15, 1922), 5567-68.

Edward C. Finney formally announced the leasing of Teapot Dome. Three days later, in response to Kendrick's resolution, Finney officially notified the Senate and sent it a copy of the contract by which Sinclair's Mammoth Oil Company had been given a lease on the entire area of Naval Oil Reserve Number Three. Under the terms of this contract the government was to receive royalties of 12.5 to 50 per cent on the production of the wells. The lease was for twenty years and, in customary oil lease language, "so long thereafter as oil or gas is produced in paying quantities from said lands." An unusual provision stipulated that the government was not to receive its royalty in oil or in cash payments, but in oil certificates. These could be exchanged for fuel oil and various petroleum products, could be redeemed in cash, or could be exchanged for oil storage tanks—all such exchanges to be with the Mammoth Oil Company.[12]

When Finney announced the Teapot Dome lease, he also indicated that Edward L. Doheny's Pan-American Petroleum and Transport Company was being awarded a contract on parts of the California oil reserves. By April 25 the terms were arranged. The navy's royalty oil from the reserves was to be exchanged for storage tanks that Doheny would construct at Pearl Harbor, along with docks, wharves, and other facilities for fueling the fleet. The Doheny contract also stipulated that if future leases should be given for any or all of the California reserve, Doheny's company would have a preferential right to the lease.[13]

The two contracts received little publicity. Finney's announcement, as did Kendrick's resolution, raised hardly a ripple outside conservation and oil circles. According to *The Oil and Gas Journal*, certain "leaders of the oil industry" were "exceedingly well pleased with the apparent reversal of the Government's policy," many oil men having "contended for years that it is more advantageous to have the petroleum reserve of the Navy stored above ground than under ground, where it may be drained by adjacent drilling." Only "conservation hysteria" had prevented adoption of such policy in the past, and even now the opposition to the new contract was being "led by certain politicians who seek to

[12] New York *Times*, April 19, 1922, p. 31; contract printed in *Leases upon Reserves* (1924), I, 6-21.
[13] *Leases upon Reserves* (1924), I, 296-98.

make the matter the 'pièce de résistance' of another Pinchot-Ballinger conservation campaign." The Democratic New York *World* merely criticized the administration's secretiveness over the new oil policy, saying: "The whole transaction lends color to the theory of underground government . . . and the Harding administration can thank only itself for standing in a bad light before the country." But the country, and evidently the press, knew little about any mysterious maneuverings in the Interior Department, or about any new conservation crusade in the offing. John Lathrop of the *World* asked Slattery for facts, "and I don't care whom they hit. . . . If you have provable facts—fire them along."[14]

Slattery, too, wanted some facts. He had a surplus of hunches, and every day was picking up rumors and opinions to support them. Soon after his talk with Admiral Griffin he made contact with Captain John Halligan, one of the naval officers he had seen earlier. Slattery described their conversation in his diary: "We had a long talk. He showed me that Griffin, [Commander Nathan H.] Wright, and [Commander H. A.] Stuart, including himself, protested Executive Order on Naval Reserves, also data showing Stuart knew nothing of Doheny deals—also letter of Stuart in protest . . . to Admiral John K. Robison, and long one to Denby. . . . This is going to be a national scandal before all is over."[15]

Slattery conveyed whatever information he possessed, as well as his fears, to La Follette. On April 21, a week after the news of the Teapot Dome lease had appeared in the *Wall Street Journal*, La Follette introduced in the Senate a resolution which, with one major addition, was almost a carbon copy of the one Slattery had suggested to him in the middle of March. Since the Teapot Dome lease had now been added to the book of suspicions, the original resolution was adjusted to include it in the call for information. La Follette asked that the Secretary of the Interior be directed to send to the Senate all the facts about the leasing of

14 *The Oil and Gas Journal*, April 27, 1922, pp. 7, 100; Jan. 13, 1922, p. 6, quoted in Robert A. Waller, "Business Reactions to the Teapot Dome Affair: 1922 to 1925" (Master's thesis, University of Illinois, 1958), 10; New York *World*, April 19, 1922; Lathrop to Slattery, April 21, 1922, Slattery Papers.

15 Extract from Slattery diary, quoted in Slattery, "From Roosevelt to Roosevelt," 87.

Naval Oil Reserves One, Two, and Three to private persons or corporations. He wanted a list of all oil leases, all executive orders and papers authorizing or regulating those leases, and all correspondence, papers, instructions, requests, arguments, and actions relating to them in the files of the Interior Department. The Senate offered no objection. This resolution called only for information, not an investigation, but, as Slattery noted, it "could not be met with any brief perfunctory reply such as had been given in response to the Kendrick resolution. Nor could the excuse be put forward that the Department did not know what information was desired by the Senate."[16]

On April 28, Josephus Daniels' Raleigh *News and Observer* offered the editorial opinion that "every day since the reserves were created there has been a well oiled propaganda to open them—and the recent action, wholly indefensible, promises to be the subject of congressional investigation." La Follette and Slattery had already set out to make the promise fact. As Slattery expressed it, "the war on Fall goes merrily on." And he wrote to Pinchot's secretary in Milford, Pennsylvania, explaining an inability to make a visit there: "I could not . . . leave [Washington] just when the Fall resolution was coming up. Confidentially, it would have completely bogged down because I know most of the facts." The "Fall resolution" about which Slattery wrote referred to the new action which La Follette was to take in the Senate, amending and amplifying his resolution of April 21. Since Fall had failed to explain or justify his recent oil leases in any way, La Follette decided that he must try to smoke him out by calling for an investigation. Just before noon on April 28, as he left his office to go to the Senate floor, La Follette said: "I am going just as far as I can in the charges I make . . . I can't prove that there has been corruption but if we get this investigation I am confident it will be shown."[17]

La Follette's afternoon speech to the Senate was an arraignment. In scathing language he charged crime and pleaded for indictment. Vice-President Coolidge was in the chair, and a

[16] *Cong. Rec.*, 67 Cong., 2 Sess. (April 21, 1922), 5792; Slattery, "From Roosevelt to Roosevelt," 84.

[17] Raleigh *News and Observer*, April 28, 1922; Slattery to H. H. Chapman, April 28, 1922; Slattery to Philip Stahlnecker, April 27, 1922, Slattery Papers; and La Follette, *Robert M. La Follette*, II, 1048.

goodly number of Republicans were in their seats when La Follette began. As he opened with a proposed amendment to his
resolution of April 21, the Republicans "promptly vacated" their
side of the chamber, and only a scattering of Democrats remained. Several administration stalwarts already had told La
Follette that they would bury his earlier resolution; ignoring the
threat, La Follette asked that the Senate Committee on Public
Lands and Surveys "be authorized to investigate this entire subject of leases upon naval oil reserves . . . and to report its findings and recommendations to the Senate." When the resolution
was read, Senator Henry Cabot Lodge, Republican floor-leader,
at once started consultation with several Republican senators.

La Follette, meantime, began to sketch a history of oil reserve
withdrawals, recalling past exploitation and subterfuges used to
gain private entry. He referred to the 1921 executive transfer of
the reserves and warned his Republican colleagues that "we cannot permit a record to be made here which will parallel the record
of Mr. Ballinger. . . . " He condemned the Interior Department
as "the sluiceway for a large part of the corruption to which this
government of ours is subjected. . . . " The transfer of the oil
reserves to this department—one "befouled under all administrations"—had come "as a distinct shock to the country." Even as
administration supporters huddled in the cloakrooms devising a
block to his resolution, La Follette tongue-lashed Republicans
Fall and Denby and asked the Senate why it should not inquire
"who were the real organizers of the Mammoth Oil Co. who were
to be favored by the Government with a special privilege in value
beyond the dreams of Croesus?" A great national policy had been
reversed, and the nation was endangered; Congress and the public should have the facts.[18]

Senator Gilbert M. Hitchcock, Democrat from Nebraska, interrupted La Follette. He pointed out that La Follette was "making some amazing revelations," but since scarcely a Republican
was present, "most of the Senate are not aware of that fact."
Would Coolidge order a roll-call? Republicans filed in for the

---

[18] *Cong. Rec.*, 67 Cong., 2 Sess. (April 28, 1922), 6041-50; Slattery,
"Story of Teapot Dome," 42-43; and Sucher memorandum, Slattery Papers
(All accounts of the Senate reception of La Follette's speech, unless other-
wise indicated, are from this manuscript.).

count, then filed out again. As La Follette continued, many of them returned and soon the chamber was filled, as he attacked Fall's justification for the leasing policy. He cited telegrams from geologists, who declared that Teapot Dome lay in a geologic saddle and could not be drained by adjacent wells; the excuse of drainage, he argued, was an old and specious plea of the exploiters. In conclusion he asked for unanimous consent that his resolution be taken up for adoption. Reed Smoot, Republican of Utah, objected; he wanted to study the proposal first. La Follette replied that it was nothing more than a request for an inquiry. Smoot still wanted to read it. On that note, the day's session ended.

The next afternoon, following a brief debate, the Senate adopted the resolution by a unanimous vote—fifty-eight to zero, with thirty-nine Republicans voting for an investigation of their party's administration. Perhaps by coincidence, that same afternoon the Senate, in further response to the Kendrick resolution, received a copy of the Teapot Dome contract from Secretary Fall himself. The conservationists at last were storming his position.[19]

[19] *Cong. Rec.*, 67 Cong., 2 Sess. (April 28, 1922), 6041-50, and (April 29, 1922), 6097. The Democrats provided the remaining nineteen affirmative votes. There were thirty-eight Senators not voting: twenty-one Republicans and seventeen Democrats.

4

Harding and Fall Depart

When the Senate adopted La Follette's resolution, the initiative for investigation passed to the Senate Committee on Public Lands and Surveys. The conservationists, having exposed Fall to the committee's scrutiny, withdrew to observe from afar. Occasionally they scurried back with aid and suggestions, but soon Teapot Dome transcended their immediate interests and aspirations.

La Follette's request that the Public Lands Committee conduct the investigation stemmed from calculation.[1] The logical choice, the Naval Affairs Committee, was weighted with administration supporters. Although the Public Lands Committee contained Reed Smoot, Irvine Lenroot, and other party stalwarts, its roster also included George W. Norris of Nebraska, Edwin E. Ladd of

[1] Belle and Fola La Follette point out that he "considered carefully whether to ask" the Naval Affairs or the Public Lands Committee to investigate. *Robert M. La Follette*, II, 1051.

North Dakota, Peter Norbeck of South Dakota—Republican in-
surgents all—and Democrats Thomas J. Walsh of Montana, and
Kendrick of Wyoming.[2] La Follette knew his men. Ladd had
ridden into the Senate on votes from North Dakota's Non-Partisan League, and in 1924 he would eschew Republican lines and
support the third party candidacy of La Follette, losing thereby
his party rank for committee assignments. Norris made a career
of insurgency, magnificently scorning party lines; as he once informed a critic who charged him with being "an enemy" to the
Republican party, "party solidarity is . . . not paramount. The
investigation of the Teapot Dome . . . was brought about by
such outcasts as you would have me be." Norbeck, an old prairie
apostle of Theodore Roosevelt, had opposed Harding's nomination to the last in 1920 and was consistently at odds with the
Harding administration. Kendrick's support for a genuine investigation was obvious. Walsh showed reluctance to investigate at
first. As a westerner, he had certain sympathy for Fall's ranch-
ing and prospecting background; furthermore, no conservationist himself, he had in the past advocated leasing the oil reserves.
But La Follette considered Walsh an able constitutional lawyer,
and he had "absolute confidence" in Walsh's integrity.[3]

Reed Smoot, rank partisan and chairman of the committee, was
La Follette's real concern. His biographer has noted that Reed
Smoot was "a Senator who would work . . . with almost monstrous
energy, and . . . always in the interest of the party program."

2 The committee did not retain this same roster throughout the investigation; some of these men remained, while others departed. La Follette, of
course, could calculate only upon the membership as it existed at the time
of his resolution.
    3 Robert L. Morlan, *Political Prairie Fire: The Nonpartisan League, 1915-
1922* (Minneapolis, 1955), 300 and *passim;* Doane Robinson, "Edwin F.
Ladd," *Dictionary of American Biography* (20 vols.; New York, 1928-37), X,
525; George W. Norris, *Fighting Liberal, The Autobiography of George W.
Norris* (New York, 1945), *passim;* David Fellman, "The Liberalism of
Senator Norris," *American Political Science Review,* XL (Feb., 1946), 27-
52; Richard Lowitt, "The Making of an Insurgent," *Mid-America,* XLII
(April, 1960), 105-15 (Norris' statement about party solidarity is in Norris
to Rev. James E. Wagner, June 11, 1924, Tray 8, Box 1, Norris Papers, Division of Manuscripts, Library of Congress); Gilbert C. Fite, *Peter Norbeck:
Prairie Statesman* (Columbia, Missouri, 1948), 94-95 and *passim;* J. Leonard Bates, "Senator Walsh of Montana, 1918-1924; A Liberal Under Pressure" (Ph.D. dissertation, University of North Carolina, 1952), 309-10; and
La Follette, *Robert M. La Follette,* II, 1052.

Although in his Senate career Smoot had given "full and complete support" to the Forest Service and to conservation policies in general, in 1922, with the administration endangered by attack, Smoot's legendary loyalty to party was to dictate his behavior. To Smoot, the party could indulge in private and internal disputes "but there must be a solid external front." Lenroot, following an early friendship with La Follette, had become a party regular only less devout and was close to Harding and Coolidge. He and Smoot were the two members most likely to carry whitewash to the committee's sessions.[4]

Hearings did not begin until eighteen months after the Senate had approved the investigation. Slattery believed that Smoot and his Republican cohorts on the Public Lands Committee delayed any investigation until after the Congressional election of autumn, 1922; however, Senator Walsh once commented: "It is scarcely fair to Smoot to charge him with the delay. . . . " Labor leader Samuel Gompers blamed the newspapers for not arousing sufficient interest to stir the committee to activity. In March, 1924, he declared that "when the lease was signed in secret the great newspapers of the country were silent. For weeks afterward they were silent. For months afterward most of them were silent." Gompers' memory, however, must have dimmed. On May 7, 1922, the New York *Times* reported: "Overnight . . . Teapot Dome has become a matter of Congressional controversy which threatens to assume major proportions. . . . Many are the charges whispered in the corridors of the Senate and House." Two days later the Santa Fe *New Mexican* reported that "the Democrats expect to use the old cry of 'Ballingerism' for all it is worth in connection with the [forthcoming] probe of the leases. . . ." On May 5, 1922, John Lathrop of the New York *World* informed

[4] The quotations and judgments on Smoot's overall partisanship are from Milton R. Merrill, "Reed Smoot: Apostle in Politics," (Ph.D. dissertation, Columbia University, 1950), preface, and pp. 101-102, 250, 498. The interpretation of Smoot's behavior during the Teapot Dome investigation in all cases is my own; for all its excellence, Merrill's study does not consider Smoot's activities in the investigation at all. A portion of Merrill's dissertation appears in *Reed Smoot: Utah Politician*, ("Utah State Agricultural College Monograph Series," I, no. 2 [Logan (?), 1953]); see also his "Reed Smoot, Apostle in Politics," *The Western Humanities*, IX (Winter, 1954-55), 1-12. On Lenroot, see La Follette, *Robert M. La Follette*, II, 942, 1015-18 1051, and especially 1058.

Slattery: "I have a story in the Sunday *World* two days hence, *re* the oil leases, etc." Then on May 13, the National Association of Oil Producers filed a protest with the Senate against the Teapot Dome lease, calling it "a return to the era of landgrabbing and carpetbagging whose hydrahead of iniquity was crushed by . . . Roosevelt almost a decade ago." This statement received wide coverage in press reports. La Follette, who submitted the protest, said that he was receiving "a large number of communications of like character." Nevertheless, the committee dallied, and the explanation for their behavior is not clear. Perhaps Smoot did procrastinate from partisan motives. Possibly feeling about Teapot Dome, except among those directly involved, bordered on unconcern. Senator Walsh himself seemed unaware of the sensations implicit in Teapot Dome, and perhaps therein lies the better explanation for the delay.[5]

Once his resolution had passed, La Follette, looking for a bellwether among the Public Lands Committee members, urged Walsh to "take the leadership in investigating." Senator Kendrick joined La Follette in his plea. Walsh, already holding more committee assignments than any man in the Senate, accepted with reluctance and hesitation. Even a year later, on the very eve of the committee's first hearing, duty, more than interest, appeared to be motivating him. To his Montana colleague, Senator Burton

[5]Slattery, "Story of Teapot Dome," 52; Walsh to Lewis Gannett, June 9, 1928, Thomas J. Walsh Papers, Division of Manuscripts, Library of Congress; *American Federationist,* XXXI (March, 1924), 244-45—Gompers also claimed that "Teapot Dome . . . was exposed to the world through the activities of the American Federation of Labor." How, Gompers did not say; New York *Times,* May 7, 1922, Sec. 7, p. 1; Santa Fe *New Mexican,* May 9, 1922; Lathrop to Slattery, May 5, 1922, Slattery Papers (Slattery, meanwhile, according to his autobiographical account, was "following the oil situation" partly through the assistance of "men like John D. Erwin of the New York Evening World, Charley Michelson of the Morning World, Gilson Gardner and others of the Scripps-Howard papers who were all following this oil story"; in "Roosevelt to Roosevelt," 84); *Cong. Rec.,* 67 Cong., 2 Sess. (May 13, 1922), 6893.

The oil industry did not neglect to discuss the Teapot Dome lease or to speculate over the delay in the investigation. See Charles E. Kern, "Teapot Dome Causes a Furor," *The Oil and Gas Journal,* XX (April 20, 1922), 81; and "Teapot Dome Drilling Contract Arouses Storm of Opposition," *National Petroleum News* (Cleveland), XIV (April 19, 1922), 23, cited in Waller, "Business Reactions to Teapot Dome," 13; Waller concludes that "Business, as represented chiefly by the oil concerns, was vitally interested [in Teapot Dome, although] the oil industry was divided within itself over the propriety of the leasing." (pp. 22-24)

K. Wheeler, he wrote: "I am handling this Teapot Dome matter at his [La Follette's] special insistence and urgent request."
Walsh realized that Smoot and other Republican members of the
committee were unsympathetic to the probe, and this helped to
persuade him to take informal command of a committee containing a Republican majority and a Republican chairman.[6]

La Follette gave Walsh all the evidence that he had gathered
on Fall. Then in June, 1922, Walsh suddenly received more material than he could handle. Fall, in response to the resolution,
sent to the Senate a truckload of documents. They arrived along
with a letter of transmittal from President Harding. Fall had notified Harding of his compliance with the Senate resolution and
had sent Harding what the President called "a full and compre-
hensive report, probably not contemplated in the resolution." It
gave, according to Harding, "the details of the handling of all
naval reserve petroleum matters up to the present . . . including
full explanation of the contracts . . . and the necessity for
[them]." Harding saw Fall's report not as "a defense of either
specific acts or . . . general policies," but as an "explanation to
which the Senate is entitled. . . . " Harding's letter of transmittal
concluded with a clear statement: Fall and Denby's oil policy
"was submitted to me prior to the adoption thereof, and the policy decided upon and the subsequent acts have at all times had
my entire approval." The letter that Fall had sent to him, massive in detail, was a voluble explanation and defense of Interior's
oil policy. Harding, whether or not understanding or even reading it, had accepted Fall's argument. The leasing of Teapot
Dome, afterwards if not before the act, had the approval of the
President of the United States.[7]

[6] La Follette, *Robert M. La Follette*, II, 1051-52; Thomas J. Walsh, "The
True History of Teapot Dome," *The Forum*, LXXII (July, 1924), 1-12;
Bates, "Senator Walsh of Montana," 309-10; Walsh to Wheeler, Oct. 10,
1923, Box 374, Walsh Papers. Walsh later wrote that he also assented
"because the Federal Trade Commission had just reported that, owing to
conditions prevailing in the oil fields of Wyoming and Montana, the people
of my state were paying prices for gasoline [higher than] anywhere else in
the Union." Walsh, "True History of Teapot Dome," *loc. cit.*

[7] Slattery, "From Roosevelt to Roosevelt," 90; Walsh, "True History of
Teapot Dome," *loc. cit.; Leases upon Reserves* (1924), 24-68; reprint of
Harding's letter of transmittal, *Leases upon Reserves* (1924), p. 25; see also
Cong. Rec., 67 Cong., 2 Sess. (June 8, 1922), 8398; Fall's letter to Harding
in *Leases, upon Reserves* (1924), 27-68.

Fall—his characteristic sarcasm showing—had pointed out to
Harding that, to meet the Senate's demand for documents, it
"became necessary to search all the files of . . . the General Land
Office; the Bureau of Geological Survey; the Bureau of Mines;
the personal files of the Secretaries of the Interior; the records of
the mails and files division of this department, etc. . . [as well as
to] check up our files and correspondence with the records of
the Navy Department." The results, in Fall's estimation, would
"aggregate between five and six thousand pages of matter . . .
delivered."[8]

Slattery had anticipated that Fall would try to swamp the committee with a mass of documents too voluminous to permit full
analysis of all items. Even so, Philip Wells, Pinchot's legal counsel, doubted that Fall had sent all pertinent material. He told
La Follette: "I have not forgotten the supression of embarrassing documents that was attempted in the Ballinger-Pinchot investigation. Only a careful study of the documents . . . sent . . .
would disclose traces of omissions." Wells supposed that "the
practical thing to do . . . is to have printed the documents now
submitted and to have them carefully studied by experts and
trustworthy persons." La Follette followed his advice. Soon after Fall's material arrived at the committee room, La Follette and
Slattery held a conference at Walsh's office, where they agreed
that Slattery would work through the great mass during the summer "and be ready for the hearings on the oil leases in the fall."[9]

[8] *Leases upon Reserves* (1924), 27-68. Fall was at home in Three Rivers
when the Senate approved La Follette's resolution. Upon receiving a wire
from the Interior Department, informing him of the Senate's action, Fall
replied: "I am wiring New York Herald answering their invitation [to] present my side of case that all documents letters etc. are being prepared for
senate committee and that I am much pleased that investigation has been
ordered." Finney Safford to Fall, and Fall to Safford, May 2, 1922, Fall
Papers. One month later, in Washington, Fall wrote to Reed Smoot: "Immediately upon being advised by telegram of the adoption of the Senate
Resolution requesting this Department to furnish information . . . , I instructed officials of this Department, by telegraph, to prepare all such data.
. . . Immediately upon my return, I gave my personal attention to the matter and we have been assiduously engaged in collecting all data called for,
as well as any other. . . . I think that copies of every memorandum, letter,
telegram, etc. . . . have been included." Fall to Smoot, June 2, 1922, Box
1, Fall Papers.

[9] Philip Wells to La Follette, June 6, 1922, copy in Slattery Papers; and
Slattery, "From Roosevelt to Roosevelt," 90.

Slattery went through the material, and occasionally La Follette also turned a hand to the analysis. But their hopes for "hearings in the fall" went astray. Instead of beginning the hearings, Walsh started what he later called "a laborious study" of the evidence. Between June, 1922, and October, 1923—a period of some sixteen months—he made what he called "a critical analysis of the lease itself"; he studied past legislation relevant to the leasing; and he sent letters to "all journals which had exhibited any special interest in the subject," asking for the sources of statements they had made in their columns. Most of this activity he crammed into the summer and fall of 1923, for Walsh was slow to become aroused, and not until then did his distrust of Fall fully develop. Slattery and Pinchot were willing to see corruption at once in any program endangering conservation. Walsh, however, had never been enthusiastic over the Pinchot doctrine, and unless Fall's policy was shaded with corruption, Walsh was not the man to oppose it. Not until early 1923 would he indicate any real misgivings over Fall's conduct; by March 12 of that year, he was becoming "very much interested" in the hearings, then scheduled to begin in the fall when the next session of Congress opened. Perhaps by then, evidence, if not Democratic demands, had begun to break through Walsh's caution.[10]

La Follette, for one, had continued to supply Walsh with information. As soon as his request for the oil investigation had been approved, La Follette, partly to assist Walsh in building a case against Fall, had called for an inquiry into another question. For some time, one of his aides, Gilbert Roe, had been gathering clues that encouraged La Follette to launch an investigation into the high prices of crude oil, gasoline, and other petroleum products and to determine "whether there is any natural reason for the change of prices . . . or whether there has been any understanding . . . between various oil companies to raise or depress prices, or [to] prevent effective competition." La Follette won co-operation from the Democrats, and on May 13, 1922, Kenneth McKellar, Democrat from Tennessee, introduced the resolution

[10] Walsh, "True History of Teapot Dome" *loc. cit.;* and Walsh to Hamilton Holt, March 12, 1923, cited in Bates, "Senator Walsh of Montana," 310. For Walsh's record on conservation, see Bates, "Senator Walsh of Montana," 29, 292-303.

to investigate. In the brief debate that followed that day, Joseph
T. Robinson, Democrat from Arkansas, supported the resolution,
which finally carried on June 5. A subcommittee, with La Follette as chairman, began work immediately. Much of what it
disclosed, La Follette turned over to Walsh early in 1923. Among
the committee's findings was evidence that Fall "had been duped
or had lied about his activities."[11]

Meantime, in August, 1922, Kendrick of Wyoming—after weeks
of silence—raised a powerful voice of accusation against Fall.
Kendrick had studied Fall's report to Harding "long and carefully" and had decided that the lease was "a shameful and un-
necessary destruction of the final reserve of the Navy; that the
terms were not only improvident but were viciously and criminally wasteful." The contract "does not, as it is claimed, promote
any real competition but on the contrary strengthens and makes
more enduring the monopolistic control of the oil industry." Furthermore, the lease could not be justified by any drainage theory,
for there "is not a single tract of privately owned land within
several miles of the Teapot field." He concluded that the contract was "so disastrous to the national interest and so outrageous
in its terms that it could never have been negotiated and executed in the open. . . ." It was a bargain that, if defended by the
Harding administration, would "forever discredit" the Interior
Department and "eventually plague and even damn that administration." Kendrick met only perfunctory challenge from the
floor; the Senators appeared ignorant, if not apathetic, over a
tempest arising among them.[12]

However much Kendrick increased the pressure for action,
neither Walsh nor the rest of the committee made any visible
moves to begin hearings. Pinchot himself was still unable to see
the oil for the forests. He had won a sensational race for the
governorship in Pennsylvania, defeating the intrenched Republican organization for the nomination, and then drubbing his Dem-

---

[11] Portion of La Follette's resolution, *Cong. Rec.*, 67 Cong., 2 Sess. (May
15, 1922), 6932; La Follette, *Robert M. La Follette*, II, 1052-53; *Cong.
Rec.*, 67 Cong., 2 Sess. (May 13 and 15, and June 5, 1922), 6867, 6893-94,
6932, and 8140; Bates, "Senator Walsh of Montana," 308. For the La Follette investigation, see U.S. Senate, *High Cost of Gasoline and Other Petroleum Products*, 67 Cong., 2 Sess. and 4 Sess. (4 vols, Washington, 1923).
[12] *Cong. Rec.*, 67 Cong., 2 Sess. (Aug. 25, 1922), 11785 ff.

ocratic opponent in the election. A week after his victory, he wrote to Harding: "I have just been . . . told that an effort will be made, with administration support, to transfer the Forest Service to the Interior Department during the coming session. . . . Nothing . . . could hurt the cause of conservation more than such a transfer." Secretary of Agriculture Wallace also heard the report, and his *Wallace's Farmer* renewed the argument against any transfer.[13]

While Pinchot and Wallace fretted over the Forest Service, Fall continued to dispose of the oil reserves at his command. On December 15, the *Wall Street Journal* reported that Edward L. Doheny had secured an extension of the earlier contract between the government and his Pan-American Petroleum and Transportation Company. In the original contract of April 25, 1922, Doheny had been granted preferential rights to further leases. In accord with his own obligations in that contract, he now agreed to drill wells in Reserve Number One to prevent drainage; he also would complete construction of fuel oil tanks at Pearl Harbor and fill them with royalty oil, as agreed to in the April contract.[14] The *Journal* had no reason to suspect that Doheny had been granted more than that. In time, however, Walsh would discover that Fall also had leased Doheny the entire Elk Hills Reserve.

As December waned, rumors spread that Fall soon would resign from the Cabinet. On December 26, the White House announced that Harding had no information on the subject. Fall, on Christmas vacation in Virginia, said nothing for publication. Then on January 2, 1923, eight months after the Senate had approved La Follette's resolution, the White House announced that Fall had entered the Cabinet at great financial sacrifice; now he was resigning, effective March 4, in order to devote his time to business affairs in the Southwest. Although he and Harding still were friends, Fall reportedly was piqued over several acts and shortcomings of the Harding administration and Congress. One source of his vexation, claimed his friends, was the "long undercover controversy" over his plan for transferring various agricul-

[13] Pinchot to Harding, Nov. 15, 1922, copy in Slattery Papers; *Wallace's Farmer*, Nov. 24, 1922, p. 6.
[14] *Wall Street Journal*, Dec. 15, 1922, cited in *Leases upon Reserves* (1924), 413; see the latter for reprint of the December contract.

ture bureaus to Interior and the failure to accomplish his plans
for reorganizing Alaskan administration.[15]

If Fall listed the pending oil investigation among his griev-
ances, the *Times* did not report it. Indeed, the oil inquiry may
have had little influence upon Fall's decision. As early as February, 1922—two months before La Follette's request for an investigation—rumors had Fall about to resign. Loss of influence in
New Mexican politics, where he had long been a power, as well
as disappointment over his relative unimportance in the Cabinet
had supposedly turned Fall's thoughts toward resignation. There
was much speculation that Fall, intending to continue as a dominant voice in New Mexico politics even after resigning his Senate post in favor of the secretaryship, had been unable sufficiently to influence such New Mexicans as Senator Holm Bursum. On
the other hand (so went the story), even while losing voice in
his home state, Fall also had been unable to fulfill his ambition
to be the dominant figure in Harding's administration. Secretary
of State Hughes, for example, had refused to listen to Fall's advice regarding foreign affairs. Finally, even his plans for Interior
policy had been largely frustrated.[16]

If William Allen White was right in his recollections of the
Harding administration, Fall may have been influenced by his
growing isolation from Harding. In the winter of 1922, White
had a talk with Harding at the White House. He recalled leaving
the White House "with a feeling that it was the scene of a terrible

[15] New York *Times*, Dec. 27, 1922, p. 29; Jan. 3, 1923, pp. 12, 19.

[16] For an early analysis of Fall's possible resignation, see the Santa Fe
New Mexican, Feb. 19, 1922, which reported that "eastern papers" for some
time had been carrying the rumor. See *ibid.*, May 20, 1922, and Denver
Post, May 20, 1922, for further expression of southwestern sentiment. Meantime, the New York *Times*, March 12, 1922, Sec. 7, p. 1, carried a special
story on Fall's differences with Harding and the Cabinet. The Santa Fe
New Mexican, no admirer of Fall, is especially rich in material on New
Mexico politics during this period. For stories on Fall as a state boss and
for some account of his waning influence in the state after becoming Secretary of Interior, see the issues of Aug. 24 and Sept. 15, 16, 20, 26, and 27,
1920; August 2 and 19, and Sept. 3, 1921, and Aug. 22 and 23, 1922. See
also George Curry, *An Autobiography*, 292-93, and Fall to Herbert B. Holt,
July 22, 1922, and Fall to C. E. Mitchell, July 31, 1922, Fall Papers. For
southwestern defenders of Fall against charges of bossism or for support
of him in general during the early 1920's, see Rio Grande *Republic*, Oct. 7,
1920, and March 10, 1921; Santa Fe *New Mexican*, April 5, 1921; and
Hutchinson, *Bar-Cross Man*, 165.

struggle. Fall was the symbol of one of the forces, Hoover of another, that was grappling for supremacy with the confused mind of the President." By now, according to White, Washington was abuzz with a "thousand little stories, rumors and suspicions of irregularity," and White was convinced that Harding, aware of the conflicts and rumors surfacing all around him, was trying to break with his sordid past. This, among other things, meant abandoning Albert Fall. White's rich imagination probably created evidence of more moral struggle than actually existed. Furthermore, when Fall did resign, Hoover wrote to him that the Interior Department had "never had so constructive and legal a headship as you gave it." And reports had it that Harding, rather than deserting Fall, had offered him an appointment to the Supreme Court. Nevertheless, between Harding and Fall the old camaraderie was missing.[17]

In Las Cruces, where Fall had first practiced law, entered New Mexico politics, and gained a great many supporters, an editor wrote of his resignation: "The fact that President Harding offered Mr. Fall a position on the Supreme Court bench proves the howls of the jackels had nothing to do with his resignation." On the other hand, a good friend and fellow New Mexican, Eugene Manlove Rhodes, saw Fall's resignation as "a monstrous, sacrificial injustice." One sympathetic New Mexico newspaper reported that Fall's resignation was "generally regretted" in the Southwest; regional reclamation projects in particular had lost "a tried and worthy friend at the seat of government." Fall's "sympathetic understanding of the difficulties to be overcome in establishing homes in the desert won for him the esteem and confidence of . . . settlers, by whom he was regarded as a real friend." On the other side of this coin, though, some of Fall's critics found fault not with his morals or abilities but with his very western orientation: "An able lawyer, with pronounced Far Western ideas as to . . . conservation, his appointment made many of the friends of conservation . . . nervous. . . . His departure will relieve a certain amount of real apprehension—due not to his gen-

[17] White, *Autobiography*, 619-20; Hoover to Fall, March 12, 1923, as quoted in David H. Stratton, "Behind Teapot Dome: Some Personal Insights," *The Business History Review*, XXXI (Winter, 1957), 389.

eral qualifications as a public man, but to his local environment."[18]

Harry Daugherty saw no relation between Fall's retirement and the pending Senate investigation: "Fall . . . was not under fire when he gave Harding his resignation. . . . He resigned to go abroad on a mission of oil development and a prospective merger." But Slattery believed otherwise: "The threat of the coming . . . investigation . . . drove Fall out of the Cabinet." Slattery was in upstate New York on his way home when he heard of Fall's resignation, and he wrote in his diary that "his demise gave me satisfaction all the way to New York." For Slattery, Fall's resignation marked "the end of one phase of the oil fight." Pinchot saw a connection between Fall's resignation and his feud with the conservationists and wrote in one letter: "I had a good deal to do, I think, with the decision of Fall to resign." Several friends wrote to Pinchot, asking him to propose various names to Harding for successors to Fall, and to one of them he replied that "President Harding credits me with having had something to do with forcing Fall's resignation, which I am by no means disposed to deny, and, therefore, any action I might take would hurt rather than help the man I would recommend."[19]

As Fall retired, he did reveal chagrin over the accusations lately thrown at him. In an article which the New York *Times* called "Secretary Fall's Soliloquy on Quitting Harding Cabinet," he wrote of the obligations facing persons in government service and the obstacles which worked against a full public understanding of their actions. By implication his own career was clearly in his thought. "The public mind," he said, without full information on decisions and actions taken, cannot "crystallize into judgments unless information is conveyed to it thereafter." To Fall, history had shown "that such information is often never acquired, or, if so [it is] after the object of this public attack has not only gone out of the public service, but has departed from life."[20]

[18] Rio Grande *Republic*, Jan. 4, 1923; Hutchinson, *Bar-Cross Man*, 170-71; Rio Grande *Farmer*, March 22, 1923; New York *Tribune* editorial, reprinted in Santa Fe *New Mexican*, March 12, 1923.

[19] Harry M. Daugherty, *Inside Story of the Harding Tragedy* (New York, 1932), 196; Slattery, "From Roosevelt to Roosevelt," 90-91, including quotations from his diary; Pinchot to John E. Ballaine, Feb. 15, 1923, and Pinchot to Marshall McLean, Feb. 5, 1923, Boxes 244 and 250, Pinchot Papers.

[20] New York *Times*, March 4, 1923, Sec. 7, p. 14.

Fall did not have to wait so long for a judgment. Not everyone had heard William Allen White's thousand little stories, not everyone had followed Fall's Cabinet career as closely as had Pinchot and Slattery; and on March 4, he left for New Mexico with colors flying and character unsullied, and later that spring he journeyed to Russia with Harry Sinclair, who was seeking an oil concession in Sakhalin. But Fall's name and his record were not entirely forgotten along the Potomac; nine months after his resignation, his reputation was to be wholly discredited.

In early February, 1923, the Public Lands Committee made a feeble gesture toward activity, when Chairman Reed Smoot asked the director of the Geological Survey for a list of "the principal geologists in the United States." Furnished with this list and with names submitted by some of its own members, the committee met to select two geologists who were "to make an examination of the Teapot Dome and report to the committee at the earliest date possible." Then in the Senate in late February, Senator Thaddeus Caraway, Democrat from Arkansas, injected Fall's name into a rambling diatribe on Cabinet members and sundry political weaknesses of the Harding administration: "Whenever the lid on the Teapot Dome blows off—and it is already stewing . . . Fall is not going to have to carry the entire responsibility for giving away all of the national wealth. He is entitled to only his part of it. The President also 'whitewashed' him." Caraway's remark was a mere parenthesis in the Senate's activity that day.[21] The senators were busy with other affairs. But the jibe, trifling as it was, marked Caraway's entry into the Fall chase; and within the year, his voice would harmonize with a great chorus of Democratic colleagues, likewise in pursuit.

As the summer of 1923 neared, while the Public Lands Committee's two geologists poked around the Teapot Dome reserve and Walsh of Montana prepared for a brief vacation, Warren G. Harding acted to strengthen his political future. He was surrounded with difficulties. Congressional elections of the past autumn had reduced the Republican majority to eight in the Senate and five in the House. The farm bloc, with its core of insurgent

[21] *Leases upon Reserves* (1924), 69-174, for reprints of the letter of instructions to the geologists, and their final reports to the committee; and *Cong. Rec.*, 67 Cong., 4 Sess. (Feb. 20, 1923), 4100, for Caraway's remarks.

Republicans, now held a balance of power in Congress that sty-
mied the administration's legislative program. And ever more
clearly White's "thousand little stories" crept along the corridors
of the capital. The Department of Justice was said to be lush with
corruption. One of Harding's "Ohio Gang," Jesse Smith, brought
to Washington by Attorney-General Daugherty, was dead, either
from murder or suicide. There were rumors also of looting by the
Alien Property Custodian and by Charles R. Forbes, Director of
the Veterans Bureau. White suggests that by now Harding "must
have been assailed by the devils of his past. Always there must
have been, in the dark periphery of his consciousness, cackling,
ribald voices . . . drunken, raucous in debauch; the high-tensioned
giggle of women pursued; the voices of men whispering in the
greedy lechery of political intrigue. . . ." On June 20, 1923, the
unhappy President left Washington on a transcontinental tour.[22]

Harding delivered speeches and eagerly showed his good fellow-
ship wherever his train paused on its journey toward the west
coast. And as his train crossed the Kansas plains, he chatted with
William Allen White, while they sat in the Presidential private
car. "I have no trouble with my enemies," the President said. "I
can take care of them. It is my . . . friends that are giving me
my trouble." In July, Harding reached Alaska, then moved down
to Seattle. By the end of the month, weary and obviously under
great strain, he was in San Francisco.[23]

[22] William Allen White, *Masks in a Pageant* (New York, 1928), 425;
James Shideler, "The Neo-Progressives: Reform Politics in the United States,
1920-1925," (Ph.D. dissertation, University of California, 1945), 155; Frederick Paxson, *Postwar Years: Normalcy, 1918-1923* (Berkeley, 1948), 370
ff.; William E. Leuchtenburg, *The Perils of Prosperity, 1914-32* (Chicago,
1958), 84-103. Paxson's book contains an unusually thoughtful summary
and evaluation of the Harding administration; Leuchtenburg's chapter is a
brief but scintillating look.

[23] The quotation is from White, *Autobiography*, 623-24. (The ellipses
do not stand for "Goddam." Harding, as quoted by White, did use the
oath earlier; White, evidently impressed by Harding's statement, quoted it
several times, with and without the expletive. White's more pungent version
has become standard for almost all discussions of Harding.) Before Harding left Washington, the White House had wired to White in Emporia:
"The President would be very glad if you could arrange to go on his train
from Kansas City to Hutchinson." George B. Christian, Jr. to White, June
20, 1923, William Allen White Papers, Box 324, Division of Manuscripts,
Library of Congress. For interpretations of Harding's mood at this time,
see White, *Autobiography*, 615-24. Coolidge, with the maddening indirec-

On August 2, Gifford Pinchot wrote to Henry C. Wallace of
Harding's recent activity. To Wallace, who had gone with the
chief executive on the Alaskan tour, Pinchot offered "as vigorous
congratulations as I ever sent to anybody on the magnificent results of your trip . . ." and gave him direct credit for a great
speech on conservation Harding had made in Seattle. To Pinchot,
Harding's address meant "that the two-year effort of the Seattle
boomers to grab the resources of Alaska has failed, that the good
old Roosevelt Alaska policy has been sustained, and that Fall and
his work so far as Alaska is concerned has been definitely and
finally repudiated." In his opinion, Harding's speech disposed
"pretty well of any danger of effective attack against the Forest
Service during the rest of this administration. . . . Altogether," Pinchot was "as cheerful as a bug in a rug."[24]

The champion of conservationism was right: from conviction or
otherwise Harding would make no further changes in the Forest
Service. As he rested in San Francisco on the night of July 28, the
President became ill, and on August 2, he suddenly died. Cause
of death was stated to be embolism. But White wondered: "How
could the doctors diagnose an illness that was part terror, part
shame, and part utter confusion!" The Kansas editor was sure
that Harding had realized how "his friends of the Ohio gang had

tion characteristic of his autobiography, wrote that before Harding left
Washington "he had discovered that some whom he had trusted betrayed
him and he had been forced to call them to account. It is known that this
discovery was a very heavy grief to him, perhaps more than he could bear."
Coolidge, *Autobiography*, 168. For an early estimate—and still one of the
best—of Harding, see Preston Slosson, "Warren G. Harding: A Revised Estimate," *Current History*, XXXIII (November, 1930), 174-79. Other contemporaries of Harding judged him largely as Slosson and White did; see, for
example, Cyrenus Cole, *I Remember, I Remember* (Iowa City, 1936), 438-
39; James E. Watson, *As I Knew Them* (Indianapolis, 1936), 226 ff.; and
Nicholas Murray Butler, *Across the Busy Years; Recollection and Reflections* (2 vols.; New York, 1939-40), I, 410-12. A friendly sketch, bordering
on sympathy, is Finley Peter Dunne, "A Look at Harding from the Sidelines," *Saturday Evening Post*, CCIX (September 12, 1936), 24-25, and
74-79. Allan Nevins, in the *Dictionary of American Biography*, VIII, 257,
offers a brief sketch of Harding without placing an undue stress on the
unattractiveness of the subject.

[24] Pinchot to Wallace, Aug. 2, 1923, Box 254, Pinchot Papers. For further praise of Harding's belated support for conservation, see Chief Forester
William B. Greeley's report to Secretary Wallace in the Department of
Agriculture, *Annual Report of the Secretary of Agriculture* (Washington,
1923), 200-201; and *Wallace's Farmer*, Jan. 11, 1924, p. 8.

led him into a sad morass." Some day, said White, America would
realize "how wickedly unfair the Republic was to pick up that
man—weak, unprepared, with no executive talent . . . and pinnacle
him in the most powerful place on earth. He was as a child in
heart and head, set down to fight the dragon, and in the end his
terror conquered him." Or as Herbert Hoover, with more sim-
plicity and perhaps more accuracy, phrased it: "People do not
die from a broken heart, but people with bad hearts may reach the
end much sooner from great worries."[25]

The rumors and suspicions that dogged Harding's conscience
as he crossed the continent and finally came to rest in San Francisco broke into tangible charges and confessions in the months
following his death. The degree of Harding's own guilt for the
scandals of his administration can hardly be fixed with any pre-
cision. Professor John D. Hicks suggests that, in a sense, "the
slanting of government during the 1920's to support whatever
stand the dominant business interests wanted was far more scan-
dalous than the merely political depravity for which the Harding
regime was noted." For this state of affairs, the Republican party
leaders themselves were, if anything, more guilty than was the
President. Their very selection of the pliable Harding was as disgraceful as any action by Harding himself. As President, Harding
was innocent of any direct transgressions; as one historian has
suggested, "though the trail of graft led all around him no one has
conclusively shown that Harding . . . knowingly touched a dishonest dollar."[26]

But if Harding himself was relatively innocent, some of his
friends were not, and he had chosen his friends. How irresponsible
they really were, how disastrous their friendship really was, he did
not live to realize. And when the scandals began to break, the
opprobrium that a living Harding might have been forced to share
with his friends fell upon them in full force. Of them all, however,

[25] White, *Autobiography*, 623-24, and White, *Masks in a Pageant*, 425
and 434; Herbert Hoover, *The Memoirs of Herbert Hoover* (3 vols.; New
York, 1951-52), II, 51. Professor John D. Hicks notes: "The various stories
that there was something strange about the President's passing are totally
without foundation. There is nothing strange about the death from apo-
plexy of a man Harding's age who had long overeaten, overdrunk, and
overworried." *Republican Ascendancy, 1921-1933* (New York, 1960), 80.

[26] Hicks, *Republican Ascendancy*, 73; and Preston Slosson, "Warren G.
Harding," *loc. cit.*

Albert Fall was to suffer the most. Whether he deserved the guilt
that the public and the courts assigned him, whether indeed he
was simply a scapegoat for the entire administration, is an insol-
uble question—but one to be touched on again in these pages.

With Harding lying dead in California, Calvin Coolidge became
President of the United States. His first thought after receiving
the news of Harding's death had been, "I believe I can swing it."
He probably meant the succession, but undoubtedly he would
seek the office in his own right in 1924; and this taciturn Ver-
monter's hand had never touched directly the corruption in Washington. From the quick tragedy in San Francisco, the Republican
party's fortunes seemed actually improved, or so thought William
Gibbs McAdoo, a Democrat from California. Soon after Coolidge's succession, McAdoo wrote to Thomas J. Walsh: "It is too
bad about Harding's death and everyone sympathizes with Mrs.
Harding but it undoubtedly relieved the Republicans of a serious
embarrassment." McAdoo saw in Coolidge "just as much of a
standpatter" as Harding, and McAdoo was "inclined to think that
he will be a more useful servitor of the interests than Harding
was." And it was "perfectly clear" that "big business and the stand-
patters" were determined to nominate Coolidge in 1924.[27]

McAdoo's letter to Walsh was no idle speculation about Republicans, but was one of the many lines that he was laying out for
himself. For McAdoo had White House aspirations.[28] This son-
in-law of Woodrow Wilson already had known political success as
well as defeat. He had been vice-chairman, then acting chairman,
of the Democratic national committee in 1912. President Wilson
had named him Secretary of the Treasury, and then, during World
War I, Director General of the Railroads. In 1920, he was the
strongest candidate at the Democratic national convention in San
Francisco, but was outmaneuvered in a struggle with James M.

[27] White, *A Puritan in Babylon,* 241; Claude Fuess, *Calvin Coolidge,* 311
(Fuess writes that several years after his succession, Coolidge, replying to
a question asked him about his first reaction to the news, recalled: "I
thought I could swing it." White, as I have done, changed the tense to
convey the thought as it first occurred); and McAdoo to Walsh, Sept. 18,
1923, Box 375, Walsh Papers.

[28] Walsh also had supporters for the Democratic nomination in 1924, and
McAdoo may have subtly parried the idea in closing his letter to Walsh,
"With warm regards and hoping to . . . be able to help re-elect you to the
Senate."

Cox. Now in 1923, as another convention neared, he began to point toward it.[29]

By summer, McAdoo had become a serious contender for the 1924 Democratic prize. In North Carolina, from the offices of Senator Furnifold M. Simmons, McAdoo's chances looked "extremely bright." The same vantage point revealed "very strong McAdoo sentiment" in Georgia and Alabama, while "the West" seemed to be "exceedingly strong for McAdoo." In mid-August, Daniel C. Roper, the leader of the McAdoo campaign, wrote to Simmons: "The situation with regard to McAdoo, according to information which I am receiving from many sections of the country, is growing apace." Roper was "satisfied [that] with proper organization and management [by] his friends, he can be nominated and elected President." In September, an editorialist in the Louisville *Post* claimed that "nearly everything" west of the Mississippi was "McAdoo territory," that Virginia, Texas, and other southern states would "go for McAdoo," and that "even in the East the anti-McAdoo men are in trouble."[30]

Personal correspondence between McAdoo supporters tended to encourage this optimism. One politician wrote to William Jennings Bryan that McAdoo would have at least half of Kentucky's votes at the national convention. A California supporter wrote McAdoo: "I was never so encouraged over a political outlook. . . . Have no fear that the [California] delegation will not be a McAdoo delegation." Josephus Daniels thought McAdoo's chances

[29] Frank Freidel, *Franklin D. Roosevelt: The Ordeal* (Boston, 1954), 60-66; William Gibbs McAdoo, *Crowded Years* (Cambridge, 1931), *passim;* Diary of Breckenridge Long, McAdoo Papers, Division of Manuscript, Library of Congress, Oct. 31, 1923 (I am indebted to Joseph C. Vance of Mary Washington College for calling this diary to my attention.); Lee N. Allen, "The Democratic Presidential Primary Election of 1924 in Texas," *The Southwestern Historical Quarterly*, LXI (April, 1958), 478.

[30] Frank A. Hampton to Judge Walter E. Brock, July 31, 1923, Furnifold M. Simmons Papers, Duke University Library (See also Hampton to McAdoo, Sept. 24, 1923, Box 284, William Gibbs McAdoo Papers, Division of Manuscripts, Library of Congress, for Hampton's statement that the "leaders of the Democratic organization in the State, following the Senator, are practically all for you."); and Roper to Simmons, Aug. 13, 1923, Simmons Papers. See also Simmons to Roper, July 11, 1923, Simmons Papers; and Daniel C. Roper, *Fifty Years of Public Life* (Durham, 1941), 212-13, 218-19. Breckenridge Long of Missouri, a major supporter of McAdoo in 1924, called Roper "the real head" of the McAdoo forces. Long diary, McAdoo Papers, Nov. 5, 1923.

in North Carolina were "good." In Deming, New Mexico, an enterprising newspaper editor polled the state's Democratic precinct committeemen and out of seventy-one replies counted fifty-seven for McAdoo. In Georgia, the editor of the Augusta *Chronicle* was "confident of Georgia and South Carolina being in line." A lawyer in Bolivar, Tennessee, informed McAdoo that "sentiment [in Tennessee] is crystalizing in your favor for the nomination." In Virginia, "rank-and-file sentiment" was reportedly "overwhelming" for McAdoo. And an official in the Brotherhood of Locomotive Firemen and Engineers informed McAdoo: "Our boys are for you first, last and all the time."[31]

Optimistic tidings—but McAdoo unknowingly had begun to lose the nomination almost as soon as he began to seek it. In 1921, McAdoo was practicing law in New York City, but he was already thinking of 1924. Perhaps at the suggestion of Daniel C. Roper, who thought McAdoo could never be nominated from Tammany-dominated New York, he moved his residence to California. Having accepted an offer as legal counsel for oil man Edward L. Doheny of Los Angeles, he told Roper: "While developing a general practice in California, I'd have the advantage of one client at the start."[32] But that client was no advantage. He was a friend of Albert Fall and a dealer in naval reserve oil, and in February, 1924, with one simple if calculated statement, he was to shatter the optimism of McAdoo and McAdoo's friends. Now, however, it was autumn, 1923, and McAdoo was confident, even as Calvin Coolidge was settling into his new quarters.

In the afternoon of the day Mrs. Harding moved out of the White House, Calvin Coolidge entered its spacious front hallway and, after a few shy moments, spoke to the head usher Ike Hoover: "I understand how things are around here . . . I want things as they used to be—before!" William Allen White judged that in

[31] Louisville *Post* editorial, Sept. 27, 1923, copy in Box 284, McAdoo Papers; Patrick Henry Callahan to W. J. Bryan, Oct. 1, 1923; J. S. Wardell to McAdoo, Oct. 4, 1923; Jack Griffin to McAdoo, Oct. 6, 1923; Thomas J. Hamilton to McAdoo, Oct. 8, 1923; C. A. Miller to McAdoo, Oct. 13, 1923; James G. Doyle to McAdoo, Oct 3, 1923; Norman R. Hamilton to McAdoo, Oct. 16, 1923, Box 284, McAdoo Papers; and C. W. Main to McAdoo, Oct. 20, 1923, Box 285, McAdoo Papers.

[32] Roper, *Fifty Years of Public Life*, 212-13; see also Allen, "Democratic Primary in Texas," *loc. cit.*, 477.

those last nine words, Coolidge "changed the whole social aspect of the White House. No more poker, no more Forbes and Fall and Daugherty . . . no more trash in the White House."[33]

Coolidge, meantime, asked a friend and former occupant of the White House what to do, now that he was President. William Howard Taft told him to "do nothing." Taft told him that he thought "the public were glad to have him in the White House doing nothing . . . in the returning prosperity people were glad to have a rest from watching Washington, and that . . . his wisest course was to be quiet." Accordingly, Coolidge remained quiet and did almost nothing for awhile. Unlike Harding, he "slapped no man on the back, he pawed no man's shoulder, he squeezed no man's hand." He wanted things as they were—before. But he took over Harding's Cabinet intact, and thereafter, except when a member voluntarily departed, he sought few changes.[34]

The choice of inertia or activity did not long remain with Coolidge. He found that he could neither do nothing, nor call things back as they were before. In early October, 1923, the Washington *Post* reported that the "first political rumblings from the opponents of the [Republican] administration are expected to be heard next week." The investigation of Teapot Dome at last had a green light, and the *Post*, displaying either dry humor or arid imagination, pointed out: "It is known here that some of the Democrats hope to see the investigation provide them with advance ammunition for the next Presidential campaign. . . ." It was not clear to the *Post* just how "political insinuations can be brought into the hearings . . . [but] there may be political possibilities concealed somewhere in a review of the circumstances connected with the lease."[35]

On October 18, four days before hearings began, national press wires carried the story that Teapot Dome's supposed productivity was a myth. A recent survey by the Interior and Navy departments had shown that the reserve contained far less oil than earlier estimates had indicated. Sharp and clear arose one inference: Fall

---

[33] White, *A Puritan in Babylon*, 247: Hoover, in a conversation with White, recalled Coolidge's comment.

[34] W. H. Taft to Horace Taft, Sept. 29, 1923, cited in Henry F. Pringle, *The Life and Times of William Howard Taft* (2 vols.; New York, 1939), II, 1019; White, *A Puritan in Babylon*, 250.

[35] Washington *Post*, Oct. 9, 1923.

had been right in his claim that Teapot Dome was draining into adjacent wells. As one newspaper commented, the "unexpected results of the recent survey are expected to have a great influence on the trend of the Senate inquiry." Harry Slattery thought that the report, "given out with a blare of publicity," was a plot by Smoot and Lenroot "to blanket the investigation."[36] If it was a plot, it failed. On October 22, 1923, hearings before the Senate Committee on Public Lands and Surveys began. Shortly thereafter, Teapot Dome began to engross a nation's attention.

[36] *Ibid.*, Oct. 19, 1923; New York *Times,* Oct. 18, 1923, p. 33; Slattery, "The Story of Teapot Dome," 61; see also Slattery's quotations from New York *Herald-Tribune* and other papers in the latter.

5

The Eruption of Scandal

The investigation of Teapot Dome had a slow start, but it remained routine for less than three months. At 10:00 A. M., Monday, October 22, Reed Smoot called the Public Lands Committee to order, in Room 210, Senate Office Building. The committee used the entire day's session to place statements and documents in the record and to hear reports from their two geologists. They testified that Teapot Dome, originally estimated to contain 135,000,000 barrels of oil, contained less than 70 per cent of this amount and that the existing reserve was draining steadily into adjacent areas.

Smoot made the most of their testimony. At the close of the day's hearing, he said: "If the reports of the experts are accepted, the theory that the Government made a mistake in leasing this . . . reserve has been exploded. The action of the Government [Fall] has been entirely justified." The New York *Times* concluded: "The hearings will be continued tomorrow, but all interest in its outcome has evaporated with the reports of the experts." This leap-to-the-wrong-conclusion reflected the lack of interest in the investigation and the unawareness of the political thunder hidden therein. Even Josephus Daniels' Raleigh paper merely reported the experts' testimony and made the negative observation that the lease nevertheless had violated conservation principles. Attempting a more positive rebuttal, Walsh protested to the New York *Times* that its coverage of the experts' testimony had left the inference that Teapot Dome was losing oil through drainage into wells outside the reserve. Actually, said Walsh, there had simply been a miscalculation earlier of the reserve's capacity.[1]

Following this lusterless opening, Fall, Denby, Sinclair, and various naval officers and government employees began appearing before the committee. Fall, who had hurried home from Europe when his friend Harding died, testified morning and afternoon for two days. In garrulous debate with Walsh, he defended his leasing policy. He claimed that since, following the Washington Conference of 1921–22, the United States and other powers were to cut down their naval strength, he had sought to "make one-half of the [United States] battleship fleet worth more than the total fleet had heretofore been" by securing royalty oil through his leases and storing it in Hawaii. This testimony by Fall was the first reference in the hearings to a theme that appeared from time to time: that a "war scare" was in the air early in the 1920's and that Doheny and Fall had patriotically responded to it by looking to the preservation of the navy's oil supply. Whether or not patriotism had motivated Albert Fall, Walsh, at dead end, could only dismiss him. The Senator imagined that "as the matter develops," he would wish to question Fall again, but he had no more questions for the moment.[2]

[1] *Leases upon Reserves* (1924), 1–174; New York *Times*, Oct. 23, 1923, p. 23; Raleigh *News and Observer*, Oct. 23, 1923; Walsh to the New York *Times*, Oct. 23, 1924, Box 200, Walsh Papers

[2] Santa Fe *New Mexican*, Oct. 4, 1924; *Leases upon Reserves* (1924), 279–80, 282. For Walsh's own comments on this early testimony, see his article in the New York *Times*, Feb. 10, 1924, Sec. 8, p. 5. The Santa Fe *New Mexican*, which seldom lost a chance to report critically on Albert Fall's activities, gave the hearings routine coverage during these first weeks.

The questioning of other witnesses, done mostly by Walsh, with occasional parrying of his efforts by Smoot and Lenroot, was dull and unproductive. From the stream of testimony Walsh tried to determine whether the Sinclair contract was sound, whether the executive transfer by Harding was legal, and whether Teapot Dome was, in fact, draining into adjacent wells.

Walsh was a lonely prosecutor during these first weeks. He found Smoot and Lenroot, if not hostile, absolutely unprepared to investigate. Kendrick was reluctant, and Daniels gave no help, even from afar. The weekly newspaper *Labor* claimed that the Associated Press had headlined the reports of drainage by "Smoot's geologists," but they had neglected testimony contrary to theirs by two other experts, who had "literally riddled" the drainage theory. Aided by the Associated Press and supported at every step by Senator Lenroot, the "Old Guard Leader from Utah" was "endeavoring to put the 'lid' on the Teapot Dome scandal." Walsh himself felt there had been some "startling" disclosures in the investigation, yet "the Press" was, he said, remaining "strangely silent." Peter Norbeck wrote to an acquaintance: "Most of the Republican members and some of the Democratic members on the . . . Committee were not very anxious to stir up that Teapot Dome business. Senator Walsh had to fight his way through all along." George Norris was a beacon-light of encouragement to Walsh, but hardly another member of the committee earned his gratitude. Several months after the hearings had begun, Walsh wrote to Norris: "Until you came I never had . . . one word of encouragement or even sympathy from the majority side, at best I guessed that Ladd and Norbeck were not unfriendly."[3]

Not for long, however, was Walsh neglected. Soon, as the political potentialities became more obvious, good men began to come to the aid of their party. In 1923, Cordell Hull was chairman of

[3] Kendrick to Walsh, Oct. 1, 1923; Walsh to D. F. Pugh, Dec. 13, 1927; Walsh to Roy E. Reed, Feb. 4, 1926; Walsh to Kendrick, Oct. 6, 1924; Kendrick to Walsh, Oct. 1, 1923; Daniels to Walsh, Oct. 6, 1923, and Walsh to Daniels, Oct. 8, 1923, Walsh Papers, all cited in Bates, "Senator Walsh of Montana," 136 ff. (Kendrick told Walsh that his livestock business and other affairs would keep him away from Washington for awhile.); *Labor* (Washington, D.C.), Nov. 3, 1923; Walsh to Thomas Arthur, Nov. 16, 1923, Box 373, Walsh Papers; Norbeck to Harry King, Feb. 2, 1924, cited in Fite, *Peter Norbeck*, 113; Walsh to Norris, Feb. 18, 1924, Box 7, Tray 7, Norris Papers.

the Democratic national committee. Years afterward, Hull recalled that as chairman, he "considered it the best strategy to attack the political opposition wherever it was most vulnerable, and where major issues could be presented. One major issue was over the tariff. . . . We made another . . . of the scandals and maladministration under Harding." Hull's memory was accurate, but he omitted some details. Late in October, 1923, Grattan Kerans, assistant director of publicity for the Democratic national committee, heard that Walsh was about to abandon his search for fraud in the leasing of Teapot Dome. Kerans learned from a newspaperman, John Erwin of the Nashville *Tennesseean* and the New York *World*, that Slattery was "familiar with many of the facts respecting these oil leases and . . . could be of assistance in prompting Senator Walsh to continue the investigation." Kerans reported this to Hull and offered to talk to Slattery. Kerans proposed to "fully identify" himself to Slattery as an employee of the Democratic national committee, and if he found Slattery's facts "useful" he would suggest that the committee "take political advantage of them but . . . use them in the public interest." Hull agreed, and Kerans, visiting Slattery, asked him for "the names of persons who had official or other knowledge of the leasing of oil lands and a hint . . . of what information they might be able to give the committee." A day or two later, Kerans called at Slattery's office, where Slattery gave him a two-page list of prospective witnesses and suggested the information each of them might possess. He urged that Walsh call these proposed witnesses "early in the hearings."[4]

Kerans submitted the names to Hull, who agreed that Kerans should take them to Walsh "and explain their probable value to him." Kerans went to see Walsh, who received him "very brusquely." A few days later, Walsh called Slattery to his office. Slattery wrote later that Walsh "said with some heat that he felt I was trying to build a fire under him. There was little I could say . . . but I went to . . . La Follette to lick my wounds." Whether or not

[4] Cordell Hull, *The Memoirs of Cordell Hull* (2 vols.; New York, 1949), I, 114-15; Slattery, "From Roosevelt to Roosevelt, 91-92; Kerans to Slattery, Oct. 29, 1931, and Slattery to Kerans, Oct. 26, 1923, Slattery Papers. Slattery listed thirty-seven names, including Josephus Daniels, Franklin D. Roosevelt, Edward Doheny, Harry Daugherty, several naval officers, and a dozen-odd employees of the Justice and Interior departments.

La Follette interceded, several days later Walsh called him again and, "as if nothing had ever happened," suggested that they discuss what Walsh called "this Navy angle." According to Kerans, "within a few days," Walsh vigorously renewed his interest and activities.[5]

Then on November 5, Hull issued a hot broadside. Sinclair had testified before the Senate Committee that he contributed to both major parties' campaign fund in 1920. Hull denied any Democratic donations, saying that Sinclair's contribution, "if any, was surreptitiously made and concealed by the agent who tendered it for him." If Sinclair gave money to the Democrats, said Hull, it was "to gain favor with some individual Democrat . . . and not to advance a cause with which he could have had no sympathy." Thus did Hull decline any affiliation with Albert Fall's friend Harry Sinclair, and to further distinguish Democrat from Republican, Hull suggested that Fall's lease had no match in any past Democratic misbehavior: "In all its history the Democratic Party has never been disgraced by such a scandal as the secret lease of the Teapot Dome."[6] Hull's reference to the Teapot Dome "scandal" is noteworthy; although perhaps a natural expression of partisanship, the phrase was now coming into general use more and more, and by others than Democratic chieftians. Rumors, if not testimony, had begun to encourage it, and soon the phrase was to be a byword.

Walsh now had abundant support. Soon he would have even more. He had found most of November unrewarding, but late in the month and early in December the trail grew warm. As he later recalled, stories began to reach him about "some significant land deals in New Mexico." Somehow, Albert Fall was involved, but the picture was vague and Walsh could get no details. He began calling in witnesses from New Mexico. A newspaper man from Albuquerque, Carl Magee, had information about Fall, which he

[5] Kerans to Slattery, Oct. 29, 1931, Slattery Papers; Slattery, "From Roosevelt to Roosevelt," 92. About this same time, Walsh informed Daniels that he was "struggling along with little help from any source except that . . . by Chester Washburne and Mr. Slattery." Walsh to Daniels, Nov. 5, 1923, cited in Bates, "Senator Walsh of Montana," 317. Hull, Memoirs, I, 115, wrote: "I came into possession, from time to time, of items of information bearing on the investigation and turned them over to Walsh."

[6] New York Times, Nov. 5, 1923, p. 19.

already had been circulating through New Mexico. Walsh brought him before the committee. Magee told how Fall, in 1923, had suddenly shown evidence of financial well-being and had made "beautiful" improvements on his ranch at Three Rivers, New Mexico. This was in striking contrast to his circumstances of several years past, when he had lived impecuniously. Following Magee came others, neighbors or acquaintances of Fall, all of them corroborating Magee. As Walsh questioned Magee and those who succeeded him, Lenroot and Smoot injected subtle queries, which, along with his responses to Walsh, revealed that in the past Magee had differed with Fall over political as well as legal issues in New Mexico. But the circumstantial evidence could not be ignored: Fall, at about the time he leased Teapot Dome, had substantially increased his fortunes.[7]

Then on November 30, J. T. Johnson, Fall's ranch manager at Three Rivers, testified that Harry Sinclair had visited Fall at the ranch around Christmas of 1921. Under Walsh's skillful prodding, Johnson stated that Fall lately had acquired several registered hogs and cows from Sinclair's farm in New Jersey. The stock transaction appeared to be a ludicrous tangent down which the committee promptly plunged for a moment, but the implication arose that Sinclair had visited Fall before his finances improved; and the hogs and cows, rather than a business deal, may have been a tiny token of gratitude.[8]

Walsh quickly learned more about Fall's livestock acquisitions. On December 3, he questioned Edward Doheny, who revealed that he had received favorable treatment from Fall during the preliminary biddings for a lease on Elk Hills. But when Lenroot asked him if Fall profited "in any way, directly or indirectly, through the making of [a] contract," Doheny replied, "Not yet." The next day, Sinclair made his second trip to the committee's witness chair. He brought along his secretary and accountant, G. D. Wahlberg, who spoke for him when Walsh asked about Fall's

[7] *Leases upon Reserves* (1924), 830-914, *passim;* William G. Shepherd, "How Carl Magee Broke Fall's New Mexico Ring." *The Worlds Work,* XLVIII (May, 1924), 29-40; New York *Times,* Dec. 1, 1923, p. 15; Walsh, "True History of Teapot Dome," *loc. cit.*

[8] *Leases upon Reserves* (1924), 860-90; New York *Times,* Dec. 1, 1923, p. 15.

"seven cows and two bulls." Wahlberg displayed an account book
showing receipts of payment from Fall for the stock. He recalled
that "some one from Three Rivers" brought a check to him in payment; otherwise, his memory seemed to be blank. Sinclair himself
simply claimed that on a visit to Three Rivers in January, 1923, he
found that Fall "did not have any milch cows, and [I] suggested
to him he better let me send him some." Fall had agreed, and Sinclair told his farm manager "to get together a bull and half a dozen
heifers and a few pigs and send them down."[9]

As the year ended, Sinclair returned to the hearings and explicit-
ly denied giving Fall a gift of any kind in return for the Teapot
Dome lease. On the same day, from his sick bed in a Washington
hospital, Fall sent to Smoot a prolix statement of his financial
condition. He declared that in order to enlarge his ranch holdings
in New Mexico, he had, in November, 1921, borrowed $100,000 in
cash from Edward B. McLean, publisher of the Washington *Post*.
McLean, said Fall, was "a gentleman" with whom he had a "plea-
sant and close personal relationship," and he had borrowed money
from him before. Sinclair had come to Three Rivers just after Fall
acquired his additional property; this, said Fall, "invited some evil-
minded persons to the conclusion that I must have obtained money
from Mr. Sinclair." He thought it needless to say that he had
never approached Doheny or Sinclair for the money to purchase
his property. In fact, he found the "entire subject . . . more or
less humiliating even to refer to."[10]

Walsh seemed immersed in trivia and getting nowhere. The
flow of witnesses—civil servants, oil men, naval officers, financiers
—continued unabated. But according to one observer, at the end
of December, 1923, "the impression in Washington was that Senator Walsh was up against a stone wall. The wise politicos of
Washington believed that he had gone as far as he possibly could
go." Obviously all the truth had not been told, and a few anti-
administration journals were insisting that the Senate inquiry was

[9] *Leases upon Reserves* (1924), 973-1016, 1018-34; New York *Times*,
Dec. 5, 1923, p. 27.
[10] *Leases upon Reserves* (1924), 1429-35; New York *Times*, Dec. 28,
1923, p. 2.

much more than "a tempest in a teapot."[11] But Denby and Fall, like Sinclair and Doheny, had denied under oath any collusion over the naval oil reserves, and Walsh apparently could not prove otherwise.

Then he heard from Palm Beach. On January 3, 1924, Edward McLean's lawyer, A. Mitchell Palmer, sent a letter to Irvine Lenroot, Smoot's replacement as chairman of the committee.[12] Palmer had read the press reports of Fall's supposed loan from McLean and had evidently discussed Fall's story with McLean, who was now in Florida for the winter and, according to Palmer, was "obliged to remain there owing to the condition of his health and that of his wife." If the committee desired it, however, McLean would give them a "complete statement" about his loan to Albert Fall. McLean had wired to Palmer: "In 1921 I loaned Fall $100,-000 on his personal note. I have never met Harry Sinclair nor . . . Doheny. There is no stock of [their] oil companies pledged with the note. It is absolutely unsecured." This message Palmer passed on to Lenroot; meanwhile, he conveyed it to Walsh, as well. Walsh hoped to subpoena McLean to appear before the committee, although at this point McLean was only one more lead for Walsh, who appeared discouraged and ready to close the hearings, once McLean testified. Smoot wanted to end them within the week, "even though . . . compelled to sit in the evenings." Lenroot, too, hoped to conclude within the week, with the possible exception of later testimony from McLean. Walsh agreed.[13]

But then McLean proved obdurate. He could not come to Washington. He was suffering from an acute sinus infection, and his physician thought it "out of the question for Mr. McLean to return North." McLean wired Lenroot that he would "most gladly answer here [in Palm Beach] all questions. . . ." Walsh did not

[11] George H. Payne, "The Political Drama of 1924," *The Forum*, LXXI (April, 1924), 504-508; W. Hard, "Tale of the Teapot," *The Nation*, CXVII (Nov. 21, 1923), 575-77; *American Federationist*, XXX (Dec., 1923), 1011-12.

[12] Smoot resigned his chairmanship, although not his seat on the committee, to become chairman of the Senate Finance Committee.

[13] *Leases upon Reserves* (1924), 1453-55 (Palmer's letter to Lenroot is reprinted on p. 1453); see also Walsh, "True History of Teapot Dome," *loc. cit.*; New York *Times*, Jan. 2, 1924, p. 19; and Payne, "Political Drama of 1924," *loc. cit.*, 504-508.

think that sinus trouble was "a desperate malady," since he had endured an operation himself for a sinus infection only a few weeks earlier, but he decided to go to Palm Beach. The committee appointed him as a subcommittee of one to take testimony and to issue subpoenas "to require the attendance before him of . . . McLean or any other witnesses."[14]

On January 12, in Palm Beach, Walsh began questioning McLean. Although the Senator "suspected that in some way" Fall's loan had come from Harry Sinclair, McLean "dumbfounded" him when he denied lending Fall the money at all. He told Walsh that in November, 1921, he was in Brownsville, Texas with President-elect Harding. There he met Fall in a hotel. Fall talked of a ranch in New Mexico that he thought would be a profitable investment. Later in the month, in Washington, Fall came to McLean's house and asked him for a loan in order to buy the ranch. McLean gave him "two or three checks, made out on different banks." Several days later, Fall returned the checks, uncashed.[15]

Fortunately for Walsh, Fall happened to be in Palm Beach. Indeed, he was the guest of Edward McLean, and host and guest had talked together fifteen minutes before Walsh interrogated McLean. Walsh, by letter, asked Fall for a statement "either orally, before me, at your convenience . . . or in the shape of a letter to the committee if you prefer. . . ." Not until Walsh threatened to turn the letter over to the sheriff for delivery would the hotel management deliver it—to McLean, who in an hour returned with a reply from Fall. Fall admitted it was "absolutely true that I did not finally use the money from Mr. McLean . . . because I found other sources." But he wished it "thoroughly understood that the source . . . was in no way connected with Mr. Sinclair or . . . Teapot Dome or any oil concession." Further than this, Fall did "not care to go." And he was, he said, "not in anything like the physical condition to stand the ordeal of an examination." He may have been reluctant to talk; yet Fall and McLean had agreed beforehand that McLean himself should "answer freely" any questions Walsh might ask. Fall told reporters that he was not un-

---

[14] *Leases upon Reserves* (1924), 1545, 1549, and 1649.
[15] *Ibid.*, 1649 ff.; New York *Times,* Jan. 12, 1924, p. 2; Walsh, "True History of Teapot Dome," *loc. cit.;* and Walsh to Fall, Jan. 11, 1924, Fall Papers.

willing to co-operate with the Senate committee and that he stood ready to appear before it when his health permitted it. But he refused to appear before the Senator at the Palm Beach hotel, saying, "I will not appear before Walsh or any other man. I think I am right in believing that on his visit here he was empowered only to examine Mr. McLean's confidential secretary. . . . As to the question of where I got the money . . . that is my own private affair. I do not feel called upon to discuss it either with Senator Walsh or any other man."[16]

The Teapot Dome inquiry, close to expiration days earlier, came alive. Any possible Republican hope for a quick demise of the inquiry fled, and Democratic comment now abounded. The Democratic national committee moved with alacrity. It issued a pungent statement, comparing Teapot Dome to "the Ballinger scandal" and stressing the profits, exploitation, and mismanagment arising from Fall and Denby's Republican administration of the people's resources. A United Press wire to Fall read: "Washington is filled with ugly rumors and gossip and newspapers throughout the country are pressing for exact information as a result of the . . . investigation and its developments." The United Press would "welcome a statement . . . at whatever lengths" from him, "setting forth where the hundred thousand dollars came from." In New Mexico, Fall's old journalistic critic, the Santa Fe *New Mexican*, editorialized: "A clean breast is due the public. Mr. Fall has got to do some tall explaining and do it now." William Howard Taft, who once had believed that the Democrats were merely trying to create campaign material out of the investigation, now admitted that "they have discovered some real pay dirt apparently in the . . . lease. Fall has lied. . . . The Democrats are going to try to embarrass Coolidge with this, but I think it is rather farfetched." Taft thought that perhaps Fall could explain things.[17]

[16] Walsh to Fall, Jan. 11, 1924, Fall Papers; Fall to Walsh, Jan. 11, 1924, in *Leases upon Reserves* (1924), 1699; and New York *Times*, Jan 12, 1924, p. 3, and Jan. 13, 1924, p. 10.

[17] Robert J. Bender to Fall, Jan. 18, 1924, Box 1, Fall Papers; Santa Fe *New Mexican*, Jan. 14, 1924, p. 4; Taft to A. I. Vorys, Jan. 3, 1924, and Taft to F. B. Kellogg, Jan. 23, 1924, cited in Pringle, *Life and Times of Taft*, II, 1020-21.

In time Fall did explain his lie. He would claim that in December, 1923, when illness kept him confined to his Wardman Park apartment in Washington, unable to testify before the Senate committee, Senators Smoot and Lenroot had begged him to tell where he had obtained his recent funds and thereby possibly end the inquiry that was damaging the Republican party's prestige. Some time later, again at his apartment, several Republican politicos, including Republican national chairman Will H. Hays, had urged him to do the same. Possibly there was a third conference between Fall and several of his friends and acquaintances in the party. Someone—and Fall claimed it was Smoot, Lenroot, and Hays—suggested during one or more of these conferences that he tell the committee that McLean had loaned him the money. Although Fall had suggested vaguely that McLean might have been the source, he actually had received the money from Doheny and wanted to say as much if and when he testified before the committee. His Republican colleagues, however, feared the truth might be even more damaging than refusal to confess at all, since critics could charge that there was, indeed, a collusion between oil man Doheny and the Harding Administration. On January 24, 1924, Doheny testified before the Senate committee that he, not McLean, had loaned Fall $100,000; but in December, 1923, and again in January, 1924, Fall concealed the fact, first by lying and then by refusing to give Doheny as the source.[18]

Doheny's statement in January that his son Edward, Jr., had

[18] For Fall's assertion that Smoot, Hays, and Lenroot suggested he name McLean as his source, as well as Smoot and Lenroot's denial of the charge, see New York *Times*, April 3, 1928, p. 1; for further statements and information about Smoot and Lenroot's actions, see *Leases upon Reserves* (1924), 1429-33, 2374 ff., and *Cong. Rec.*, 68 Cong., 1 Sess. (Feb. 28 and 29, 1924), 3230-33 and 3319-20. Fall gives a fuller account of his loan from Doheny in one of a series of articles that he wrote for the North American Newspaper Alliance, printed in New York *Times*, July 15, 1931, p. 5; Doheny's testimony that he loaned Fall the money is in *Leases upon Reserves* (1924), 1771 ff. Fall's old New Mexico acquaintance George Curry, who was in attendance at one of the December meetings between Fall and his various confreres, claimed that Fall was trying to protect Doheny (*Autobiography*, 303). Doheny, however, in 1925 told a reporter that Fall's lie about the loan was the one incident in a long friendship for which he could not "forgive" Fall; New York *Times*, July 1, 1925, p. 14. David Stratton, "Behind Teapot Dome," *loc. cit.*, 296-99, contains a helpful account of the Fall-McLean episode; see also his dissertation, "Albert B. Fall and the Teapot Dome Affair," 289-98.

carried to Fall's office $100,000 in cash, "in a little black bag," was to be a sensation. In December, Fall's admitted lie was equally dramatic. And whatever his motives—misguided concern for his party's interests, an attempt to shield his old friend Doheny, or simply confusion brought on by illness and by unethical pleas from his Republican confreres—his letter to the committee in December, 1923, giving McLean as the source of a $100,000 loan, was perhaps the most fateful statement he ever uttered. It was one he deeply regretted the remainder of his life. Whatever the truth in December might have gained him, his McLean story dogged him and undoubtedly blackened him in the subsequent months of the investigation. His critics would never allow Fall to forget his lie, which, no matter how explained, merely bolstered the rampant suspicion that Secretary of the Interior Fall somehow had been involved in scandal.

As Walsh returned to Washington from Palm Beach, however, the public and the committee (possibly excepting Smoot and Lenroot) knew only that Fall had not received $100,000 from Edward McLean. Walsh still was probing an enigma. As yet he had proved no positive scandal involving the naval oil reserves. Indeed, the staid Boston *Evening Transcript*, which some Democrats viewed as Coolidge's "court paper," declared that Walsh, up for re-election, was "making a frantic effort to besmirch reputation . . . in order to save himself. The indications are, however, that the whole thing will prove a political dud," since Fall was out of the Cabinet, Sinclair had "sunk money in Teapot Dome instead of taking it out," and Harding was dead. On the other hand, the New York *World*, although reporting that the Coolidge campaign headquarters had "no doubt . . . that the President will walk off with the nomination," found also a "phenomenon of Democratic confidence in success . . . growing in volume." Democrats expected Teapot Dome to reveal "government by favoritism and friendship, which the American people have always resented."[19]

At the same time, in the Senate, Thad Caraway of Arkansas rose to attack and revealed more and more clearly the campaign vistas that lay ahead for his Democratic party. Harding, said

[19] Boston *Evening Transcript*, Jan. 21, 1924; New York *World*, Jan. 15 and 19, 1924.

Caraway, had issued an illegal executive order, and Fall—whom
Caraway found much more infamous than Benedict Arnold, who
"wanted to sell only a rocky fortress on the Hudson River"—had
"parted with the last gallon of America's naval reserve fuel." Now
Fall and McLean pleaded illness. Caraway had "known more
robust constitutions ruined by criminal courts than by all other
plagues combined." Whatever Fall should say, "No lawyer can
ever add to or take away from Fall's positive declaration that 'I
got the cash from . . . McLean.'"

Caraway, along with Senator Pat Harrison of Mississippi, already had a reputation as "jeer leader" of the Democrats; even so
the New York *Times* called his speech "one of the most bitter the
upper House has heard in years." Josephus Daniels' Raleigh *News
and Observer* called it a speech "dripping with invective and bitter ridicule," but pointed out that no Republican rejoined, although
Smoot, "chief defender of the leases," was present throughout the
speech. Fall, in New Orleans on his way home from Florida, did
rejoin, saying: "Senator Caraway . . . has shot his senseless shafts
repeatedly in the past, before the oil matter came up." But Caraway, senseless or not, was going beyond ridicule. Already he, as
Walsh before him, had proposed cancellation of the oil leases.
On January 21, he picked up his shafts once more; noting that Fall
had said, "I'm out of politics," Caraway suggested, "Why, God
bless his soul, if he does not mind, he is going to put all of his
friends out, also."[20]

Calvin Coolidge, no doubt, would have disclaimed Fall as
friend, but Caraway's sentiment was applicable to him, be he
soiled or not by Fall's machinations. And Democrats were not
alone in suggesting the President's guilt by association. Shortly
after Senator Hiram W. Johnson, Republican of California, announced his candidacy for the 1924 Presidential nomination, his
eastern campaign manager, George Henry Payne, claimed to have

[20] *Cong. Rec.*, 68 Cong., 1 Sess. (Jan. 16, 1924), 1033-34; *ibid.* (Jan.
21, 1924), 1202; New York *Times,* Jan 17, 1924, p. 19, and Jan. 18, 1924,
p. 21; Raleigh *News and Observer,* Jan. 17, 1924. Caraway seemed to de-
light in refuting almost every public utterance Fall made. Referring to
Fall's denial to reporters in New Orleans that he had not been "hiding out"
while in Palm Beach, Caraway noted: "I do not know what he calls 'hiding
out.' Nobody could find him." *Cong. Rec.*, 68 Cong., 1 Sess. (Jan. 21,
1924), p. 1202.

—Darling in the New York *Tribune*

THE FIRST GOOD LAUGH THEY'VE HAD IN YEARS

"visited six States in the last two weeks and in every one of them numerous men voluntarily expressed their opinion that . . . Teapot Dome . . . has absolutely put an end to . . . Coolidge's possibilities as a . . . nominee." Denby, who also signed the lease, was still in the Cabinet, said Payne, and Coolidge himself, who "sat in the Cabinet meeting in which the leases were discussed," had as yet made no move to assist the Senate inquiry.

Payne displayed no proof that the Cabinet had ever discussed Teapot Dome, but his thoughts were not unique with him. Harold Ickes made essentially the same analysis privately to Gifford Pinchot: "Teapot Dome is going to be a heavy load for Mr. Coolidge

to carry. His position is not improved by the circumstance that
he sat in . . . the cabinet when the deal was considered and approved." Also, said Ickes, Coolidge had retained in cabinet and
administration men who "didn't know enough . . . to protect the
public interests against a bunch of crooked oil operators." Senator Walsh, even before his interview with Fall in Palm Beach,
wrote optimistically to an acquaintance in Montana: "All our
Democratic friends here [in Washington] regard the situation as
most promising and from time to time it leaks out that the Republican leaders are altogether despondent." Walsh felt that if
only the party could nominate "the right candidate" for the presidency, "it ought to be relatively easy to elect every man nominated
on the Democratic ticket next fall." Gifford Pinchot, sometime
after the investigation had begun but before Walsh's trip to Palm
Beach, suggested that the "outcome" in the 1924 Republican convention was "going to depend mainly on whether or not the under-
lying Republican authorities think they can win with Coolidge."
In late January, 1924, the New York *World* reported that Republican politicos believed Coolidge could remain detached from whatever revelations emerged out of the "unsavory mess," but in any
case they were "anxious for an investigation," since they preferred
facts to the "sinister suspicions" and "present charges and insinuations" in the air.[21]

The Democratic national committee was not awaiting further
revelations. It began carrying its version of Teapot Dome to what
the Democratic Raleigh *News and Observer* described as "thousands of women's clubs and individual voters." About January 21,
the committee released a booklet, *The Lands Ye Possess*, which
attempted to show how conservation had flourished under Democratic and progressive Republican administrations, whereas the
Harding-Coolidge caretakers had brought forth "the rape" of Teapot Dome.[22]

[21] Payne, quoted in New York *Times,* Jan. 20, 1924, p. 21; Ickes to Pin-
chot, Jan. 23, 1924, Box 248, Pinchot Papers; Walsh to Byron E. Cooney,
Jan. 2, 1924, Box 373, Walsh Papers; Pinchot to William Kent, Dec. 4, 1923,
Box 249, Pinchot Papers; and New York *World,* Jan. 22, 1924.

[22] Raleigh *News and Observer,* Jan. 21, 1924; Marion Banister, *The Lands
Ye Possess* (Washington, 1924)—see copy of the latter, which Slattery helped
to prepare, in Printed Material, Slattery Papers.

Then on January 21, Archie Roosevelt, Theodore's son, voluntarily testified before the Senate committee, and the Democrats inherited more riches. Since August, 1919, Roosevelt had been employed by the Sinclair Consolidated Oil Company. The day before he testified, he had resigned, "due firstly" to the "amazing testimony" turned up by the committee. "Secondly," he continued, "I had learned some things in the office which, while not proven facts as yet, at least corroborated my suspicions. Thirdly, I noticed . . . that two . . . people most concerned with the naval leases had left the United States in a great hurry." Archie had told his brother Theodore, Jr., of his suspicions, and he, in turn, had advised him to testify. Archie now told the committee that Sinclair, the day after Walsh questioned McLean in Palm Beach, had asked Archie to buy him a ticket on the steamship *Paris*, departing for Europe in three days. Meantime, G. D. Wahlberg, Sinclair's private secretary, told Archie of "a payment made to a foreman of Mr. Fall's; that the payment was $68,000, and that [Wahlberg] had the cancelled checks." This transaction had Wahlberg worried and unhappy and was Archie's "main reason" for testifying and was, he concluded, "the thing that took my breath away." Wahlberg, distraught and nervous before Walsh's rapid questioning, followed Archie in testifying. In utter seriousness, he explained that Archie had misunderstood him; Wahlberg claimed to have referred to "six or eight cows, and [Archie] probably understood that to mean $68,000 in some manner," hearing "thous" instead of "cows."[23]

Wahlberg's explanation may have been pure drollery to his listeners, but he persisted, and Walsh could draw from him no admission that Fall had received money from Sinclair, only cows. Fall, questioned in the Roosevelt Hotel in New Orleans on the same day that Archie Roosevelt testified, flatly denied receiving a single penny from Sinclair. His denials scarcely punctured the cloud of suspicion that now hovered closer and closer to him. Daily newspapers began to spread their coverage of the hearings

[23] *Leases upon Reserves* (1924), 1713-17. Archie explained that he knew "all the officials" of the steamship company and could get tickets, since his brother Kermit was with the company. Archie mistakenly believed that Doheny, as well as Sinclair, had left the country; *ibid.*, 1713-16. The New York *Times* reported on Jan. 22, 1922, that Sinclair had just sailed "secretly" for Europe on the steamship *Paris*.

over the front pages. For the first time, the committee room in the Senate Office Building became thronged with reporters and on-lookers. Walsh believed that "the country" became "fully aroused" when Roosevelt told his "lurid story." After Roosevelt's story, Daniels' Raleigh paper printed a scorching editorial, "Murder Will Out," elucidating for the obtuse and the nonpartisan that "Republican control of the public domain has nearly always been marked by scandal and dishonest surrender of the reserves of the West" and that bad administration "reached a climax under Fall." On January 22, on the New York Stock Exchange, Sinclair Oil securities encountered heavy selling.[24]

During the Senate's months of inquiry, journalists frequently tried to chart the rise and fall in the Teapot Dome investigation's torturous course, trying to find various "turning points." After Archie Roosevelt's testimony, the Washington correspondent of the Boston *Evening Transcript* commented: "The exposure came just in time, for before Archie Roosevelt testified the Republican management was counting Walsh a dead duck." A New York *Times* correspondent believed that Roosevelt "turned what had been a somewhat tiresome investigation into a national sensa-tion."[25] This, however, gave Archie too much credit. Although Walsh himself thought Roosevelt's testimony added much mo-mentum to the inquiry, it seems clear that Walsh's interview with McLean in Palm Beach was the first major "turning point" in the Senate investigation.

Meanwhile, from the White House, after weeks of silence and—according to Democratic critics—neglect and unconcern, Calvin Coolidge at last began showing official awareness of Teapot Dome. In late January, he directed Harry Daugherty "to have a competent member of [the Attorney General's] staff attend the hearings . . . and prepare [the] Department to take such steps as are necessary to protect the financial interests of the . . . Govern-ment, and the integrity of any Department, should the evidence disclosed show the need of any such action." Daugherty himself

[24] Fall, quoted in New York *Times*, Jan. 22, 1924, p. 1 and 2; Walsh, "True History of Teapot Dome," *loc. cit.*; Raleigh *News and Observer*, Jan. 22, 1924; *Wall Street Journal*, Jan. 23, 1924.

[25] Boston *Evening Transcript*, Jan. 25, 1924; New York *Times*, Jan. 27, 1924, Sec. 8, p. 1.

was to "examine all evidence disclosed at the hearings in the most careful manner, and make any additional investigation suggested by any discloseures or discrepancies in such evidence, in order to take any appropriate action for the same purpose."

Although Coolidge issued his directive only two days after Roosevelt testified before the Senate committee, it was not Roosevelt's testimony that broke into the solitude and inaction of the White House. Coolidge's letter to Daugherty confirmed "verbal instructions given some time ago," and Daugherty's acknowledgment of Coolidge's order showed further evidence of past discussions between the two about Teapot Dome: "As I have informed you," wrote Daugherty, "the Department of Justice, from the beginning of this investigation, has been giving careful attention to [it]. Since our conference, Mr. Holland, Assistant Attorney-General, has attended all the meetings." Daugherty assured Coolidge that his "instructions and desires" would "meet with hearty and cordial support and . . . be thoroughly and conscientiously carried out."[26]

Harry Daugherty, however, had sat in the Harding Cabinet, where—according to critics—Fall's leases may have been aired and approved. Here was a serious political liability for Calvin Coolidge. On the very day Coolidge sent his instructions to Daugherty, the Washington *Star* reported that members of the Cabinet "are keenly alive to the indirect discredit that public opinion . . . already is inclined to cast upon them as a whole." For this reason, Coolidge would "leave no stone unturned to get to the bottom of the . . . business," because, claimed the *Star*, he detested "anything remotely savoring of corruption in public office." Since he was aware that in this election year of 1924, the Democrats could create much thunder over "any evidence of Republican 'pussyfooting' in dealing with Teapot Dome," the country could "confidently await the right kind of action at the right time by Calvin Coolidge."

[26] Coolidge to Daugherty, Jan. 24, 1924, and Daugherty to Coolidge, Jan. 24, 1924, Justice Dept. General Records, Records of Naval Oil Reserve Investigations, 1924-29, Box 107, National Archives; see also New York *Times*, Jan. 23, 1924, p. 1. On January 23, Daugherty told newsmen that the Department of Justice had "been observing" the Senate investigating committee's proceedings and had "made some investigations on its own account"; *ibid.*

THE FINGER OF SUSPICION

—Spencer in the Omaha *World-Herald*

WEATHER-VANE, WASHINGTON

The *Star's* prediction of presidential activity would prove to be correct, but for a while Coolidge waited and thought and made his plans, and the cry went unabated that Teapot Dome must have been discussed in Cabinet meetings. Harry Slattery claimed that obviously "questions which vitally affect an administration . . . are discussed in Cabinet meetings." It was nonsense "to say the Cabinet did not know of the oil leases. . . . Washington, for months before the story broke in the newspapers was rife with the whole subject." Coolidge himself, however, claimed never to have heard the leases discussed during any of Harding's Cabinet meetings; and he in time penned the dry autobiographical observation that "much went on in the departments under President Harding, as it did under me, of which the Cabinet had no knowledge."

Herbert Hoover, Secretary of Commerce in the Cabinet, recalled that "our political opponents" became so persistent in their charge that "Secretary Hughes . . . and I found it necessary to denounce them"—and Hoover pointed out that Fall resigned "six months before any hint of wrong doing had been exposed." According to one account, when the Teapot Dome revelations began to emerge, Secretary of State Charles Evans Hughes "was just as much surprised as anyone else. . . . The question of oil leases had never come up in the Cabinet." Furthermore, Hughes had "little or no association with some of the members of the Cabinet, among them Fall." Hughes "scarcely saw them except at Cabinet meetings." On January 31, 1924, Hughes issued to the press a statement that the leases "were never brought before the Cabinet for its decision. My opinion . . . was never sought or expressed either in or out of the Cabinet." The same day, Hoover said that he could "confirm Secretary Hughes' statement." If, said Hoover, the Cabinet "were asked for their views on the oil leases, I was not aware of it." Secretary of War John W. Weeks followed Hoover with a declaration: "My recollection is exactly the same as expressed by Secretary Hughes. There may have been some discussion . . . but if there was I don't remember it, and I have missed very few Cabinet meetings in the last three years." Daugherty, the Cabinet member most likely to decide on the legality of the leases, insisted that his legal opinion on them "was never given, verbally or otherwise," and he "knew nothing about the . . . leases until the matter came up for investigation."[27]

Denials of Cabinet complicity were hardly sufficient to quell the joyful noises from certain critics of the administration. Without pausing for final reckoning on this subject, Thad Caraway raised another one. On January 23, he took the Senate floor and,

[27] Washington *Star*, Jan. 24, 1924, excerpt reprinted in *Cong. Rec.*, 68 Cong., 1 Sess. (Jan. 28, 1924), 1518; Slattery "Story of Teapot Dome," 93; Coolidge, *Autobiography*, 164 (see New York *Times*, Jan. 26, 1924, p. 2, for his disclaimer in 1924); Hoover, *Memoirs*, II, 55; Henry C. Beerits, memo on "The Fall Oil Scandals," Folder 45, Container 173, Charles Evans Hughes Papers, Division of Manuscripts, Library of Congress—Beerits arranged and catalogued the Hughes Papers, and from the papers and from interviews with Hughes he compiled memoranda on several subjects related to Hughes's career; all of these memoranda are in the Hughes Papers; Hughes, Hoover, and Weeks are quoted in these memoranda. Daugherty, *Inside Story*, 200. Daugherty wrote that Harding had "issued the order

in scathing sentences, denounced Fall as a traitor and demanded
that Congress cancel the leases. When McKellar of Tennessee
suggested that Denby was equally guilty of giving away the reserves, Caraway replied that "a man cannot be held liable unless
he has understanding enough to know what he does." McKellar's
remark was a portent of an ordeal that still lay ahead for Denby,
but Caraway's rejoinder was the substance of the judgment eventually rendered upon him. Walsh, returning the debate to modera-
tion as well as to the point, claimed that the leases could be cancelled only by the courts. Only Congress, he said, could authorize
the President "to institute proper suit to annul and cancel the
leases." And this Coolidge should do by appointing special counsel to investigate and prosecute, since Attorney-General Daugherty was an old political associate of Fall and was himself under
suspicion and criticism.[28]

Clearly, Coolidge and his Republican party were in jeopardy,
and their opposition was showing them little mercy. Apart from
any sincere desire to seek the truth and to punish the guilty, Democrats had sensed the campaign potentials in Teapot Dome. Coolidge had not revealed any readiness to create a strategy for over-
coming the stigma, and, by their silence, Republican spokesmen
appeared equally bereft of imagination. In truth, they seemed
overcome with the sudden outburst of revelation and insinuation.
The Coolidge administration's position seemed in peril, and its
future status in doubt.

Into this atmosphere of Democratic optimism and Republican
gloom, Edward Doheny dropped a calm confession. On January
24, he returned to the large, oblong room where the Public Lands
Committee sat for its hearings. By now the investigation had

---

without hesitation and without consulting me, either personally or as
Attorney-General. He had implicit faith in Fall's ability as a lawyer and
expert on oil lands. No man had ever questioned [Fall's] honesty." Daugherty accused Fall of "a gross betrayal" of Harding's confidence; by not telling Harding that he had received a loan from Doheny before making the
leases and by not admitting that he had asked for no competitive bids, Fall
"allowed his chief to send to the committee a letter of endorsement"
(Daugherty, *Inside Story*, 194).

[28] *Cong. Rec.*, 68 Cong., 1 Sess. (Jan. 23, 1924), 1309 ff.; New York
Times, Jan. 24, 1924, p. 1.

turned into what one reporter called "the most poignant play in Washington" since the Ballinger-Pinchot affair. In the presence of a throng of newspaper men, senators, and mere spectators, the dapper little millionaire confessed in his thin, inassertive voice that he had been the source of Albert Fall's $100,000.

In a prepared statement which he read to the committee, Doheny declared that he believed Fall had "been making an effort to keep my name out of the discussion for the reason that a full statement might be misundersood." Doheny himself had not revealed the loan during his previous testimony because, he claimed, "such statement was not pertinent in answer to any of the questions asked . . . by the committee, and to have done so would have been volunteering something in no way connected with the contracts [that Fall] made with Pan American Petroleum and Transport Company." Doheny had been asked before whether Fall had profited by any contract, directly or indirectly. Doheny had denied profit then; he denied it now. He loaned Fall $100,000 on November 30, 1921, "upon his promissory note to enable him to purchase a ranch in New Mexico." The money was Doheny's, and did not belong to Pan American; and the loan had no relation to the Elk Hills lease of 1922. Doheny and Fall had been friends for over thirty years, had prospected for gold together in the West years ago. Fall had suffered recent troubles; Doheny had become quite rich. He willingly lent Fall $100,000, sending it to him in cash. His son Edward Doheny, Jr., took the money, "in a little black bag," to Fall a day or so after Fall asked for it.

Doheny claimed that Pan American received its lease on the Elk Hills reserve simply because it made the best bid. Still, he suggested that a "board of experts" study the contract, and if it should report that the terms were "not wise, desirable, and advantageous for the Government to make and the very best that the Government could have obtained," he would "reconvey to the Government all interest" in the contract, "receiving in return only just compensation for . . . expenditures . . . made by the company under the contract, without profit." Finally, since certain skeptics on the committee wished to see the check Doheny had cashed to obtain the $100,000, as well as Fall's promissory note to him, Do-

heny agreed to look for them and place them before the committee when he found them.[29]

As though Edward Doheny had not sufficiently entwined Albert
Fall in a circumstantial net, J. W. Zevely, a lawyer for Harry Sinclair, testified the day following and added another strand. He
recalled that in 1922, when Sinclair asked Fall to go with him to
Russia, Fall needed $25,000 for personal business affairs. Sinclair
had told his secretary G. D. Wahlberg to give Zevely "$25,000 or
$30,000 in bonds," if Fall should ask Zevely for it. Fall "asked
for it," said Zevely, and Wahlberg sent the bonds to Fall's bank
in El Paso.[30]

By now, even Coolidge and Republican party spokesmen seemingly had had enough. If heretofore they had been at all willing
to shield Albert Fall and his transactions—and certainly individual
Republicans had been vocal in his defense and others eloquent in
their silence—testimony now had carried him beyond rescue. The
party must protect its interests. It may have been at about this
point that Coolidge sent for Harry Slattery to come to the White
House. Coolidge said he had been told that Slattery was familiar
with the details of "this whole oil incident." He asked Slattery to
tell him "the complete story." Slattery recalled: "I stated the details of the oil case beginning back in the early part of the Harding
administration." Coolidge made an inquiry about Fall's motive;
later he asked about Theodore Roosevelt, Jr. "It was evident,"
said Slattery, that Coolidge "did not know very much about the
whole case nor was he familiar with the background or phrase-
ology of it." When Slattery had told his story and answered Coolidge's questions, the talk promptly ended. As William Allen

[29] *Leases upon Reserves* (1924), 1771-1823, *passim*. Doheny was on the
stand for three hours. Some of the above testimony was from Doheny's prepared statement; some was from his responses to questions from the committee. For a vivid description of Doheny's testimony and of the committee
room atmosphere, see William Hard, "Oil Speaks," *The Nation*, CXVIII
(Feb. 6, 1924), 133-34; see also New York *Times*, Jan. 25, 1924, p. 1. See
New York *Times*, Jan. 27, 1924, Sec. 8, p. 1, and Feb. 17, 1924, Sec. 8, p.
3, for articles about Doheny and his fabulous activities in the oil industry.

[30] *Leases upon Reserves* (1924), 1831; New York *Times*, Jan. 26, 1924,
p. 1.

White observed, Coolidge now "knew the worst. He had nothing more to ask."[31]

White also noted that after Coolidge talked to Slattery, "an honest critic of Coolidge's slothful attitude," the President began —with circumspection—to move into action. The noted newspaperman probably had in mind administration behavior of late January. By this time, "administration leaders" were reported to be greatly worried over the political effect of Teapot Dome, and a Presidential spokesman asserted that the Cabinet, discussing the situation "carefully," had agreed that the government should "take positive and assertive steps that the guilty in the several transactions . . . be proceeded against criminally and the leases restored to the Government." Coolidge was quoted as not wishing to "jump to conclusions," but he did feel that the evidence brought out by the committee "requires explanation" and also "points to criminal action." When the Department of Justice was sure it had a case, it would present it to a grand jury.[32]

Concurrently, Frank Kent, a political analyst for the Baltimore *Sun*, reported that "brows of the Coolidge counselors for the first time are furrowed with care." Since Fall was not a member of the Coolidge administration and "no personal blame" could in any way be attached to the President for what Fall had done, Teapot Dome would not hurt Coolidge personally; however, wrote Kent, Teapot Dome did "hurt his party, and that hurts him politically." Kent pointed out that "concededly, this is the worst scandal in the Government in many decades. It is an exposure directed by Democrats of a Republican Administration and forced upon a Republican Senate and . . . committee. The facts have been

---

[31] Slattery to William Allen White, May 4, 1933, Slattery Papers; White, *A Puritan in Babylon*, 276. White, *A Puritan in Babylon*, 275, in later quoting Slattery's remark about Coolidge's lack of information, suggested: "All his life . . . Calvin Coolidge would rather appear foolish than to be a fool." White placed Slattery's visit "in the early spring of 1924." From his correspondence with Slattery, White was justified in making such an estimate, for Slattery was misleading, even contradictory, about the date. But he did tell White of seeing Coolidge "when the oil case first broke, at his request." Slattery to White, April 25, 1936, Slattery Papers. Several other letters and Slattery's autobiography tend to confirm the January date.

[32] White, *A Puritan in Babylon*, 276; New York *Times*, Jan. 26, 1924, pp. 1 and 2.

brought out by a Democratic Senator—Walsh—and the Democrats can be counted upon to make the most of it in the coming campaign." Kent had been told, however, that Coolidge did not "propose to permit the Democrats to murder him politically" because of Teapot Dome and that Coolidge would act "when the time comes, in such a way as to . . . nullify the Democratic attack." Moreover, concluded Kent, "the machinery of the Republican National Committee is in motion."[33]

Evidence for Kent's latter observation already existed. The *National Republican*, official paper of the Republican national committee, appeared the day after Doheny's testimony and editorialized that "the guilty in the oil reserve leases ought to be punished." The disclosures, in what the paper called "the Fall case," were "in a sense discreditable to the . . . Senate and to the Harding Administration, for . . . Fall was a member of both." The disclosures did not, however, "involve the integrity of the Senate or of the Harding Administration as a whole. Guilt is personal and dishonesty is a characteristic that has been noted in men of all parties." The *Republican* believed that "ultimate good will come out of the exposures of the Fall case—to the betterment of legislation and administration."[34]

Republicans, evincing recovery from their earlier depression, were compiling their rebuttal in the Fall case, better known by the Democratic prosecution as the Teapot Dome scandal. Whether the jury on election day in November would accept their defense remained to be seen. If the majority of voters reacted to the politics of Teapot Dome as Senator George W. Norris did, Coolidge and his party would lack ardent support. Norris was "not at all satisfied with Coolidge . . . a partisan more than anything else." Also, Norris had found "a good many prominent Republicans continually [throwing] water on this investigation. They have . . . in many cases and in many ways tried to prevent the full disclosure of the truth." Not that they had been dishonest, "but they have always seemed to be anxious to find excuses and protect anyone who was a Republican." Norris admitted, however, that Democrats had been "trying to do the same thing. . . ." In-

[33] Frank Kent, Baltimore *Sun*, Jan. 27, 1924.
[34] *The National Republican*, Jan. 26, 1924, copy in Slattery Papers; see also a summary in New York *Times*, Jan. 26, 1924, pp. 1 and 2.

deed, "partisan leaders in both parties" had been "exactly the same."[35] Norris' remarks were an apt summary of partisan activity through the first months of the investigation, and they remained valid as the great debate surged on into the spring of 1924.

While revelations from the hearings began to pile up, public criticism arose in proportion. Slattery and a group of fellow conservationists made plans to use the press again, this time to prevent any attempted "whitewash," as they called it, of the Senate hearings. Fall's perennial critic in Santa Fe editorialized, "How Are the Mighty Fallen," and suggested that Fall had the distinction of being "the hero of the greatest scandal that ever involved an American cabinet officer." The Chicago *Tribune* suggested that the "Fall scandal" may "outrun the famous Ballinger blight." Despite such evidence of indignation, however, Fall still had supporters. An old acquaintance from Las Cruces, New Mexico, wrote to Fall: "It is with deep regret that I note the many mean things being said . . . none of which I can believe to be true. I have talked to many of your old friends here and they all feel as I do, that you will come forward when you believe the time right and correct this affair to your credit." Another southwesterner, a business and political associate of Fall's, wrote that among "a great many people in New Mexico, Texas, and Arizona" not one had "criticized or condemned" him for borrowing money from Doheny. Even those critical of Fall's "misstatement" about McLean were "sympathetic and understanding," although "holding that it was wrong." If Fall would "sit steady," in time he could regain whatever confidence he had lost among southwesterners.[36]

Meanwhile, whatever the sentiments of Fall's friends, Democratic leaders increased their oratorical attacks on Teapot Dome. Senator J. Thomas Heflin, the "Don Tom" from Alabama, although himself never deficient in words, liked a New York *World* editorial

[35] Norris to Rev. B. F. Eberhart, March 8, 1924, Tray 2, Box 1, Norris Papers.

[36] Matthew F. Boyd to Slattery, Jan. 27, 1924, Slattery Papers; Santa Fe *New Mexican*, Jan. 18, 1914, also Jan. 23, 25, 28, 29, and 31, 1924; Chicago *Tribune*, quoted in Santa Fe *New Mexican*, Jan. 22, 1924; Charles C. Lee to Fall, Jan. 29, 1924, and W. A. Hawkins to Fall, Feb. 6, 1924, Box 1, Fall Papers. See also Curry, *Autobiography*, 300-91, and Hutchinson, *Bar-Cross Man*, 304, for further evidence of southwestern support of Fall at this time. The Fall Papers contain numerous letters from supporters of Fall.

enough to have it read into the *Congressional Record*. The editorial matched Heflin's own customary harangues. It viewed the "Fall scandal" as "the natural heritage of the recent Republican political philosophy of materialism." There was justifiable suspicion for "every act with which Fall and others in the Cabinet had any official connection." The "evil political growth" of Republican policies had yielded its "first rotten fruitage," and the harvest had only begun. With this contribution, if not before, Heflin joined Caraway of Arkansas as vocal pace-setter in senatorial criticism of the great Republican scandal. Democratic national chairman Cordell Hull was far from quiescent. On January 26, he issued a grossly partisan pronouncement, calling Teapot Dome "the greatest political scandal of this or any other generation." Although the time "would seem ripe for a housecleaning" of this and a dozen-odd other scandals, Coolidge gave no promise of action. According to Hull, the only way to clean house, punish the evildoers, and expose the scandals still concealed was to elect to office in 1924 the Democratic party, which had "an unblemished record of honest and faithful public service for more than a hundred years."[37]

While partisan debate thus swelled and the hearings went on, the principals involved responded to Teapot Dome in individual ways. Albert Fall was reported to be "very sick" at his home in New Mexico. In Paris, Harry Sinclair dodged reporters by moving to Versailles. And from the White House, Calvin Coolidge, detecting a loud pulse-beat from the Midwest and possibly reading—as was his custom—the editorials in the New York *World*, prepared to make a quiet but dramatic gesture, one that buoyed Republican hopes and raised cries of pain from the Democratic opposition.

On Saturday, January 26, five Republican congressmen from Kansas jointly telegraphed to Coolidge: "Believe situation demands vigorous action by President in oil lease matter. Public amazed by developments and nothing could increase confidence in administration like use of 'Big Stick' without delay. Think it

[37] *Cong. Rec.*, 68 Cong., 1 Sess. (Jan. 28, 1924), 1547, including editorial from New York *World*, Jan. 27, 1924; Hull, quoted in New York *Times*, Jan. 27, 1924, p. 2; Ray T. Tucker, "Don Tom of Alabam'," *North American Review*, CCXXVI (Aug., 1928), 148-57, for brief comment on Heflin's rhetoric.

important hit at once and hit hard." The same day, in the Senate, Tom Heflin of Alabama promised to try for a vote Monday on Thad Caraway's earlier motion to cancel the lease of Teapot Dome. Then late that afternoon, the Public Lands Committee met in executive session. During this session Walsh told the committee that he intended on Monday to call up the Caraway resolution and then to offer a substitute for it, one authorizing Coolidge to bring suit immediately to annul the leases, to enjoin further extraction of oil, and to appoint special counsel to prosecute the litigation. According to Walsh, the committee agreed not to reveal the terms of his resolution until he brought it before the Senate on Monday.[38]

Evidently the terms leaked almost at once to Coolidge, who was aboard the presidential yacht, the *Mayflower*, sailing on the Potomac. Coolidge had on board with him Senator George W. Pepper of Pennsylvania, his close friend and adviser William M. Butler from Massachusetts, and Chief Justice Arthur P. Rugg of the Massachusetts Supreme Court. They talked about Teapot Dome. According to Pepper, Coolidge did not know of the agreement reached in executive session by the Public Lands Committee. Whatever the President knew, whatever his thoughts of the day's pressures and problems, he turned that night from meditation to oral action. At seven o'clock, from the *Mayflower*, he wired his secretary C. Bascom Slemp to meet him later at the White House. At nine o'clock, Coolidge, Rugg, and Butler reached the White House, where Coolidge talked with acting Attorney-General Augustus T. Seymour and Rush Holland, the Justice Department's observer at the Senate hearings. Between nine-thirty and midnight, a statement from the President gradually took form. Newspapers and press associations then received it orally, by telephone. They gave it the best of care; those able to print it in late Sunday editions placed it in individual blocks on page one. Coolidge's statement was crisp and subtle:

It is not for the President to determine criminal guilt or render judgement in civil causes; that is the function of the

[38] Raleigh *News and Observer*, Jan. 27, 1924 (wire signed by J. H Tincher, Homer Hock, D. R. Anthony, Jr., J. C. Strong, and Hays B. White); *Cong. Rec.*, 68 Cong., 1 Sess. (Jan. 24, 1924), 1389-92; New York *Times*, Jan. 28, 1924, p. 2.

courts. It is not for him to prejudge. I shall do neither. But when the facts are revealed to me that require action for the purpose of insuring the enforcement of either civil or criminal liability such action will be taken. That is the province of the Executive.

Acting under my direction, the Department of Justice has been observing the course of the evidence which has been revealed at the hearings . . . which I believe warrants action for the purpose of enforcing the law and protecting the rights of the public. This is confirmed by reports made to me from the committee.

If there has been any crime, it must be prosecuted. If there has been any property of the United States illegally transferred or leased, it must be recovered.

I feel the public is entitled to know that in the conduct of such action no one is shielded for any party, political or other reasons. As I understand, men are involved who belong to both political parties, and having been advised by the Department of Justice that it is in accord with the former precedents, I propose to employ special counsel of high rank drawn from both political parties to bring such actions for the enforcement of the law. Counsel will be instructed to prosecute these cases in the courts so that if there is any guilt it will be punished; if there is any civil liability it will be enforced; if there is any fraud it will be revealed; and if there are any contracts which are illegal they will be cancelled.

Every law will be enforced. And every right of the people and the Government will be protected.[39]

The statement was filled with implications. It was clear that Calvin Coolidge was grabbing for the reins before the investigation ran away, leaving him and his party smeared and scorned. He admitted no crimes and he carefully recalled that men of both parties were involved, but his indirect slap at Harry Daugherty was manifest. Democrats would be quick to exploit it. Daugherty, in Miami on vacation, received notice Saturday night that

[39] New York *Times*, Jan. 28, 1924, p. 1; *Cong. Rec.*, 68 Cong., 1 Sess. (Jan. 28, 1924), 1537-41, 1611 for the statement and the background to it.

Coolidge intended to take the investigation out of his department. Just before midnight, he wired the President, urging him to appoint special counsel to "at once take up all phases of the oil leases." Daugherty did not wish to evade any responsibility, but, he said, "considering Mr. Fall and I served in the Cabinet together, this would be fair to you, to Mr. Fall and the American people, as well as to the Attorney General." Daugherty did not wish to be consulted about the appointments, but he did offer the aid of the Justice Department to them and to Coolidge, if they wanted it.[40]

Daugherty apparently was trying to make the best of a bad situation. According to Democrats, so was Coolidge. In his midnight broadside, Democrats saw only political calculation. On Sunday, Walsh charged that Coolidge had been told of the Public Land Committee's confidential agreement, the implication being, as Lenroot phrased it Monday in the Senate, "that the President's action was actuated by what the committee did in executive session." But Lenroot claimed that Coolidge had called him to the White House Saturday night at ten-thirty, that when he arrived "the statement . . . had been prepared," and that Coolidge at the time had "no information from me, and I am advised from no other person, concerning the action of the committee." In the House on Monday, Joseph W. Byrns, Democrat of Tennessee, suggested during debate over appointment of Coolidge's special counsel that the President had anticipated a Democratic move to call for cancellation of the leases and appointment of the counsel.[41]

To this and other Democratic taunts, Republicans in the House replied with a sober plea for unity in the face of tragedy and urged that Teapot Dome was bigger than any party. And from Republican floor leader Nicholas Longworth of Ohio came a foretaste of the tactics that Republicans, gradually regaining morale

[40] *Cong. Rec.*, 68 Cong., 1 Sess. (Jan. 28, 1924), 1537-38, for reprint of wire.

[41] Washington *Post*, interview with Walsh, Jan. 28, 1924; *Cong. Rec.*, 68 Cong., 1 Sess. (Jan. 28, 1924), 1520, 1577, and 1582-83. Byrns's Tennessee colleague, Finis J. Garret, recalled an historic parallel to Coolidge's midnight statement: The "case of the Philipian jailer who held one of the early Christians in prison and about midnight there came the rumble of a great earthquake and he began to cry out, 'What shall I do to be saved?' " *Ibid.*, 1577.

if not the initiative, would adopt in the weeks ahead. Longworth, deploring the partisanship being shown by some members of the House, said that he would not let this influence his own remarks, since he bitterly condemned and greatly regretted "the frauds which seem to have been perpetrated." But, he continued, he must correct a general impression that seemed to be current among Democrats, that Edwin Denby "is responsible for the legislation under which these leases were made." The Democratic gentlemen were wrong: "Secretary Daniels was responsible for taking these oil reserves out of the public domain and permitting them to be leased to private individuals." Under immediate fire from the Democratic gentlemen, who quite properly challenged his inference that Daniels was responsible for Teapot Dome, Longworth admitted that Daniels was entirely innocent; but, he still insisted, so was Denby. Despite the clarification, Daniels, Navy Secretary during a Democratic administration, now had been associated, however vaguely, with Teapot Dome. Republican spokesmen were subsequently to revive that association.

As the day's debate neared a close, James F. Byrnes, Democrat of South Carolina, noted that Edward Doheny had contributed $25,000 to the Republican campaign fund in 1920; whereupon, Longworth recalled that "Mr. Doheny was the largest contributor to the Democratic campaign fund in 1912." To this, Byrnes replied, "In 1912 he was honest." After the play of wit, the House passed by nearly unanimous vote a resolution to appropriate $100,000 to pay for Coolidge's special counsel.[42]

Cries of administration hypocrisy arose, too, from newspapers and magazines. One journal regretted that "Mr. Coolidge, in his midnight statement, betrays no indignation, no alarm, at the facts revealed. . . . He is content to declare that 'every law will be enforced'—after his hand has been forced." Another was cynical of the "outburst of moral indignation which has followed recent revelations." From Raleigh, the *News and Observer* accused Coolidge of undue partisanship. In Boston, Coolidge's "court paper" saw only statesmanship in his announcement. The Baltimore *Sun*, revealing more objective judgment and analysis, admitted that although Coolidge had adopted "a strong and admirable position,"

---

[42] *Cong. Rec.*, 68 Cong., 1 Sess. (Jan. 28, 1924), 1574-85.

the suddenness of his action did suggest "that his hand was forced by the thickly gathering storm."[43]

One conclusion was evident. Calvin Coolidge, in one calm and calculated move, had stolen much Democratic thunder. Undoubtedly he would pilfer more before election day in November.

[43] *The Nation*, CXVIII (Feb. 6, 1924), 130; Paul Y. Anderson, "The Scandal in Oil," *The New Republic*, XXXVII (Feb. 6, 1924), 277-79; Raleigh *News and Observer*, Jan. 28, 1924; Boston *Evening Transcript*, Jan. 28, 1924; Baltimore *Sun.*, Jan 28 ,1924.

6

The Onrush of Scandal

As January, 1924, neared an end and Coolidge began his search for counsel, Teapot Dome continued to make news. On the twenty-eighth, shares of Pan-American and of Sinclair Consolidated dropped sharply on the New York Stock Exchange. From Cheyenne, Wyoming, came word that Harry Sinclair had spent about $25,000,000 on Teapot Dome but would be delighted to give up his lease if he were reimbursed for this expenditure, since the area had not yielded according to the experts' calculations. On the twenty-ninth in the House, Byrns of Tennessee placed a wire from Josephus Daniels in the *Record*. Daniels, replying to Nicholas Longworth's criticism associating him with the Teapot Dome lease, declared: "My uniform and militant position was to preserve the oil in the ground for the exclusive use of the Navy. The leasing by [Fall] . . . overturned the policy I maintained." The same day, the Senate Public Lands Committee learned that Fall, scheduled to testify, was too sick to appear. Instead, his attorney presented a statement, signed by four physicians, that Fall should not leave his residence, but that he could endure a bedside inquiry. His attorney added that Fall was "on the verge of a nervous breakdown." The committee decided to hear the four physicians testify before them on the subject the next day. Also on January 29, Coolidge selected his special counsel, Silas H. Strawn of Chicago, a Republican, and Thomas W. Gregory of New York City, a Democrat. Both men accepted the appointments, subject to Senate approval.[1]

On this same busy day, Edwin Denby stood on the White House steps after a Cabinet meeting and told reporters that he had no intention of resigning, despite growing demands in the Senate that he do so. He thought that the oil leases were legal and wise. He resented intimations that he was guilty of malfeasance, and he challenged all senators who thought otherwise to place their sentiments on record. "I want a record vote in the Senate," he said. The day before, in the Senate, Walsh had criticized Denby for surrendering the reserves to Fall and for negligence in his duty; and unless Denby's resignation was in Coolidge's hands before sundown, Walsh promised to "ask action by this body appropriate to the occasion." This hard, clear statement contrasted sharply with a massive array of comical and partisan harangues during the day from Thad Caraway and Joseph T. Robinson of Arkansas, and Tom Heflin of Alabama, who drew retorts in a similar vein from Republican hecklers. Robinson, however, did manage during one of his perorations to introduce a resolution calling on Denby to resign. Although Democratic techniques varied, Denby was for the moment their common target. Not for long would he bear up under the attack.[2]

[1] *Wall Street Journal,* Jan. 29, 1924; New York *Times,* Jan. 29, 1924, p. 2; *Cong. Rec.,* 68 Cong., 1 Sess. (Jan. 29, 1924), 1639; *Leases upon Reserves* (1924), 1907-1909; New York *Times,* Jan. 30, 1924, pp. 1 and 2; and Charlotte *Observer,* Jan. 30, 1924.

[2] New York *Times,* Jan. 30, 1924, pp. 1 and 2; *Cong. Rec.,* 68 Cong., 1 Sess. (Jan. 28, 1924), 1518-49, *passim.* Although he had his imitators and his supporters, Senator Heflin in particular exercised his wit and his considerable oratorical skills during these Senate dialogues in January and February of 1924. From moment to moment caustic, humorous, and grandly rhetorical, Heflin's interest wandered over the political landscape as he

On January 29, the Senators debated six hours, this time over the leases. Lenroot used up most of the session himself. With certain qualifications, he supported Walsh in declaring the leases illegal, but he deplored the political propaganda that Democrats were making of a serious national problem. Lenroot wanted the Senate to express, in a resolution, merely a doubt that the oil contracts were legal, in contrast to Walsh, who wanted them declared positively illegal. In harsh debate the following day, the Senate refused to soften the Walsh resolution. George Norris had "no party to condemn" but did suggest that the committee had found from the beginning of its investigation an utter disregard for law. To Norris, the contracts were void, and the government should bring suit to annul them. He thought that the leasing was "deep, disgraceful fraud and corruption." After Norris, interminable charges and accusations echoed across the gallery, sometimes laden with scriptural plagiarisms, and rarely free from blatant partisanship. The Senate finally rejected Lenroot's proposed resolution, the vote reflecting party alignment with great clarity. Then on January 31, the senators, this time in complete unanimity, adopted and passed the Walsh resolution, directing Coolidge to begin suit to cancel the oil leases and to hire special counsel for doing it.[3]

Coolidge's recent behavior to the contrary, Walsh and the critics of Teapot Dome still appeared to hold the initiative. Out in the grass roots, one Democratic organization bubbled with confidence, as well as imagination: the party committee in Clackamus County, Oregon placed an order for ten thousand miniature aluminum teapots.[4] Teapot Dome, however, knew no political bounds, and suddenly it diminished the glee of numerous Democrats who were

---

harangued the Republicans, quoted scripture, denounced the rich, and jibed at the administration's incompetency. Republicans often rose to his bait. When he faltered—which was not often—his Democratic colleagues rescued him with timely barbs or reminders of other tacks his speeches had not yet taken.

[3] *Cong. Rec.*, 68 Cong., 1 Sess. (Jan. 29, 30, and 31, 1924), 1592 ff., 1688 ff., and 1728. The vote on Lenroot's resolution is on p. 1685; there were thirty-eight ayes, all Republicans, and forty-six nays from thirty-eight Democrats, two Farmer-Labor Senators, and six Progressive Republicans. The vote on the Walsh resolution was eighty-nine yeas, no nays, with seven not voting.

[4] New York *Times*, Jan. 31, 1924, p. 2.

promoting William Gibbs McAdoo for the presidential nomination in 1924.

On the morning of February 1, 1924, McAdoo appeared to be
the man to beat for the Democratic presidential nomination. In
mid-January, McAdoo himself had written to a correspondent:
"My friends give me the best sort of reports from all parts of the
country, and I am inclined to think that they are not over-opti-
mistic." William Jennings Bryan privately expressed the opinion
that McAdoo was "the strongest force for the leadership of the
Party," although Bryan cautioned that conditions could change
before the June convention assembled. Senator Furnifold M. Simmons wrote McAdoo of "an overwhelming sentiment in the country for you. . . . The only way you can be defeated is by jockeying
you out of votes to which you are entitled." And Simmons' secretary, Frank Hampton, reported to McAdoo from Washington that
"the conviction is growing here . . . even among the correspondents of metropolitan newspapers . . . heretofore not . . . friendly
to you that the opposition to your nomination is fast breaking up."
Hampton thought it "not too much to hope for" that McAdoo
would control the necessary two-thirds votes before the convention assembled.[5]

Analyst Frank Kent, on January 15, reported great optimism at
the Washington meeting of the Democratic national committee.
"On the surface," McAdoo seemed to have the nomination "all but
'sewed up'." A poll of the committee showed that more than 60
out of a total of 106 were for McAdoo. Atmosphere in the Washington hotel lobbies "was a McAdoo atmosphere and the McAdoo
control of the committee was conceded." Yet Kent saw one flaw
in the complacency. Conceding the McAdoo domination of the
national committee, there was still "a powerful and bitter minority"

[5] McAdoo to Frederick I. Thompson, Jan. 16, 1924, Box 292; Roper to
McAdoo, Jan. 22, 1924, and Simmons to McAdoo, Jan. 26, 1924, Box 293,
McAdoo Papers; Hampton to McAdoo, Jan. 3, 1924, Simmons Papers. For
more detailed analyses of McAdoo's strength—and likewise expressions of
optimism—see Carl Vinson to McAdoo, Jan. 15, 1924, Box 294, and M. L.
Fox to McAdoo, Jan. 23, 1924, Box 293, McAdoo Papers. Vinson offered
a state-by-state estimate of McAdoo's strength in the South, where his
principal rival for the nomination was Senator Oscar W. Underwood of
Alabama. Fox, secretary of the McAdoo for President Committee, believed
that by late January, 1924, Underwood had " 'shot his wad' in the South."
Cf. Allen, "The Democratic Primary in Texas," loc. cit.

among the Democratic leaders who were against McAdoo and who gave "every evidence of a determination to stay against him to the end."[6]

Senator James A. Reed of Missouri, for one, opposed McAdoo, since Reed wanted the presidential nomination himself, and it was Reed who first set McAdoo on the bitter path toward political downfall. On January 31, in the Senate, Reed asked that Doheny be recalled for further testimony before the Public Lands Committee. Reed knew precisely what he wanted from Doheny and what the committee should ask him. They should, said Reed, ask Doheny "whether he has ever . . . given or contributed any money to any person at the time holding a public position . . . or whether he has, immediately or shortly after discontinuance in office of any such public official . . . , contributed or given any money to him." Lenroot agreed to subpoena Doheny immediately, and he assured Reed that "if no one else asks the question he desires, the Chairman will do so."[7]

Chairman Lenroot carried out his promise. The next day, February 1, he asked Doheny: "Have you employed any . . . Cabinet officer [other than Franklin K. Lane] subsequent to his retiring from the Cabinet?" Doheny replied that he had hired several. One was Wilson's Attorney-General, Thomas W. Gregory, the Democrat recently nominated by Coolidge as one of his special counsel. Another was Wilson's Secretary of the Treasury, William Gibbs McAdoo. McAdoo was a member of the law firm of McAdoo, Cotton, and Franklin, which Doheny claimed to have employed "to represent us in Washington in connection with Mexican matters." This was while Wilson remained in office; afterwards, McAdoo "represented us in Mexico." Doheny testified that he paid McAdoo "about $250,000."[8]

During his testimony, Doheny also produced a mutilated note, which he claimed was the one signed by Albert Fall when he re-

---

6 Frank Kent, in Baltimore Sun, Jan. 15, 1924.

7 Cong. Rec., 68 Cong., 1 Sess. (Jan. 31, 1924), 1740.

8 Leases upon Reserves (1924), 1936-40. Doheny later corrected this figure, when he learned from his records that "on November 20, 1919, there was paid to the law firm of McAdoo, Cotton and Franklin the sum of $100,000." Also, beginning on March 1, 1922, McAdoo had "been in receipt of an annual retainer at the rate of $25,000 per year." Doheny to Lenroot, Feb. 2, 1924, ibid., 1969.

ceived the $100,000 loan; but Fall's signature was torn off. Do-
heny said that he had torn it from the note himself, since, if he
should die before Fall could repay the loan, Fall might be pressed
for repayment to the Doheny estate at an inconvenient time. He
gave the signature to his wife, so that the two together still held
Fall's entire note. Edward Doheny, Jr., knew of this arrangement,
and in case Doheny and his wife should die, he could "get a new
note from Mr. Fall by asking for it."[9]

This latest rigmarole simply elaborated an already weird tale,
but the McAdoo revelation brought fresh incriminations to the
political scene. The scandal that had been almost exclusively Republican now had smeared a Democrat. By pure association
McAdoo was linked fast to Teapot Dome. In South Carolina, one
newspaper editor wrote to another: "I threw McAdoo over immediately [after] the oil touched him. . . . It would be impossible
for the Democrats to capitalize the oil scandals to anything like
their productive value with McAdoo as leader, and that would be
blessed relief to the Republicans." Harry Slattery did not think
that the Democrats would "be such fools as to try a go with
[McAdoo]." Frank Hampton, McAdoo's strong supporter in North
Carolina, now feared that McAdoo's "availability has been much
injured." Not that McAdoo had done anything wrong, "for he has
not," wrote Hampton, but "the people will not understand. . . . It
appears that we will have to get another candidate." Breckenridge Long, McAdoo's stalwart supporter in Missouri and one
who already despised Senator Reed, was dismayed with the Doheny testimony: "Just as everything had been arranged for Mc-
Adoo, a bomb was thrown into the camp—engineered by Reed.
He is a shrewd devil." Long telephoned Colonel E. M. House,
another early McAdoo supporter, to suggest that Doheny had
damaged McAdoo's candidacy "perhaps beyond repair." Nevertheless, he and House agreed to "stick to McAdoo till we could
discover the reaction of public thought."[10]

[9] Ibid., 1919 ff.

[10] T. R. Waring, editor of Charleston (S.C.) Evening Post, to W.W. Ball,
editor of The State (Columbia, S.C.), March 25, 1924, W. W. Ball Papers,
Duke University Library; Slattery to John Grace, April 5, 1924, Slattery
Papers; Frank Hampton to E. J. Smathers, March 6, 1924, Simmons Papers;
Breckenridge Long diary, Feb. 2, 1924, McAdoo Papers.

—Marcus in the New York *Times*

"You Splash Me — I Splash You"

That reaction was not immediately encouraging. In the New York *World*, Charles Michelson wrote of "the present dismay of the Democrats," who were "as bewildered at the political consequences [of Doheny's testimony] as the Republicans have been since the first explosion." To Michelson, Doheny had "seemed to take a vicarious revenge . . . and Senator Lenroot, smarting like the rest of the Republicans . . . , saw to it that [Doheny's] testimony was brought out in its entirety." The Coolidge court paper in Boston commented tersely: " 'McAdoo 'll do' is proposed as the Democratic slogan—but it looks now as if they were ready to make it 'McAdieu.' " The New York *Times*, offering a more extended analysis, reported that in the opinion of most political observers in Washington McAdoo had "been eliminated as a formidable contender for the Democratic nomination." Doheny's testimony had not involved McAdoo in scandal, but since the

Democrats proposed to make the oil lease an issue in the campaign, it would be embarrassing to nominate a man who had accepted "lucrative employment" with Edward Doheny. Frank Kent, in the Baltimore *Sun*, pointed out how the Democrats had built up a powerful issue in Teapot Dome and "were equipped for an aggressive fight." Then came the Doheny story. "At once," wrote Kent, "the issue disappears if the candidate remains." For it would be "a joke" to see McAdoo on the stump denouncing his own employer's bribery of Albert Fall.[11]

Kent had found that "nearly everybody" in Washington agreed that Doheny had eliminated McAdoo "but they do not agree about whom it helps." One man certain to profit, however, was Senator Robert M. La Follette, who gained for his third party candidacy votes that McAdoo lost for himself. McAdoo, until Doheny wounded him, appeared to be an ideal candidate of the unions, especially the railroad brotherhoods, which had not forgotten his friendly attitude toward labor during the war. But when the Conference for Progressive Political Action met in February, 1924, at St. Louis, William H. Johnston, chairman of the CPPA executive committee, declared that McAdoo, hitherto favored by railroad men, had been rendered ineligible by Doheny's testimony. With his name scratched, Progressives had to turn to third party candidates; among these, only the name of La Follette was outstanding.[12]

[11] New York *World*, Feb. 1, 1924; Boston *Evening Transcript*, Feb. 2, 1924; New York *Times*, Feb. 2, 1924, p. 5; Baltimore *Sun*, Feb. 3, 1924. George Creel, chairman of the Committee on Public Information during World War I, had also been listed by Doheny as one of the former government officials employed by his company. Creel wrote to Josephus Daniels: ". . . of all the things that have been said about me, the Doheny lie hurt worst." Two weeks before his testimony, Doheny had offered to make Creel "a rich man if I would quit urging Mexican recognition [by the United States]." When Creel told Doheny what he thought of him, Doheny, said Creel, "flew into one of his maniacal rages and nearly had an apoplectic fit." Creel did not doubt that Doheny then tried to maneuver him into an untenable position, for it was "not possible to overestimate that creature's cunning." Creel to Daniels, Sept. 12, 1924, Box 583, Daniels Papers.

[12] Baltimore *Sun*, Feb. 3, 1924; Kenneth McKay, *The Progressive Movement of 1924* (New York, 1947), 74; James H. Shideler, "The Neo-Progressives: Reform Politics in the United States, 1920-1925," (Ph.D. dissertation, University of California, 1945), 217. Johnston later denied making the statement that Doheny's testimony had rendered McAdoo ineligible; Santa Fe *New Mexican*, Feb. 11, 14, 1924.

McAdoo, despite his affliction, refused to collapse; indeed, he clearly had not been injured beyond recovery. If some of his former labor supporters now began to fade away, others remained even more articulate in his defense. Johnston turned from McAdoo to La Follette, but various other railroad brotherhood leaders did not. Soon after Doheny's testimony, the assistant president of the Brotherhood of Locomotive Firemen and Enginemen in Cleveland, Ohio, wrote to McAdoo: "A word of encouragement to a man who is fighting to protect and preserve his name and honor. . . . I think I can safely say that every true and loyal laboring man in the country realizes that the whole scheme to associate your name with this scandal is a 'frame-up'. . . . I am sure the railroad workers of America are behind you to a man."[13]

Numerous other wires and letters of encouragement came to McAdoo, expressing continued loyalty and deploring—as the writers saw it—the underhanded tactic of Doheny and those who had encouraged him. Judge Walter E. Brock of Winston-Salem, North Carolina, an early supporter, wired McAdoo on February 2, 1924, that "all realize that republicans are trying to cover their own shame by undertaking to draw you and exsecretary daniels into the matter. . . ." An angry supporter in Denver, Colorado, wrote: The "vultures who thrive on false unjustifiable and character annihilating propaganda cannot dethrone you from your high pedestal in the confidence of the American electorate." Many of these statements undoubtedly were the natural responses of McAdoo enthusiasts, telling their candidate what they felt he now needed to hear. But privately, Breckenridge Long expressed a more gloomy outlook: "It is unmistakable that the McAdoo forces are crumbling." Thomas Love of Texas, who had been "his ardent supporter," was now "out for [the Governor of Indiana, Samuel] Ralston for President," wrote Long. Joseph Tumulty was now favoring Senator Walsh. Bernard Baruch, who had been helping to finance the McAdoo campaign, was now turning toward another candidate. "When Love, Tumulty, and Baruch . . . desert

[13] McKay, *Progressive Movement*, 103 n.; Timothy Shea to McAdoo, Feb. 9, 1924, Container 295, McAdoo Papers.

him," suggested Long, "it means a great deal. It means he is gone."[14]

Yet Long would not abandon the cause. His own analysis was quite simple: "One of the arguments of his friends . . . is that his availability as a nominee has been damaged. But who else is there?" And within less than two weeks after Doheny's testimony, Long had recovered some of his original optimism. "We are beaten today," he said, "but in a week will be even and in two weeks will be again in the lead." At the same time, McAdoo himself blazed with righteous indignation; Long described him as being "mad . . . full of fight. He is swearing mad . . . cussing and swearing, damming every opponent and every obstacle." From Los Angeles he issued a statement declaring that Doheny was "wholly without justification of any sort" in mentioning his name during testimony on the oil leases; and he wired Walsh, asking for a chance to testify before the committee.[15] On February 11, the committee heard his defense. But by then, other themes and characters had appeared in the bizarre unfolding of Teapot Dome.

On January 28, before a packed gallery, the Senate debated at length Senator Joseph T. Robinson's resolution asking Coolidge to remove Denby as Secretary of the Navy. Senator Royal S. Copeland, Democrat from New York, said the Senate should demand Denby's resignation. Senator Duncan Fletcher, Democrat from Florida, found Denby incompetent because he had exonerated Richard A. Ballinger in 1911. Rare was the Republican who defended Denby, although frequent was the charge that Democrats were playing politics with his name. Senator George H. Moses, Republican from New Hampshire, deplored the "partisan and miasmatic air" of the Senate chamber and supposed that "the manhunt" would go on, that the Senate would "find sick chambers invaded by a jazz band, . . . and partisan snipers making a rifle pit

[14] Brock to McAdoo, Feb. 2, 1924, Container 294; Thomas Arthur to McAdoo, Feb. 3, 1924, Container 294; Breckenridge Long diary, Feb. 2 and 8, 1924, McAdoo Papers. In his entry for Feb. 8, 1924, Long noted that even Dan Roper, "his supposed chief advisor and supermanager" was "awfully wobbly."

[15] Breckenridge Long diary, Feb. 8, 1924, and Feb. 13, 1924, McAdoo Papers; New York *Times,* Feb. 2, 1924, p. 11.

of the grave of Warren Harding." With this ill-timed remark, Moses threw up a new target for partisan crossfire, since Democrats could also find in sick-rooms and former presidents a fruitful argument. Heflin promised to speak on the latter subject the next day.[16]

Harry Daugherty, another target for Democratic charges, continued to show an aggressive defense of his virtue. On February 1, he telegraphed seven Republican senators, six Republican congressmen, and Coolidge, informing them that he "was never consulted by anybody as to the wisdom [,] merits or legality of the leases . . . nor was the Department of Justice ever asked for an opinion or consulted."[17] But Harry Daugherty would not escape political exile by a mere protestation of innocence—accusing fingers continued to point him out.

Then in the Senate, on February 1, Democrat Henry F. Ashurst of Arizona, and Heflin—as he had promised—took up the charge made by Senator Moses the day before. Ashurst recalled a visit made to President Wilson's sick room in December, 1919, by a delegation of Republicans, including Senator Albert Fall, who reportedly pulled back the covers from the bed to see if Wilson truly was ill. Heflin suggested that Fall could not complain that Democrats had so invaded his own sick room; even if he should, he could say: " 'The thorns which I have reap'd are of the trees I have planted; they have torn me, and I bleed.' " Heflin's remark may have been pure buffoonery, but the little Senate debate took on tragic irony when the next day's headlines announced that Wilson was dying. At the same time, from the hearings came a report that three physicians, appointed by the committee to ex-

[16] *Cong. Rec.*, 68 Cong., 1 Sess. (Jan. 28, 1924), 1729 ff.; New York *Times*, Jan. 29, 1924, pp. 1 and 2.

[17] General Records of Justice Dept., Records of Naval Oil Reserve Investigation, Box 107, National Archives. Daugherty's wires went to Senators Frank B. Willis and Simeon D. Fess of Ohio, David A. Reed of Pennsylvania, Frank B. Brandagee of Connecticut, Henry Cabot Lodge of Massachusetts, Charles Curtis of Kansas, and Reed Smoot of Utah; to Representatives George S. Graham of Pennsylvania, Richard Yates of Illinois, Frederick H. Gillett of Massachusetts, and John L. Coble, Israel M. Foster, and Nicholas Longworth, all of Ohio. See also *Leases upon Reserves* (1924), 1969, for copy of the telegram, which Daugherty also sent to Chairman Lenroot.

amine Fall, found him in suitable condition to appear before the committee.[18]

The New York *Times* reported rumors that Fall, now forced to testify, would "hold nothing back" and that "leaders of both parties admittedly were awaiting his testimony with ill-concealed nervousness and . . . apprehension." The Chicago *Tribune*, looking over all the "Hullabaloo at Washington," asked: "Isn't it about time for one of our statesmen to get out on a balcony and in the historic words of Garfield on the assassination of Lincoln, assure us that 'God reigns and the Government at Washington still lives'?" The *Tribune* admitted that disclosures thus far were "sordid and omniously ambiguous," but criticized the "strident demands for instant action and the ludicrous scramble to get into the limelight," as being "plainly cheap politics." But the Santa Fe *New Mexican* noted: "The oil lease probe is spreading. The deeper you get into it the more bottomless it appears. . . . There is nothing to do but see it through." *The Nation* suggested that "we are only at the beginning of the revelations," that the country was "getting a delightful picture of what a business government really is and exactly what Mr. Harding had in mind when he declared for a return to 'normalcy.'" And *The New Republic* suggested that because of the Harding administration, the nation would "have to undergo another process of muck-raking and stable-cleaning."[19]

---

[18] *Cong. Rec.*, 68 Cong., 1 Sess. (Feb. 1, 1924), 1804; and *Leases upon Reserves* (1924), 1911. In December, 1919, the Senate Foreign Relations Committee, seeking Wilson's views on certain foreign policy problems, appointed Fall and Nebraska's Senator Gilbert M. Hitchcock, as a subcommittee to visit Wilson, who was bedridden at the time. The two Senators went to the White House and saw Wilson. Democratic accusations that Fall, during this visit, pulled the covers from Wilson's bed recurred from time to time, until November 2, 1929, when Senator Bronson Cutting of New Mexico showed evidence to the contrary. Cutting was, by his own admission, Fall's "political antagonist for nearly 20 years," but he offered his evidence "in the interest of accuracy and . . . justice." Cutting had communicated with Hitchcock and with Wilson's physician, who also was in the room during the visit. Both men said that Fall had not pulled away the covers. See *Cong. Rec.*, 71 Cong., 1 Sess. (Nov. 2, 1929), 5105; see also David Stratton, "President Wilson's Smelling Committee," *The Colorado Quarterly*, V (Autumn, 1956), 164-84.

[19] New York *Times*, Feb. 2, 1924, p. 1; Chicago *Tribune* editorial, reprinted in Boston *Evening Transcript*, Feb. 2, 1924; Santa Fe *New Mexican*, Feb. 14, 1924; *The Nation*, CXVIII (Feb. 27, 1924), 220; *The New Republic* XXXVII (Feb. 13, 1924), 297-98.

In the midst of the hullabaloo, Albert Fall appeared before the committee and refused to answer questions on the ground that his answers might tend to incriminate him. The next day, Thomas Gregory withdrew as a nominee for Coolidge's special counsel, stating that his firm's connections with Edward Doheny, "however indirect and however small," made it inappropriate for him to act as counsel. In his place, Coolidge nominated Atlee Pomerene, former Democratic Senator from Ohio.[20]

Gregory's resignation and Fall's retreat behind the Fifth Amendment hardly cleared the atmosphere. Frank Kent reported that "neither Republican, Democrat nor insurgent leaders have the least idea which way the 'cat is going to jump. . . .' All over Washington there is a feeling that the worst is yet to come." Albert J. Beveridge, expressing sympathy with Gifford Pinchot over some recent ear trouble, concluded: "Maybe it is a good time to be deaf—Lord! but the country is howling." In Worcester, Massachusetts, newspaper publisher Frank Knox, reacting to the clamor, called for an administration "distinctively and peculiarly Coolidge's own." The entire Cabinet should resign, allowing Coolidge to accept or reject their resignations, and thus acquire a Cabinet of his own choosing.[21]

Whatever he thought of a mass Cabinet resignation, Walsh insisted that at least Denby should go. In the Senate, while the noise increased and Denby's name rose above the din, Walsh denied any personal malice toward him and disclaimed any wish "to develop political capital" out of the charges against Denby. It was, said the Montana Senator, reserved for Lenroot, upon Senator James Reed's instigation, "to travel outside the [committee's] lines" and to ask Edward Doheny entirely unrelated questions, "for the perfectly obvious purpose of ruining the prospects of the leading candidate for the Democratic nomination." Walsh would not, as some had suggested, impeach Denby; "stupidity," he said, was not a ground for impeachment. Walsh's disclaimer of parti-

[20] *Leases upon Reserves* (1924), 1961-63; Gregory to Coolidge, in New York *Times*, Feb. 4, 1924, p. 1.
[21] Kent in Baltimore *Sun*, Feb. 5, 1924; Beveridge to Pinchot, Feb., 1924, Box 244, Pinchot Papers; Knox's speech reported in New York *Times*, Feb. 7, 1924, p. 4.

sanship aside, the Senate on February 11, by a quite partisan vote, passed Robinson's resolution that Coolidge demand Denby's resignation, because of his complicity in the leasing of the reserves.[22]

Coolidge declined to obey the Senate's request. Four hours after the resolution passed, the White House issued a statement from Coolidge: As soon as special counsel had advised him on the legality of the leases, and had assembled for him "the pertinent facts in the various transactions," the President would "take such action as seems essential." He would "not hesitate to call for the resignation of any official whose conduct . . . warrants such action," but dismissal of an officer of the government other than by impeachment was "exclusively an executive function." Coolidge quoted James Madison and Grover Cleveland on the necessity of the executive maintaining his rights inviolate and of the three branches of government remaining separate and distinct. He assumed full responsibility for his conduct and would "act upon the evidence and the law" as he found it. He would "deal thoroughly and summarily with every kind of wrong doing," but he did not propose to "sacrifice any innocent man" for his own welfare.[23]

While presiding over its deliberations during his vice-presidential days, Coolidge had learned to respect the Senate. Perhaps, as President, he felt differently toward senators. He told William Howard Taft that "the Republican senators are a lot of damned cowards." Apparently, he thought that he, if not his party's senators, would weather the partisan storm by defying, rather than yielding to, Democratic charges. The day after his reply to the Senate action, he wrote to George Harvey: "I do not know why I have been put in this hard place; but here I am, and am trying to straighten it out, observe the law, and close it up. . . . I think things are fairly good, but we lack organization in Congress. I am

[22] *Cong. Rec.*, 68 Cong., 1 Sess. (Feb. 11, 1924), 2055-68, 2245. Thirty-five Democrats, two Farmer-Labor, and ten Republican Senators (mostly from the Farm Bloc) voted for the resolution; thirty-five Republicans and a single Democrat (William C. Bruce of Maryland) voted against it. Harry Slattery called the vote "a square lineup of 36 Democrats and 11 Progressive Republicans in favor, and 34 Administration Senators against the resolution." Slattery, "Story of Teapot Dome," 81 (Slattery dropped two nay votes somewhere in his calculations).

[23] Coolidge's statement, New York *Times*, Feb. 12, 1924, pp. 1-2.

looking for a reaction from the hysteria that holds sway just now."[24]

Hysteria was the word. Bruce Bliven, in *The New Republic*, wrote of Washington "wading shoulder-deep in oil." Newspaper correspondents, he continued, wrote of nothing else, and in hotels, on the streets, and at dinner tables, oil was the only subject of discussion. "Congress has abandoned all other business. . . . No one knows what each day may bring forth. . . ." Bliven thought that "nobody cared about Teapot Dome when it was a question of conservation; only when it became a scandal of personalities and corruption" did the public "suddenly wake up and lick its lips."[25]

Into this charged atmosphere strode William Gibbs McAdoo, fighting for his reputation and his political life. He already had sent Lenroot an eloquent plea for vindication, asking to appear before the committee promptly, because the newspapers throughout the land "have blazoned my name on the front pages in glaring type in the most unfair and libelous manner as though I were involved in some way in this nauseating scandal." McAdoo "indignantly" protested sharing "any taint of any kind." His work with Doheny had been, he claimed, strictly within his rights as a lawyer. On February 11, when he testified, his remarks and the questions from the committee revealed few surprises and offered little food for political thought not already available. McAdoo defended his record; the committee, Republicans in particular, showed him deference.[26]

Several of McAdoo's supporters had tried to persuade him to go before the committee and there announce his withdrawal from

[24] Coolidge, *Autobiography*, 161-62; Taft to Horace Taft, Feb. 16, 1924, cited in Pringle, *William Howard Taft*, II, 1021; Coolidge to Harvey, Feb. 14, 1924, cited in W. J. Johnson, *George Harvey* (Boston and New York, 1929), 400.

[25] Bruce Bliven, "Oil Driven Politics," *The New Republic*, (Feb. 13, 1924), 302-303. One journal about this time spoke of "the mire and dirt of the oil scandal," of the "stifling atmosphere of the Senate Committee room, with its sordid stories," and of the need for "all that we have of faith in human integrity and incorruptibility"; *The Christian Advocate*, Feb. 21, 1924, pp. 219-20. See also "Sinister Shadows Behind the Oil Scandal," *The Literary Digest*, LXXX (March 1, 1924), 1-9, for reports on hysteria and concern over Teapot Dome in the public press.

[26] McAdoo to Lenroot, Feb. 7, 1924, Container 295, McAdoo Papers; reprinted in *Leases upon Reserves* (1924), 1970-72; McAdoo's testimony, *ibid.*, 2059-70.

the race for the Democratic nomination. McAdoo, however, insisted upon clearing his reputation. Preceding his testimony before the committee, he told a conference of his supporters, "I
cannot withdraw under fire or while there is any suspicion. . . .
But after that is cleared up . . . I must consider the welfare of the
party." McAdoo thought that "a frank, vigorous statement of the
actual facts" would be all that was necessary "to clear it up." Yet
it is conceivable that McAdoo, if anything, added to the onus of
Teapot Dome by his tactics. Historian William E. Dodd, who supported McAdoo and who was very much "hurt" by the "blight"
of Doheny's testimony, wrote to McAdoo suggesting certain historical parallels to the situation that McAdoo faced. "Be sure,"
suggested Dodd, "that statesmen err and err greatly in always assuming that they are right and have ever been right." Men do not,
wrote Dodd, "blame a great leader for making a mistake; they
blame him for refusing to acknowledge it." Another supporter of
McAdoo's suggested: "You should not have accepted this thing as
a personal attack; . . . it would have been much better to have
taken the attitude that you couldn't be harmed by any of this
petty political trickery. . . ."[27] But the customary messages to
McAdoo sounded an entirely different note and agreed that Mc-
Adoo had acted in a manner that was not only necessary but wise.

Whether or not McAdoo could have minimized the effects of
Doheny's testimony by other tactics, the fact remains that he accepted head-on the challenge of the Doheny smear. To some observers, these tactics paid off. Following his testimony, the Mc-
Adoo stock rose. *The Literary Digest* reported that the applause
which greeted him in the committee room, "the gentleness of his
inquisitors," and his "air of confidence and rectitude, all, in the
opinion of Washington correspondents, combined to create a reaction against the feeling that McAdoo was dead politically." The
Christian Advocate believed that his appearance before the committee "won for him complete vindication in the minds of those
present who were not partisan." The New York *Times*, less trust-

[27] McAdoo quoted in Breckenridge Long diary, Feb. 8, 9, and 11, 1924,
William E. Dodd to McAdoo, Feb. 8, 1924, Container 295; and Harold
Jacobs to McAdoo, Feb. 9, 1924, Container 295, McAdoo Papers. Dodd
believed that "if Wilson could only have brought himself to say in 1919 that
he had not been wholly victorious at Paris but that he had done the best he
could, . . . he would have carried the treaty."

ing of surface sweetness, saw calculation in the polite treatment
of McAdoo by Republican committee members: "It almost seemed
as if they did not want to do anything which might interfere with
his nomination. . . ." But from Montana came encouraging Mc-
Adoo news. A friend wrote to Walsh that he had secured ten interviews from Democrats of Helena "to the general effect that they
had read McAdoo's statement . . . before the senate committee
and that [they believed] he had no connection with the oil interests in securing leases and that there is nothing in his . . . record
that should deter him from seeking any public office. . . ."[28]

From Josephus Daniels and others came more somber reports.
Daniels was "distressed about the effect upon our friend McAdoo."
Although Walsh was right in saying McAdoo was "not touched
by the oil scandal," Daniels still was "depressed" that McAdoo
should have "accepted big fees for services in Washington during
the Wilson administration. . . ." Walsh shared Daniels' "appre-
hensions" about the effect of the revelations on McAdoo. Senator
Nathaniel D. Dial of South Carolina, surveying the Democratic
field, concluded that "we have a good chance to win in the [pres-
idential] election if we have discretion enough to form the right
platform and then nominate the right man." But the party "would
be on the defensive the moment they would nominate McAdoo.
. . . The people are terribly disgusted with the republicans, therefore, we should . . . present something . . . constructive."[29]

McAdoo, meantime, sought a definitive showdown. He called
for a meeting in Chicago of his supporters, to decide whether or
not Teapot Dome had eliminated him from the list of Democratic
hopefuls. On the eve of the meeting, the New York *World* found
only optimism for his chances prevailing among McAdoo's followers. There was "no oratory or sentiment in the negative. There
appears to be no issue for the conference to wrangle over. A wide
inquiry fails to find one delegate who will arise and declare Mr.
McAdoo is not now available. . . ." The next day, the conference
assembled and unanimously declared that Teapot Dome had not

[28] *The Literary Digest*, LXXX (Feb. 23, 1924), 13; *The Christian Ad-
vocate*, Feb. 21, 1924, p. 233; New York *Times*, Feb. 19, 1924, p. 14; and
J. Burke Clements to Walsh, Feb. 12, 1924, Box 374, Walsh Papers.
[29] Daniels to Walsh, Feb. 22, 1924, and Walsh to Daniels, Feb. 28, 1924,
Box 374, Walsh Papers; Dial to W. W. Ball, Feb. 23, 1924, Ball Papers,
Duke University Library.

—Orr in the Chicago *Tribune*

THE ANXIOUS WAITER

affected McAdoo's candidacy; whereupon he decided to remain in the race. Breckenridge Long, in attendance, claimed that "from the beginning there was no doubt of the ultimate decision. Everyone was for McAdoo continuing the fight. There was no other answer possible. There is no other man." And Long, ever more confident now, following his earlier depression, concluded: "We have a hard fight—but expect to win."[30] McAdoo, in fateful Feb-

[30] New York *World*, Feb. 18, 1924; New York *Times*, Feb. 19, 1924; Breckenridge Long diary, Feb. 20, 1924, McAdoo Papers. According to Long, the Chicago conference was instigated by McAdoo's supporters, who wanted such a public showdown. McAdoo himself evidently didn't think the conference necessary. "In all of these hard days," wrote Long, "Mc-

ruary, 1924, displayed tenacity and courage in attempting to overcome the sudden blight visited upon his ambitions. Whether he
also showed political sagacity remained undetermined.

Calvin Coolidge, meanwhile, was showing similar tenacity in
his own ordeals created by Teapot Dome. His refusal to oust Edwin Denby brought him much Republican praise, mixed with expressions of pious regret from Democratic spokesmen over his
stubborn persistence in retaining a man smeared with oil. Although for the moment retaining Denby, Coolidge also continued
to search for special counsel. When Lenroot notified him that the
Senate Public Lands committee would report adversely on Silas
Strawn, Coolidge withdrew his name. Pomerene remained a candidate, but Coolidge still had to find a partner for him.[31]

But even the search for bipartisan counsel was not free from
political play. Every name that Teapot Dome touched seemed
to pass eventually through a political cauldron. According to
Senator George W. Pepper, "Walsh and his Democratic associates
were going to be suspicious of anybody whom the President proposed. They wanted action but they also wanted the political
prestige to be gained from directing it." Pepper finally suggested
to Coolidge the nomination of Owen J. Roberts, a practicing Philadelphia lawyer, as the Republican counsel. Coolidge called
Roberts in for questioning and found him satisfactory. On February 15, he sent Roberts' name to the Senate. Walsh did not care
for the Roberts nomination. The more he reflected on it (he
wrote to George Norris) "the more outrageous it seems. . . . Roberts may be a good lawyer . . . but the country knows nothing of
him [nor does] the President." The Senate knew only what Pepper told it about Roberts, and, continued Walsh, "Pepper never
contributed a thought toward the exposure that has been made,
either before or after its odor smelled to heaven." Pinchot, a

---

Adoo has been fine. His greatest trouble came from his leading friends.
He had to fight them first—and his conference idea is a concession to their
point of view." To Long, these friends were "the victims of hysteria." Yet
among these friends were Bernard Baruch and Wall Street speculator Thomas Chadbourne, who were helping to finance McAdoo's campaign. "Who,"
asked Long, "is going to put up the money if they don't?" B. Long diary,
Feb. 9, and 13, 1924, McAdoo Papers.

[31] *The Literary Digest*, LXXX (Feb. 24, 1924), 14; New York *Times*,
Feb. 13, 1924, p. 14, and Feb. 15, 1924, pp. 1 and 3.

friend of Roberts, also opposed his nomination. He told Roberts:
"I have the highest regard for your ability and your integrity. . . .
My fear is that you will find yourself . . . in somewhat the same
situation that I would be in if I, a forester, were asked to undertake the work of a botanist or an engineer."[32]

Others reasoned as Pinchot did. In the Senate, bitter and aggressive debate raged over confirmation of the nominees. C. C.
Dill, Democrat from Washington, claimed that Walsh, after much
work, was "tired and worn out. He needs attorneys." But Dill
thought that neither Pomerene nor Roberts knew enough about
public land law. George Norris thought it "a disgrace" that Coolidge had not consulted Walsh before choosing Pomerene and refused to vote for him until he heard Walsh's opinion.[33] Walsh opposed both nominees. Pomerene did not have "the experience
or the training as a lawyer," he said, and neither man knew
enough about public land laws and issues. Lenroot, supporting
both Roberts and Pomerene, said that legality of a contract, not
land law, was their problem. Key Pittman, Democrat from Nevada, asked if the Senate expected the President to go into the West
and pick an oil lawyer; Pittman favored immediate confirmation,
for while Senators dallied, the oil flowed, and only civil action
brought by government attorneys could stem the production.
Finally, the Senate approved Pomerene's nomination, but made
no effort to vote on Roberts; two days later, with Walsh absent
and little opposition arising against a supporting speech by
George Pepper, the Senate confirmed Roberts as counsel. On
February 19, Coolidge handed commissions to Roberts and Pomerene, granting them unlimited authority to handle prosecution
of the oil leases.[34]

[32] Pepper, *Philadelphia Lawyer*, 197-98; Walsh to Norris, Feb. 18, 1924,
Box 7, Tray 7, Norris Papers; Pinchot to Roberts, Feb. 18, 1924, Box 253,
Pinchot Papers.
[33] Walsh felt deep gratitude for this support from Norris and wrote to
him afterwards: "I wanted to grasp your hand and to thank you in person
that you might know how very keenly I felt your commendation and praise
. . . . I never hoped in my wildest dreams of distinction to be so signalized.
I thank you not alone for what you said . . . but for the confidence in my
judgement and discretion as to the course . . . to be pursued." Walsh to
Norris, Feb. 18, 1924, Box 7, Tray 7, Norris Papers.
[34] *Cong. Rec.*, 68 Cong., 1 Sess. (Feb. 16, 1924), 2547-65, and 2637 ff.
Twenty-six Democrats and thirty-three Republicans voted for Pomerene;
seven Democrats, four Republicans, and the two Farmer-Labor Senators

Harry Daugherty, studiously ignoring the insult to his office, wired Roberts and Pomerene, offering to help them. If they did not care to attend the Public Lands Committee hearings themselves, Daugherty would gladly offer them the services of his assistant attorney-general, who had been "in constant attendance since January 22, 1924, at all hearings before the committee." Undoubtedly, Congress would provide Roberts and Pomerene money for their work. "Notwithstanding this," Daugherty felt that they may need the assistance of the Justice Department, which he placed at their disposal. He also offered them his own services.[35] They accepted none of his offers. Harry Daugherty was not yet a pariah to his party, but his nadir was near.

Denby already had reached his own. On February 18, he sent his resignation to Coolidge, who accepted it. It would "always be a gratifying thought," wrote Denby, that neither Coolidge "nor anyone else [Republican?] has at any time advised me to resign." Denby had held out for many difficult weeks. Now he departed with bold protestations of innocence. He insisted that the leases were legal and in the government's interest; he was remaining in office until March 10, which left Congress abundant leeway for impeachment. Denby challenged investigation of his record, saying: "I am able to fight my own battles, but I cannot fight slander

---

voted against him. Thirteen Republicans and eleven Democrats did not vote. All the negative votes but two came from Senators living west of the Mississippi, which may have reflected the criticism of Pomerene's supposed ignorance of western land laws. In the vote on Roberts' confirmation, the nays came from western senators, all of whom had voted against Pomerene. Their mixed party affiliations—three Democrats, three Republicans, and Farmer-Labor Senators Shipstead and Johnson of Minnesota—suggest, as at least one motive for their votes, fear of an easterner's ignorance of western land law and problems.

Coolidge asked Slattery to accept appointment as assistant to Roberts and Pomerene. Slattery declined, but agreed to Coolidge's request to "give them any aid I could." Slattery, "From Roosevelt to Roosevelt," 95-96. Slattery told Amos Pinchot: "At the direct request of the President, I spent two days going over the case and records with Roberts and Pomerene, just after their appointment." Slattery felt that neither man had a good conservation record: "Pomerene when in the Senate, blew neither hot nor cold . . . . Roberts' attitude . . . is a similar one." Slattery to Pinchot, Dec. 22, 1926, Slattery Papers.

[35] Daugherty to Roberts and Pomerene, Feb. 19, 1924, photostat in General Records of Justice Dept., Naval Oil Reserve Investigation, Box 107, National Archives.

protected by Senatorial immunity." To Coolidge, Denby expressed "deep appreciation" for his "strong message in regard to
the Robinson Resolution. No one appreciates better than I how
difficult your situation has become." In fact, Denby claimed to
be resigning only through fear that continuance in the Cabinet
would increase Coolidge's "embarrassments." Coolidge replied:
"It is with regret that I am to part with you. You will go with the
knowledge that your honesty and integrity have not been im-
pugned. I treasure and reciprocate your expressions of friendship."[36]

Reactions to Denby's resignation showed a noticeable correlation with political affiliation. Herbert Hoover, in retrospect, wrote
that Denby "was a good and able man; and he was driven from
the Cabinet by political persecution and public hysteria." The
Boston *Evening Transcript* saw wisdom in Denby's resignation;
his motives and honesty were "questioned in no responsible quarter," but for him to remain as secretary, while Coolidge probed
to the bottom of "the mess," would be embarrassing. Daniels'
News and Observer was less charitable: There was no charge of
personal gain lodged against Denby, but "it was his signature that
made [the leases] possible. He was asleep at the switch, and the
infamy that comes to those negligent of a public trust must be
laid at his door for that reason." Walsh, vacationing in Pinehurst,
North Carolina, told a reporter that the resignation was "a con-
sumation devoutly wished [for]."[37]

With Denby gone, the heat from Teapot Dome turned upon
Harry Daugherty in full force. Senator Burton K. Wheeler of
Montana told the Senate that "everybody" knew Daugherty to
be a friend of Edward McLean, Harry Sinclair, and Edward Doheny. Furthermore, "not one scintilla of evidence" had his Justice

[36] Denby to Coolidge, Feb. 17, 1924, Box 98, Calvin Coolidge Papers,
Division of Manuscripts, Library of Congress; Denby's memorandum for
the press, dated Feb. 18, 1924, from Navy Dept., copy in Box 98, Coolidge
Papers; Denby to Coolidge, Feb. 17, 1924, and Coolidge to Denby, Feb. 18,
1924, Coolidge Papers. When Denby offered to stay away from all Cabinet
meetings held before his resignation took effect, Coolidge replied: "I am
certain that I and all of . . . the Cabinet wish you to attend until the end
of your term." Denby to Coolidge, Feb. 19, 1924, and Coolidge to Denby,
Feb. 21, 1924, Coolidge Papers.
[37] Hoover, *Memoirs*, II, 54; Boston *Evening Transcript*, Feb. 18, 1924;
Raleigh *News and Observer*, Feb. 19, 1924.

Department offered to the Public Lands Committee during its investigation. Daugherty had protected crime and criminals and had sold immunity from prosecution. Wheeler offered anew a resolution calling for an investigation of Daugherty. When Wheeler suggested the members for an investigating committee, Frank Willis of Ohio and Henry Cabot Lodge of Massachusetts declared he had insulted the President of the Senate, who always designated committee personnel. But Lodge did not defend Daugherty; in fact the day after Wheeler's speech, Lodge and Pepper, acting for a group of Republican senators, went to the White House and told Coolidge that Daugherty should retire for the good of the party. John T. Adams, chairman of the Republican national committee, and a coterie of national committeemen opposed the maneuver, and talk of a split in the Republican party broke forth.

Coolidge, in character, for the moment did nothing. Daugherty's fate, and perhaps the party's, waited on his decision. But Coolidge had little choice. Powerful Republican voices, if not Democratic ones, would force him to act, even had he chosen to hold Daugherty back from exile. In the Senate, Borah of Idaho hammered away with Robinson of Arkansas in demanding his dismissal. No Senator challenged them, but Daugherty scorned them. He refused to resign without what he called "a fair hearing." Coolidge himself continued to stall, although according to the New York Times he had "approached the matter subtly and suggested in nearly every interview that [Daugherty's] resignation would be acceptable."[38]

Denby and Fall had now departed. Daugherty obviously would be the next to go. All three had suffered loss of respect, for, justifiably or not, they were tainted with oil. All three were Republicans, but already, as with McAdoo, Teapot Dome had shown its impartiality. As February neared a close, Democrats Walsh and Daniels faced Republican accusers, when the Republican national committee issued a claim that Walsh had "fathered" the leasing act under which Denby and Fall leased the reserves and that

[38] Cong. Rec., 68 Cong., 1 Sess. (Feb. 19, 1924), 2769 ff.; New York Times, Feb. 22, 1924, pp. 1 and 4; Daugherty, Inside Story, 281 ff.; Cong. Rec., 68 Cong., 1 Sess. (Feb. 23, 1924), 2981-82; C. O. Johnson, Borah of Idaho (New York, 1936) 288-89; and New York Times, Feb. 28, 1924, pp. 1 and 3.

Daniels had written the section of the law under which Denby acted in signing the leases. Daniels fumed in reply: "If the Republican Committee has any information that I leased or recommended leasing a single foot of naval reserve oil land when the oil could be retained in the ground, that information is manufactured. . . ." Daniels claimed that he had asked for the legislation of June, 1920, "exclusively to conserve oil in the ground." Walsh, too, replied to the charge at once. The Republican committee had referred to the general leasing law of February 25, 1920. Walsh pointed out that the leases had been made under an amendment to the naval appropriations act of June 4, 1920. Smoot verified Walsh's statement from the Senate floor, but the Republican national committee persisted: "Daniels wrote the [June] amendment and Senator Walsh supported it when it came before the Senate." Walsh promptly denied this charge also, saying that he "had nothing at all to do with" the act of June 4. Smoot and Lenroot agreed. Still, the accusations were in the record, and Republicans were to voice them again before election day in November[39]

Meanwhile, a pair of Republicans were forced also to fend off partisan imputations, when the quick political eye of Tom Heflin found in the Washington *Herald* a story that he promptly related to the Senate. Senators Lenroot and Smoot, reported Heflin, had "held a secret conference with . . . Fall last Christmas, about which the committee has never been told." The two had supposedly gone at night to Fall's apartment in the Wardman Park hotel in Washington. Heflin, sprinkling insinuations, wondered why they had met there. Lenroot replied that Heflin was "about as accurate as he usually is," and he explained to the Senate that late in December, 1923, Smoot learned that Fall was in Washington at the

[39] Republican national committee, quoted in Washington *Post*, Feb. 25, 1924, as reprinted in *Cong. Rec.*, 68 Cong., 1 Sess. (Feb. 25, 1924), 3046; Daniels, quoted in Bates, "Daniels and the Oil Reserves," *loc. cit.* (this latter is a strong defense of Daniels' record as an oil conservationist; see also "The Counter-Attack on Oil," *The New Republic*, XXXVIII [March 26, 1924], for a favorable view of Daniels); *Cong. Rec.*, 68 Cong., 1 Sess. (Feb. 25, 1924), 3046, 3135. Later, in April, Walsh asked Commander H. A. Stuart, an oil expert formerly in the Bureau of Engineering, to write for publication a letter describing Daniels' policy. In a letter of April 9, Stuart defended Daniels' policy of retaining "as much oil in the ground as possible." See Bates, "Daniels and the Oil Reserves," *loc. cit.*

Wardman Park, but was too sick to appear before the committee. Smoot suggested to Lenroot that they go to see Fall. Lenroot agreed. They visited Fall for about half an hour. They told him that he "owed it to the committee, . . . to himself, [and] to the country to come before the committee and make a full disclosure concerning the source [of his new wealth]." Lenroot understood Fall to say that Edward McLean was the source. Soon after the conference, Fall sent the committee his letter naming McLean as the source. "That," said Lenroot, "is the only conversation that I ever had with Mr. Fall upon this . . . or any other subject since the investigation began. . . . Of course, Mr. Fall misstated to us . . . the source." Lenroot, meanwhile, claimed to have repeated "the substance of this conversation" to two Democratic members of the committee. Smoot agreed with Lenroot, although he denied hearing Fall mention McLean's name during the conversation. Heflin asked Smoot why he did not ask Walsh to accompany him to Fall's apartment. When Smoot said that it did not occur to him, Heflin rejoined: "Just you two Republicans went . . . ?" Smoot resented the insinuation, and the next day, Lenroot appealed to Walsh's fair judgment. Walsh agreed that there was "no impropriety" in the visit. Heflin disagreed; he thought it had been "very reprehensible."[40]

Heflin's insinuations may have been a last straw to Lenroot. About this time, he served notice that he might have to resign from the committee chairmanship. On March 11, from Southern Pines, North Carolina, where he sought recuperation from a nervous breakdown, he sent to the Senate his resignation as chairman and member of the Committee on Public Lands and Surveys. Senator Ladd of North Dakota succeeded him as chairman.[41]

The Smoot-Lenroot episode, as did the Walsh-Daniels one before it, repeated a familiar theme. Teapot Dome long since had displayed a capacity to implicate public men and to soil reputations. But as one realistic observer, Stanley Frost, pointed out:

[40] Heflin, commenting on story in Washington *Herald*, Feb. 27, 1924, *Cong. Rec.*, 68 Cong., 1 Sess. (Feb. 28, 29, 1924), 3229; Lenroot and Smoot, Walsh and Heflin, *ibid.*, 3229-33, 3319-26.
[41] *Ibid.* (March 13, 1924), 4073; New York *Times*, March 12, 1924, pp. 1 and 4.

—Smith in the Oneonta (N. Y.) *Star*

THE GORMAND

"We might as well prepare to live from now till election day in an atmosphere filled with oil and mud and reverberant with drums." In Frost's view, "political Washington" had "settled down to a Presidential campaign devoted chiefly to proving that the pot is blacker than the kettle, or that it isn't—such a campaign of vituperation as has not been known for more than a generation." By March, 1924, major newspapers over the country had begun to editorialize about political immorality, about panic among political leaders and anger among the voters; more than one deplored the lynch spirit adrift in both parties. Said the New York

Herald-Tribune: "No one above ground or below ground [is] beyond the reach of innuendo."[42]

From his quiet retirement in Indiana, Albert J. Beveridge looked out upon the political scene with consternation. To a friend he wrote: "I am gravely concerned about the state of the public mind. Out in this neck of the woods, ordinary citizens are [concluding] that nobody is straight about anything." He was "alarmed at the course" Republicans had taken. If they thought the leases right

[42] Stanley Frost, "Oil, Mud, and Tom-Toms," *The Outlook*, March 12, 1924, pp. 423-25; *The Literary Digest*, LXXX (March 1, 1924), 1-9, for press comments. Tom Heflin and Henry Cabot Lodge—implausible duet though they were—one day in early March provided the Senate with a moment of comic relief from the bitter partisan haranguing. Despite its comedy, their stunt suggested the state of mind that many people seem to have reached in the spring of 1924. Heflin, rambling away in an attack on Doheny, suddenly produced and read a poem called "The Golden Fleece":

> Abou Dough Heenie (may his tribe increase)!
> Awoke one night from a deep dream of peace
> And saw within the moonlight in his room,
> Making it rich and like a lily in bloom,
> A Senator writing in a book of gold.
> Enormous wealth had made Dough Heenie bold;
> And to the Senator in his room he said:
> "What writest thou?" The statesman raised his head,
> And with a look which made Abou boil
> Answered, "The names of those who seek for oil!"
> "And is mine one?" said Abou. "We will see!"
> Replied the Senator; but Abou Dough cheerily
> Responded in a still and softer tone,
> "Write me as one who loves to make a loan."
> The Senator wrote and vanished. The next day
> he came again—it looked like CARAWAY—
> And showed the names of those whom Fall liked best
> And lo! Dough Heenie's name led all the rest.

Lodge, "the Republican . . . litterateur of the chamber," as the New York *Times* called him, was quick to reply. As the Senate chamber and galleries roared, Lodge, from a typewritten sheet in his hand, replied with a parody on Longfellow:

> Absolute knowledge have I none.
> But my aunt's washerwoman's sister's son
> Heard a policeman on his beat
> Say to a laborer on the street
> That he had a letter just last week—
> A letter which he did not seek—
> From a Chinese merchant in Timboctoo,
> Who said that his brother in Cuba knew
> Of an Indian chief in a Texas town,
> Who got the dope from a circus clown,
> That a man in Klondike had it straight

and wise, they should have defended them; if they thought them
rotten, "then our men should have led the attack—beat the Democrats to it." Instead, they had "shilly-shallied, side-stepped, dilly-
dallied, etc., until members of our party out here think that we are
all in the wrong."[43]

Beveridge in Indiana was not isolated in his gloom. Late in
February, George Lockwood, secretary of the Republican national committee, offered some unpalatable truths to Coolidge. Lockwood informed him that "the situation on Capitol Hill from a Republican standpoint during the last few weeks has been pitiable."
Correspondence "from the rank and file of the party in all stations
of life throughout the country" proved to Lockwood that "the
great call of our party membership is for courageous and even
audacious leadership." This the party had not supplied. "There is
a feeling that we have not effectively defended ourselves in the
face of an assault which is recognized as insincere and prompted
only by the basest partisan motives." Lockwood had "a good many
letters expressing approval" when the national committee met
attack with attack; he had had no letter expressing disapproval.
Republicans "throughout the country" felt encouraged by the
national headquarters' recent display of bravery in the face
of Democratic assault, and Lockwood would choose not to "surrender, retreat, or show . . . weakness." He delicately hinted
that, in the past, courage had "most commended" Coolidge to
the public; the President's reputation would not diminish, should
he continue to stand quietly by his position, ready to "take whatever action the welfare of the country and the credit of the party

---

> From a guy in a South American state,
> That a wild man over in Borneo
> Was told by a woman who claimed to know,
> Of a well-known society rake,
> Whose mother-in-law will undertake
> To prove that her husband's sister's niece
> Has stated plain in a printed piece
> That she has a son who never comes home
> Who knows all about the Teapot Dome.

According to reporters, "the august Senate listened in better temper than
it had enjoyed for several weeks." New York *Times*, March 5, 1924, pp.
1-2; see *ibid.*, and *Cong. Rec.*, 68 Cong., 1 Sess. (March 4, 1924), 3525,
for poems.

[43] Beveridge to Worthington C. Ford, Feb. 25, 1924, quoted in Claude
Bowers, *Beveridge and the Progressive Era* (Cambridge, 1932), 537.

may require." Coolidge, in reply, was laconic and ambiguous, but grateful. Failure to discuss Lockwood's full and frank analysis, wrote Coolidge, indicated "no lack of interest in your views or considerations of the action . . . you believe should be taken."[44] Coolidge must think awhile, before he acted again, but act eventually he would.

Beveridge was more explicit about future action, perhaps because he was beyond political ambition, perhaps because he was morally aroused. He told Pinchot that "the nasty mess in Washington must be cleaned up and the whole place fumigated and sterilized." The investigations "positively must go on until every last person—I don't care who he is—who has been faithless to the public interest is at least exposed and, if possible, punished."[45] Beveridge may have had Daugherty, among others, in mind. Certainly Coolidge and uncounted other Republicans carried his name around in their conscience and uttered his name in varying degrees of scorn or admiration.

Coolidge had more than one chance to cast off his political burden, but he chose, for a time, to endure it. Soon after Coolidge became President, Daugherty had offered to resign as Attorney-General. According to Daugherty, Coolidge "refused to consider it for a moment, arguing that any withdrawal would weaken his administration and give the impression that Harding's friends no longer supported him." Perhaps then, Coolidge possessed, besides political motives, a good opinion of Daugherty. On the journey from Marion after the Harding funeral, he had told Herbert Hoover that he planned to make no cabinet changes. "Had he known," Hoover later reminisced, "what bugs crawled about under the paving stones of the Harding regime, he would not have been so inclusive." Hoover felt that from Daugherty's "long-time character, he should never have been in any government."[46]

[44] Lockwood to Coolidge, Feb. 27, 1924, and Coolidge to Lockwood, March 3, 1924, Box 48, Coolidge Papers.

[45] Beveridge to Pinchot, March 7, 1924, Box 244, Pinchot Papers. Pinchot earlier had sounded a familiar refrain for Beveridge: "So far as the Interior Department is concerned, all this crookedness is the direct result of an effort to break down the conservation policy. . . . The grabbers ought to be a little sick of their efforts up to date." Pinchot to Beveridge, March 5, 1924, *ibid.*

[46] Daugherty, *Inside Story*, 280; Hoover, *Memoirs*, II, 53.

Some Republicans felt otherwise, and intense pressures swirled around Coolidge as he postponed any demand for Daugherty's resignation. One member of the Republican national committee wrote to Coolidge's secretary: "to use a rough expression, if I were the President, I would see that Democratic gang in Washington in Hell before I asked for Mr. Daugherty's resignation. . . . It would only be an inducement for them to be more destructive." No one had shown Daugherty to be guilty of "a single act even of indiscretion." Coolidge had stood by Denby; he should do the same for Daugherty. Senator Willis of Ohio sent to Coolidge a large batch of telegrams he had received, all of them protesting Daugherty's resignation. John T. Adams, chairman of the national committee, told Coolidge: "I am confident that the majority of the real Republicans throughout the country would support the President in standing by [Daugherty] until the facts are made known."[47]

The candid Lockwood, meantime, gave Coolidge a reasoned and detailed analysis of the problem. Daugherty was no particular friend of his, claimed Lockwood, "or of this headquarters organization." Daugherty had, in fact, been unco-operative and critical of him in the past, and Lockwood did not share Coolidge's belief in the strength of the administration that Harding had bequeathed to the party. Lockwood felt that some of Harding's "personal appointees, including . . . Daugherty," should have been dropped. But now, by February of 1924, a new situation had arisen. Lockwood saw the Democrats "long and deliberately" hatching a plan "entirely for campaign purposes, the objective being to discredit the administration and the Republican party." First, they had attacked Denby. It was "unfortunate that he resigned." Now they were after Daugherty. When he had gone,

[47] C. A. Reynolds, (Winston-Salem) North Carolina national committeeman to Coolidge, Feb. 23, 1924, Box 48, Coolidge Papers; Willis to Coolidge and reply, Feb. 28, 1924, *ibid.* (Coolidge replied, in part: "Thank you very much for . . . the copies. I have looked them over with a great deal of interest, and appreciate your kindness in having them copied in such convenient form."); and Adams to Coolidge, Feb. 28, 1924, *ibid.* Adams sent Coolidge "a few samples of the response" to the committee's statement that Daugherty was entitled to a "fair hearing." Coolidge, according to his secretary, was "greatly interested" in these. *Ibid.*, and Slemp (?) to Adams, March 1, 1924, *ibid.* Calvin Coolidge was a cautious—some would say a cagey—man.

"they will attack door after door until the citadel is reached." To yield now, said Lockwood, would be only to increase the Democrats' vigor and effectiveness. The country had "admired greatly" the President's stand during the Denby assault; now the people did not expect him to abandon Daugherty before he had his day in court. After Daugherty had "passed through his trial," Lockwood thought it might "be well for him to step out in a decent, orderly, and regular way," thus robbing the Democrats of "the supposed issue of his unpopularity."[48]

Lockwood's plan, accepted or not by Coolidge, failed to work. Daugherty had his trial, but he chose not to depart in a decent and orderly fashion. On the last day of February, a bevy of Democratic senators, without restraint and without mercy, verbally flayed Daugherty and the administration that sheltered him and the oil scandal that had enveloped him. Except for Willis of Ohio, Republicans sat in silence, as the Democrats made their charges. After the sound and the fury, the Senate, on March 1, passed the Wheeler resolution to investigate Daugherty for his failure to prosecute Fall, Sinclair, Doheny and other reputed grafters of the Harding administration. On March 12, the special investigating committee began its hearings. The featured witness was Miss Roxy Stinson of Columbus, Ohio, divorced wife of Daugherty's late, close friend Jesse Smith, dead from his own or someone else's hand since the spring of 1923. Roxy, and others who followed her, put together a shoddy tale: mysterious deals and pardons, permits for liquor, speculation in oil stock, illegal transportation of fight films, and a host of other charges and suggestions. Running through the testimony, as a unifying and motivating force, was the name of Daugherty, who supposedly held scheming conferences in a little green house on K Street, Washington, D. C.[49]

As the stories mounted, so did the pressure upon Coolidge. Even before the Daugherty hearings began, he had received grass-roots pleas for action. Presidential secretary C. Bascom Slemp sent to Nebraska for suggestions from the campaign director of a

[48] Lockwood to Coolidge, Feb. 27, 1924, Box 48, Coolidge Papers.
[49] *Cong. Rec.*, 68 Cong., 1 Sess. (Feb. 29, 1924), 3299 ff., 3410; and Senate Select Committee on Investigation of the Attorney-General, *Investigation of the Attorney General* (68 Cong., 1 Sess., [Washington, 1924]), Parts 1-9, *passim.*

Coolidge for President committee. The reply came back that "it is much more important to us that . . . Coolidge should be . . . reelected than that some member of the Cabinet, who appears to be temporarily in disgrace, should haggle about technicalities and . . . vindication." Contact with "a good many voters" had revealed to the Nebraska chairman "a slacking up in the enthusiasm for the President because of apparent inaction at Washington." All protests to the contrary, people saw only "a disposition to protect those . . . suspected of wrong doing."[50]

But Calvin Coolidge, at least to the public press, revealed no hopes or feelings, beyond an "intimation" that he was seeking a successor to Daugherty. According to Daugherty himself, "pressure on the President was terrific," as Daugherty's "enemies laid siege to the White House." Senators Lodge and Pepper, both supposedly holding "personal grudges" against Daugherty, called on Coolidge and demanded the Attorney-General's resignation. Borah of Idaho, in Daugherty's presence, urged Coolidge to force Daugherty out. Once during the storm, Charles Evans Hughes told Coolidge: "If it will . . . aid . . . you in displacing Daugherty, I'll arrange to have the entire Cabinet resign." Coolidge refused, saying, "Don't you do it! I should be left alone with Daugherty." But when Hoover and Hughes finally went to Coolidge and asked him to remove Daugherty, the President, according to Hoover, "asserted that he had no definite knowledge of wrong doing by Daugherty and could not remove him on rumors."[51]

Perhaps Coolidge finally decided there was substance in Roxy Stinson's stories; perhaps he finally admitted that Daugherty was a dead weight on the party and the President, with convention and election time standing near. His taciturn lips revealed little,

[50] F. P. Corrick to Slemp, March 3, 1924, Box 48, Coolidge Papers. In February, W. B. Wheeler, General and Legislative Superintendent of the Anti-Saloon League, advised Coolidge to keep Daugherty, since he had been "clean-cut and courageous from the beginning" on prohibition. From the United Brotherhood of Carpenters and Joiners of America, Local 286, Danville, Illinois, came a request to fire Daugherty because of his "inactivity" during the Teapot Dome investigation (Box 48, Coolidge Papers). See also a story in New York *Times*, March 17, 1924, p. 1, concerning opinions of Daugherty.

[51] New York *Times*, March 6, 1924, p. 1; Daugherty *Inside Story*, 281-91; Johnson, *Borah*, 289; Beerits Memorandum, Hughes Papers; and Hoover, *Memoirs*, II, 54.

and survivals from his pen offer less. But on March 19, Slemp
dropped a note to his Nebraska correspondent: "I think you may
look forward pretty confidently to some developments which will
indicate a purpose of bringing . . . matters to a conclusion . . . and
returning to the . . . real business of the campaign." On March
27, rumors sped about Washington that Daugherty was about to
go; he and Coolidge had just talked together several times. On the
same day, Daugherty received a blunt note from Coolidge's secretary, telling him that "the President does not understand the delay
in complying with his request. He directs me to notify you that
he expects your resignation at once." Calvin Coolidge had made
up his mind at last. Once he did, all procrastination dissolved.[52]

Daugherty resigned. During a Cabinet meeting on March 28,
he tendered his resignation, telling the President that he did so
"solely out of deference to your request and in compliance there-
with." On April 4, Coolidge named an old Amherst college class-
mate, eminent Harlan Fiske Stone, to succeed Daugherty. In
stark contrast to the solicitous and friendly note replying to Denby's resignation, Coolidge informed Daugherty: "I have your
letter. . . . I hereby accept your resignation effective at once."
Daugherty did not, however, depart in the spirit for which George
Lockwood had hoped. Having resigned, he sent Coolidge a six-
page letter, explaining and justifying his record. He denounced
his tormentors and declared that principles should never give
way to party expediency. And in a backward glance several years
later, Daugherty wrote: "To my dying day I shall expect Mr.
Coolidge to make an explanation of his action."[53]

But the explanation was obvious. Daugherty never faced court
charges for any wrongs committed as Attorney-General; neverthe-

[52] Slemp to F. P. Corrick, March 19, 1924, Box 48, Coolidge Papers;
New York *Times,* March 28, 1924, p. 1; and Slemp (?) to Daugherty,
March 27, 1924, unsigned copy in Box 98, Coolidge Papers. Despite
Coolidge's blunt directive, it is hardly accurate to say that he "threw him
[Daugherty] out in a panic." Alpheus Thomas Mason, *Harlan Fiske Stone:
Pillar of the Law* (New York, 1956), 142. Whatever criticisms one can
make of Calvin Coolidge, he never panicked over anything.

[53] Daugherty to Coolidge, March 28, 1924, and Coolidge to Daugherty,
March 28 ,1924, Box 98, Coolidge Papers; Mason, *Harlan Fiske Stone,* 142-
47; Daugherty to Coolidge, March 28, 1924, Box 98, Coolidge Papers (The
New York *Times,* March 29, 1924, p. 1, contains a copy of this letter.);
Daugherty, *Inside Story,* 291.

—Harding in the Brooklyn *Eagle*

"WHAT A RELIEF!"

less, Teapot Dome (along with Roxie Stinson and her fellow witnesses) forced Coolidge, for his own and his party's well-being, to drive Daugherty from his Cabinet. The party, as the President, must perforce be clean of oil. Coolidge, in his fashion, had turned to cleaning up the party, but for awhile, during the first weeks of March, he was still to see his own purity and political future endangered.

7

Teapot Dome and the Presidency

On February 25, 1924, after a ten-day recess, the Public Lands Committee resumed its investigation. Principal witness was Coolidge's private secretary, C. Bascom Slemp, appearing in response to a direct request from Walsh. Almost at once, Coolidge became involved in the testimony, although not through the choice of Slemp, who was wise in his political ways and who intended to protect himself, as well as Coolidge. Slemp had been in Palm Beach during January, 1924, when Walsh was there questioning Edward McLean. Although he claimed to have been there "for health and recreation," Slemp admitted seeing both McLean and Fall during his stay. He had "no personal, private, confidential talk" with either of them and knew nothing about the $100,000 loan, apart from what the committee knew. Walsh asked if he had communicated with the White House while he was at Palm

Beach; Slemp replied that "all communications that I would make to the White House I would have to reserve as confidential."[1]

Walsh did not press the point. But during the days immediately following Slemp's testimony, one more enigmatic, weird episode of the Teapot Dome story emerged, one that bristled with political potentials. Slemp had revealed to the committee practically nothing that was not already known. But then Walsh produced a series of telegrams taken from two Washington telegraph offices. These messages had passed between McLean in Palm Beach and various individuals in Washington. They showed that McLean had desperately tried to forestall being questioned by the committee in January. Some of the messages were in an old Justice Department code. Unravelling the ridiculous spelling and surmising what term stood for what public figure provided an exciting pastime to those not already satiated with scandal. One wire to McLean read: "Jaguar baptistical stowage beadle 1235 huff pulsator commensal fifful. Lambert conation fecund hybridize." "Jaguar" turned out to be Walsh. In one code, Fall was "officialize," in another "Appl." McLean was variously "TKVOUEP," "the Count," and "the Chieftain."[2]

Among the wires submitted to the committee were two from Coolidge to McLean. One told McLean: "Prescott is away. Advise Slemp with whom I shall confer. Acknowledge." The other told McLean: "Thank you for your message. You have always been most considerate. . . ." On the surface, the wires hardly convicted Coolidge of any wrong, but the surface of American politics had been stirred by suspicion for many months past. Then a McLean employee identified some of the persons in Palm Beach to whom messages had been sent in code or in deliberately im-

[1] Guy Hathorn, "The Political Career of C. Bascom Slemp" (Ph.D. dissertation, Duke University, 1950), 211-12; Leases upon Reserves (1924), 2343-48. Walsh asked Slemp on Saturday, Feb. 23, to testify on Monday. "I asked him what he wanted to draw from me," Slemp later recalled, "because I realized any slip I might make would be given publicity and injure me personally as well as the administration." Slemp to William Allen White, April 22, 1939, cited in Hathorn's dissertation, 211. Walsh did not tell him what to expect, but Virginia Congressman Walter Moore did; thus Slemp had a chance to meditate on his answers before he appeared. Ibid., 211-12.

[2] Leases upon Reserves (1924), 2371-81, 2479-2551.

precise phrases. Secretary Slemp was among the recipients he identified.[3]

Implications rose up, misty, but dangerous for their very ambiguity: Slemp was in Palm Beach, near if not with McLean; Slemp had received telegrams from McLean's people in Washington and in turn had communicated with Coolidge in messages he chose to keep confidential. And one message to McLean from a Washington employee had stated: "To expedite matters . . . , have arranged with Smithers at the White House, to have our end of the private wire opened at 6 o'clock tonight." An explanation of the private wire quickly came out. McLean, during his uncomfortable Palm Beach days, leased a private wire—one end of it placed in his Washington *Post* newspaper office, the other in his Palm Beach cottage. He hired E. W. Smithers, chief operator at the White House, to operate the wire for him. Smithers took the job to supplement his meager government salary. Unfortunately for Walsh, neither Smithers nor anyone else could or would produce file copies of the messages sent over the private wire.[4]

McLean appeared before the committee and underwent searching examination, but offered little illumination on the telegrams. As a witness, McLean made a favorable impression, but neither he nor anyone else gave away any testimony that could link Calvin Coolidge to Teapot Dome's complex intrigues. Nor did any direct evidence ever appear showing that Slemp had gone to Florida specifically to talk with Fall or McLean. After enduring a week of accusations and innuendos, Coolidge broke his silence on the affair and explained the two McLean telegrams, showing them to be routine and above board.[5]

Nevertheless, numerous Democrats persevered in this, their best

[3] Coolidge to McLean, Jan. 12, 1924, and Feb. 12, 1924, reprinted in *ibid.*, 2520-21; *ibid.*, 2653-54, for testimony.

[4] *Ibid.*, 2383, 2671-76.

[5] The first one concerned a political appointment Coolidge must fill in Washington. Samuel J. Prescott, the usual conferee on such a task, was absent; Coolidge wanted to know from Slemp with whom to talk. The second one was an acknowledgement of a congratulatory note which McLean had sent, following Coolidge's refusal to dismiss Denby. Hathorn, "Political Career of Slemp," 214-15; New York *Times*, March 7, 1924, pp. 1-3.

GEE,—IF WE COULD ONLY GET SOMETHING ON COOLIDGE

PARTISAN POLITICAN DISGUISED AS A RAG PICKER

WHITE HOUSE   WHITE HOUSE

ACTIONS   APPOINTME   CORRESPONDEN   PAST LIFE   SPEECHES

—Reid for *The Bell Syndicate, Inc.*

POOR PICKING

opportunity to date, to link Coolidge to the Teapot Dome scandal. For awhile, the Presidents reputation underwent a fierce buffeting. One Washington newspaper felt that it would be "both irrational and illogical" for the Senate committee to ignore a telegram "ambiguous in text, sent by the Chief Executive to one of the most important figures in the . . . investigation." To a Philadelphia paper, the telegrams conveyed "a strikingly clear impression of the unwholesome atmosphere which has pervaded the . . . Capital." But the Boston *Evening Transcript*, loyal as ever to the President, found that all attempts to involve Coolidge in Teapot Dome had been "abortive." And the New York *Times* found it "humiliating to think that we have come to the point where every

idle tale and gratuitous suspicion about the President . . . must
be given resounding publicity." Fortunately, no one would "be so
foolish as to accuse Mr. Coolidge of any complicity. . . ."[6]

By such a standard, more than one Democrat played the fool.
In the Senate, the perennial critics Heflin and Caraway, Pat Harrison of Mississippi, and others in spectacular fashion poured out
their scorn for the explanations of the Coolidge telegrams. Only
Henry Cabot Lodge defended Coolidge. He insisted that the
President should not be attacked in the Senate; such behavior
lowered the tone of the chamber and showed disrespect for the
chief executive. With this deliverance, Lodge brought down a rain
of reminders from shocked Democrats. Had Lodge forgotten
Wilson and the League? Did Lodge not recall "the vicious, mean,
determined attacks" of 1919, "charging . . . Wilson with almost
every offense in the calendar?" Heflin, grandly mixing his metaphors, said it made a great difference whose ox was gored; the
shoe now was on the other foot. And Caraway insisted that he
was not criticizing the President, but was just talking about him.
The New York *World* found more biting words: "The record for
Senator Lodge from January, 1919, to March 4, 1921, withers the
cant of this utterance with the satire of opposed facts."[7]

Lodge appeared to have caught some of the spleen originally
generated for Coolidge, as argument over the telegrams veered
off into this and other realms and thereby followed the pattern
now familiar to the point of weariness in the history of Teapot
Dome. The Coolidge reputation profited by the deflection, perhaps, but more helpful was what certain students of the public
pulse called a growing reaction against "the prevailing tendency
to tear down honorable reputations through the circulation of
rumors and open accusations. . . ." The revulsion was not against

[6] *Cong. Rec.*, 68 Cong., 1 Sess. (March 5, and 10, 1924), 3614, 3679-80,
and 3867-69, for Senatorial comment on the telegrams; Washington *Daily
News*, March 7, 1924, editorial reprinted in, *Cong. Rec.*, 68 Cong., 1 Sess.
(March 14, 1924), 3876; Philadelphia *North American*, March 14, 1924,
cited, *ibid.*, 4405; Boston *Evening Transcript*, March 20, 1924; New York
Times, March 7, 1924, p. 14. For numerous examples of press reactions to
the Coolidge telegrams and to the Senate's criticisms of them, see *Cong.
Rec.*, 68 Cong., 1 Sess. (March 18, 1924), 4401-4407, 4423-24.

[7] *Cong. Rec.*, 68 Cong., 1 Sess. (March 6, 1924), 3679-98 (Senator Kenneth D. McKellar of Tennessee asked Lodge the question about Wilson);
New York *World*, editorial, March 8, 1924.

testimony helping to uncover corruption, but against "the extra-legal efforts to demolish character for the attainments of partisan ends." George W. Norris, however, felt that certain Republican characters were quite susceptible to criticism. During the investigation, "many things" had happened to convince Norris that Coolidge "should not be President," but his association with McLean was reason enough. McLean was "one of the most disreputable characters in . . . Washington—a man who has lived a life of continual debauchery. . . ." Still, Norris thought Coolidge "was bound to be nominated, . . . not because the people want him . . . , but because the . . . Republican party is in the hands of men whom he controls."[8]

If a columnist in *The Nation* could be believed, Coolidge himself was far from maintaining such close command of his own and his party's fortunes. Visitors to the White House supposedly were finding not "the cool, austere man of legend . . . , resolute and alert to meet and subdue any large emergency," but "a rather huddled up little figure, much dismayed, wondering and asking what he should do." Even McLean's Washington *Post* began to mourn the lack of leadership in the Republican party: Republicans throughout the United States were "dazed and shamed" by the Democrats' ability to defy, insult, and vilify the administration. "Paralysis has overtaken Congress. . . . Government is unable to function." The rank and file could not follow men who lacked the courage to defend their party. Through the lack of stalwart leadership, the Republican party was going into the approaching campaign "as if it were a criminal on the way to execution." The New York *World*, explaining the hysteria and the excesses of the investigation, blamed the President's inaction. The people had looked to him "for proof that . . . in the President himself, there exists the will and the power to attack and destroy the evil." But Calvin Coolidge sat in his seclusion, "silent, judicious, and on the defensive."[9]

Other observers saw Coolidge acting a different role. Walsh

[8] New York *Times*, March 10, 1924, p. 1; Norris to B. F. Eberhart, March 8, 1924, and Norris to Joseph Polcar, March 27, 1924, Box 1, Tray 2, Norris Papers.

[9] *The Nation*, CXVIII (March 12, 1924), 269; Washington *Post*, March 24, 1924; New York *World*, March 24, 1924.

thought that Coolidge actually had received too much credit for what had been exposed, and he suggested that party chairman Cordell Hull utilize a recent article in the Brooklyn *Eagle* which played up the President's passive record. Whatever Coolidge's past record, he was, as the Springfield *Republican* pointed out, the Republican party's one hope. Unless the party could be saved through him, it could not be saved at all. If, said the *Republican*, Coolidge had not "in his patient, cautious way" played an heroic role, if he had let slide opportunities for bold and dramatic action, the Republican party "must still recognize that he is the ship and all else is the sea. The bottom drops out if public confidence in him cannot be maintained."[10]

The perceptive Stanley Frost, analyzing the Republican situation, also saw in Coolidge the party's sole strength. Reports from "all parts of the country" agreed that Coolidge still held "the full trust of the nation, indeed, that he has even grown stronger through his calmness and stability in the midst of the uproar. . . ." Teapot Dome had discredited the Republicans, as a party, while Coolidge had remained clean. The future of the party thus rested with him alone, and his willingness to lead in his own fashion.[11]

Whatever presidential qualities Coolidge possessed, the fact remains that he emerged from the McLean episode with no noticeable tarnish on his reputation. In the early spring of 1924, while the Teapot Dome investigation swept on, his and the party's chances for continued political control beyond November appeared to be no worse than they had been before Walsh produced his batch of telegrams.

In contrast to Coolidge, William Gibbs McAdoo continued to find Teapot Dome an ominous barrier. Veteran newspaperman Richard V. Oulahan, in late February, commented that McAdoo's forces should begin crumbling soon. The stock of others, claimed Oulahan, had risen accordingly, with Senator Oscar W. Underwood of Alabama standing foremost. If McAdoo or Underwood failed, other candidates might prevail—among them Senator Samuel M. Ralston of Indiana, Governor Alfred E. Smith of New York,

[10] Walsh to Hull, March 7, 1924, Box 374, Walsh Papers; Boston *Evening Transcript*, March 5, 1924, reprinting editorial from Springfield *Republican*.
[11] Stanley Frost, "The G.O.P. at the Bar," *The Outlook*, March 19, 1924, pp. 471-73.

or John W. Davis of West Virginia. The New York *World*, which had taken no clear editorial stand on McAdoo after the Doheny blow, on March 4 put forth a muted statement that McAdoo had "been made unavailable by his own acts since leaving office in a Democratic Administration." About the same time, the Detroit *News* punned: "It seems to be interpreted here and there that . . . the McAdoo candidacy remains, with emphasis on the remains."[12]

Opinions from within the party were even more disheartening. Breckenridge Long found "a general feeling abroad" that the Democratic nominee would win, but, he lamented, "the general opinion is that McAdoo cannot be nominated. Walsh feels so. [Senator Claude A.] Swanson [of Virginia] feels so. Everyone I see feels the same. . . . The McAdoo case is beginning to assume the aspects of utter helplessness." Even after McAdoo carried several state primaries, Long remained pessimistic, for there was still "much opposition among the leaders." He talked with financial backer Bernard Baruch in late March. Baruch thought McAdoo could not be nominated. "He will not," wrote Long, "give any more money nor raise any."[13]

Meantime early in March, from the McAdoo headquarters in Chicago, Frank Frazier, an assistant to Judge David L. Rockwell, McAdoo's campaign manager, wrote a confidential letter to Judge Walter Brock, a McAdoo manager in North Carolina. He told Brock: "Up to one week ago although the mail had dropped off almost completely and the daily callers . . . almost to zero, I hoped that a reaction favorable to our great leader would set in. I am now convinced that this . . . will not materialize." Frazier reported that during the past few days, "we have learned that the sentiment among our former supporters in many States is crystallizing towards favorite son or uninstructed delegations." To Frazier the "Progressive wing of the Democratic party," which was "almost solidly behind" McAdoo before Doheny testified, "faces a crisis and a grave responsibility." The wing was "becoming disorganized" because it had not selected a leader to replace McAdoo. The Democratic party had "never before been in a better position

---

[12] Oulahan, in New York *Times*, Feb. 24, 1924, Sec. 8, p. 1; New York *World*, March 3, 1924; the Detroit *News*, quoted in Boston *Evening Transcript*, March 5, 1924.
[13] Breckenridge Long diary, March 18, 21, 26, 1924, McAdoo Papers.

to win," provided it gave the convention a progressive candidate, who could take the offensive and make the most of the issue handed to him by the Republicans on "an oily silver platter." Frazier enclosed for Brock a memorandum that had, he said, been sent to McAdoo. It read, in part: "You have been cleared by Walsh and by Chicago conference. . . . You have fought a great fight, but as a presidential candidate you are a victim of circumstances . . . [and] cannot be nominated. Come out . . . with a statement that you are joining the ranks with the rest of us. Rockwell would give you a similar statement if he had the heart. . . ."[14]

Hampton's immediate reaction was to accuse Frazier of trying "to submarine Mr. McAdoo." Frazier had quit the McAdoo campaign; this, Hampton admitted, he had every right to do, but he had "no right at all to undertake . . . a treacherous blow upon the [Headquarters] stationery." Hampton wanted no further letters from him. Hampton himself, a week earlier, had admitted that "it appears we will have to get another candidate." But he also pointed out that this opinion was "strictly confidential," and he did not want to "get into any publicity at the time" about McAdoo's candidacy. Evidently, Hampton did not disagree with Frazier's analysis; he simply preferred to hang on for awhile, hoping McAdoo could weather the storm. When McAdoo trounced Oscar W. Underwood in the Georgia primary, Hampton's hopes rose again: "While we expected Mr. McAdoo to carry Georgia, the magnitude and completeness of his victory there has . . . rather surprised us . . . it shows clearly that while the politicians became frightened by the conspiracy to destroy Mr. McAdoo the people themselves never wavered at all."[15] Hampton's views in the spring of 1924, varying between hope and despair, neatly chart the conflict within the minds of a goodly number of McAdoo supporters from the time Doheny testified in February until the Democratic convention in June.

McAdoo's campaign manager David Rockwell wrathfully denied Frazier's analysis. Rockwell wired to Hampton, who had sent him the exchange of correspondence with Frazier: "Am amazed

---

[14] Frazier to Brock, March 9, 1924, mimeographed copy, Simmons Papers.
[15] Hampton to Frazier, March 15, 1924; Hampton to E. J. Smathers, March 6, 1924; Hampton to E. J. Smathers, March 6, 1924; Hampton press statement, March 20, 1924, Simmons Papers.

—Harding in the Brooklyn *Eagle*

"WILLIE, YOU CAN'T GO WITH THAT PATCH ON!"

at . . . letter discharged clerk of this office has sent and delighted at your reply. . . . This is basest treachery of vilest character. . . . Campaign was never in better shape."[16] Rockwell may have been whistling in the political dark, or he may have lacked the heart to tell even himself that McAdoo had been deeply wounded.

The question of Frazier's "treachery" aside, his analysis of the situation cannot be discredited, for other men at the time were voicing similar feelings. Walsh had lately changed his mind about McAdoo; when he did, he wrote to McAdoo, telling him why. Doheny's testimony, he said, was "no reason whatever for withholding or withdrawing my support of your candidacy." But then McAdoo disclosed the fact that his law firm had appeared in tax

[16] Rockwell to Hampton, March 17, 1924, Simmons Papers.

cases before the Treasury Department soon after he retired as Secretary of the Treasury. This record, in addition to the Doheny handicap, was "too heavy" for McAdoo to carry. Walsh laid out his sentiments in precise language: "I may be quite wrong . . . , but I give you my candid judgment that you are no longer available as a candidate; at least, that the oil scandal issue would be lost to us if you should be nominated." The "lay mind," continued Walsh, would be unable to make the necessary distinction be- tween McAdoo, who was clean, although linked with Teapot Dome, and Coolidge, who was not so pure. More cryptic than Walsh was Rockwell. On April 7, now less sanguine than he had been with Hampton, he wired Judge Brock: "We are exerting every effort but are ourselves tremendously crippled."[17]

McAdoo himself laboriously tried to justify continuing the race. He sent Walsh a voluminous reply, defending his record. He wondered why "some people, chiefly Republicans and my enemies in the reactionary wing of our Party, [are so] super-sensitive [about my activities as a lawyer], when no complaint is ever made against others who have practiced in precisely the same way." In the past two months, said McAdoo, he had spoken in thirteen states and had "found no evidence anywhere" that the ordinary citizen would be unable to properly distinguish his from Coolidge's association with Teapot Dome. McAdoo, believing that his "ene- mies" in both major parties were "making common cause to im- press . . . the belief" that his law practice could be properly criti- cized, insisted that the people did not "care a continental" for his law practice. McAdoo felt it his duty to stay in the race in order that the party convention itself could decide whether or not he was "the most available candidate." If the convention turned him down, he would not complain.[18]

[17] Walsh to McAdoo, April 3, 1924, Box 375, Walsh Papers; Rockwell to Brock, April 7, 1924, Simmons Papers. Walsh felt sure that McAdoo would not believe that this changed attitude sprang from "any latent ambition har- bored by me [for the nomination]. I entertain neither desire nor hope of the nomination. . . ." Several weeks later, Walsh wrote to a Montana cor- respondent: "McAdoo seems to be holding his own wherever he was strong. before the disclosures . . . , but I find no one here who feels that he can make the grade, or that, under the conditions confronting us, his nomination would be wise." Walsh to J. T. Carroll, May 15, 1924, Box 374, Walsh Papers.

[18] McAdoo to Walsh, April 26, 1924, Box 375, Walsh Papers. McAdoo cited Charles Evans Hughes, who, a few months after retiring from the

Thus privately McAdoo voiced his desperate hopes. Publicly another interpretation had appeared. According to the New York *Times*, "unprejudiced leaders in his campaign" already had admitted that the nomination was beyond McAdoo's reach. Doheny and "other factors" had so weakened him that his race now was one for control of the convention rather than for the nomination.[19] No matter whether his own views or those of his "unprejudiced leaders" prevailed, Teapot Dome had dealt harshly—and some would say fairly—with the once bright political aspirations of William Gibbs McAdoo.

Through March and April, men in both parties continued to point toward convention and election time, and Coolidge's special counsel readied their cases for trial; meanwhile, as the Senate hearings droned on, Walsh, on March 8, made one last bold stroke in his efforts to find bedrock for a Teapot Dome conspiracy. In the middle of February, Walsh had written to Pinchot, asking him for information about a rumor that "the oil scandal comes of a conspiracy antedating the [1920 Republican] convention." Walsh had heard that during the convention, after General Leonard Wood gave up the race, he told Pinchot: "If I had agreed to turn over to private exploitation the public natural resources I could have had the nomination rather than the man who is to get it." Walsh claimed that the "political aspects" of this story did not interest him; he simply felt it a "duty to probe to the depths" and wanted whatever help Pinchot could give him. With this cast for information, Walsh began to unwind one more fanciful story.

Pinchot replied to Walsh that he had "no recollections of such a conversation with General Wood," and he was "very strongly

---

Supreme Court, argued cases before the court. McAdoo might have noted the remark of one editorial writer who pointed out that McAdoo had a "pathetic . . . inability to sense political values." McAdoo criticized people for trying to disqualify him because he made money rapidly, because he accepted technically legitimate business; but "what Mr. McAdoo fails entirely to see is that the standards he thus sets up for himself can never be set up for a lawyer who is also a candidate for the presidency. A great deal of money may be earned legitimately by an attorney in activities which automatically bar him from the White House." New York *Tribune* editorial, reprinted in Santa Fe *New Mexican*, Feb. 15, 1924.

[19] New York *Times*, March 31, 1924, p. 1. At about the same time, Breckenridge Long remarked: "We may not nominate him—but we can control the convention by keeping his forces together even if we cannot nominate him." Entry of Breckenridge Long diary, March 26, 1924, McAdoo Papers.

inclined to believe that the alleged conversation never took place."
Encouragement came to Walsh, however, from another quarter.
On March 7, a newspaper story appeared in Washington that
"certain oil interests" had sought an agreement with General Wood
at the 1920 convention. In return for oil support, General Wood
(according to his son, quoted in the story) was to have appointed
as Secretary of the Interior one Jake Hamon, Republican committeeman from Oklahoma and prominent oil man sometimes associated with Harry Sinclair. Walsh could not subpoena Hamon,
for Hamon had been killed in 1921 by Mrs. Clara Smith Hamon,
a woman living with him in bigamy. But Walsh did subpoena the
general's son, Leonard Wood, Jr., the source for the story. He also
called in an array of other witnesses, including Al Jennings, an
ex-train robber from Oklahoma. Jennings, on his journeys to
Washington from California, his newest residence, issued per-
iodic broadsides suggesting that his testimony would "rock the
country."[20]

Before the committee, Jennings declared that Hamon told him
"that Harding would be nominated . . . , and it had cost him a
million dollars." In their conversation, Hamon had, said Jennings,
"brought out in some way" that Daugherty and Republican national chairman Will Hays, as well as "somebody else from Ohio,"
had agreed in return to make Hamon Secretary of the Interior.
As Mark Sullivan suggests, once Jennings' testimony was in the
record, "a considerable portion of the male population of Oklahoma had to be called, some to support the tale, others to denounce it as a fantastic yarn." Sullivan noted that the "residium
of truth seemed to be adequately described by one witness who
said that 'when Jake had a few drinks of scotch he talked pretty
big.' "[21]

Jennings had implied that Will H. Hays, Republican national
chairman in 1920, received a portion of Hamon's "million dollars."

[20] Walsh to Pinchot, repeating Wood's supposed remark, Feb. 16, 1924,
and Pinchot to Walsh, Feb. 25, 1924, Box 254, Pinchot Papers; New York
Times, March 8, 1924, pp. 1-2; and March 22, 1924, p. 1. Jennings had
taken his story to a captain of detectives in Long Beach, California, who in
turn contacted Walsh.

[21] Leases upon Reserves (1924), 2995; Mark Sullivan, Our Times, VI,
339. For examples of the testimony by Oklahomans, see Leases upon Reserves (1924), 3037-94, passim.

ALBERT B. FALL

HARRY A. SLATTERY

GIFFORD PINCHOT

ROBERT M. LA FOLLETTE

THOMAS J. WALSH

Courtesy Underwood & Underwood

Mr. and Mrs. Edward L. Doheny being congratulated by Frank J. Hogan, Chief Defense Counsel.

Courtesy Underwood & Underwood

Harry F. Sinclair (right)
with H. F. Stanford, general counsel for the Sinclair Consolidated Oil Corporation.

William G. McAdoo

Courtesy Library of Congress

Hays at once denied it. He wired to Chairman Edwin Ladd: "Never at any time, for any purpose, did I receive from Jake Hamon $25,000 or any other sum, directly or indirectly, personally or on behalf of the Republican national committee or otherwise." Jennings' story and Hays' protest merely complicated the puzzle of what went on at the 1920 Republican convention. The New York *Times* lately had published a report that 75,000 shares of Sinclair oil stock had helped the Republican national committee to erase a huge deficit incurred during the 1920 campaign. John T. Adams, successor to the 1920 chairman Will Hays, promptly labeled the story "ridiculous." He claimed that "about 10,000 contributions from nearly every state . . . made up the [deficit]." Adams disclaimed any contribution of oil stock or "easy money of any kind." Hays testified before the Senate committee on March 22 and admitted that Harry Sinclair had contributed $75,000 to the Republican national committee to meet the 1920 campaign deficit. He denied that the gift was in the form of oil stock. He also denied knowing anything of the oil leases until he read about them in the papers "a month or more" after he had resigned as Harding's Postmaster-General. During his tenure in the Cabinet, Hays had heard nothing about the leases.[22]

More witnesses followed Hays, as Walsh sought to pin down the rumors of campaign contributions. But as April gave way to May, no new political skeletons materialized; not until the eve of another presidential campaign, in 1928, would the Senate committee uncover really incriminating evidence of oil money in the Republican party. Now, in May of 1924, Teapot Dome was buried deep in the inner pages of the daily press. The elaborate newspaper reports, the detailed magazine articles and analyses, the extravagant accusations on editorial pages and from the floors of Congress—all had diminished or disappeared. At the hearings, the storm of fruitful testimony had died away, and only a dreary overcast of suspicion remained. Monotonous questioning of geologists and oil experts replaced the earlier sharp examinations of cabinet officials and sundry political figures. The committee was trying once more to establish some truths about drainage and

[22] Reprint of wire, Hays to Ladd, March 27, 1924, in *Leases upon Reserves* (1924), 3003; New York *Times,* March 22, 1924, p. 1; *Leases upon Reserves* (1924), 2900-13.

productivity of the oil reserves. Attendance at the hearings shrank away; not a single spectator attended on May 8, when the Director of the Bureau of Mines testified on Teapot Dome's geological features.

The end of the inquiry now was in sight. On May 2, Senator Frances E. Warren, chairman of the committee on appropriations, told the Senate that the Teapot Dome investigation, up to April 16, 1924, had cost $32,808.03. On May 14, Walsh suggested to the Public Lands Committee that they adjourn, subject to the call of the chairman. Walsh intended to prepare a report and submit it for the committee's consideration and then ask for its adoption. Senator Selden P. Spencer of Missouri stated that he, too, had a report, but he would not present it if he and the committee could agree upon the one prepared by Walsh; as soon as Walsh had drawn it up, Spencer would like to see it. Chairman Edwin Ladd adjourned the committee.[23]

With the Senate committee inactive, the initiative passed to the President's special counsel, Owen Roberts and Atlee Pomerene. They had been at work since early March, preparing for legal action. On March 11, they left Washington for Cheyenne, Wyoming, to file application for an injunction to restrain Sinclair from operating Teapot Dome, while they sought a decision on their application to cancel the lease. From Cheyenne, they went to Los Angeles, and there filed similar action against Doheny. As Roberts and Pomerene left Washington for the West, so did Doheny and Sinclair, the latter accompanied by six attorneys. Both oil men declared that they would contest the government action.[24]

[23] *Cong. Rec.*, 68 Cong., 1 Sess. (May 2, 1924), 7667; *Leases upon Reserves* (1924), 3586. The inquiry's total cost included clerical salaries and expenses, counsel fees and experts' salaries, expenses of witnesses, stenographic reporting, and miscellaneous expenses.

[24] For a general narrative of the civil and criminal trials arising out of the oil reserve leases, see Francis X. Busch, *Enemies of the State* (Indianapolis and New York, 1954), 117 ff. A valuable legal study is Charles G. Hagland, "The Naval Reserve Leases," *Georgetown Law Journal*, XX (March, 1932), 293-328; for the trials and decisions concerning the Elk Hills Reserves, see, pp. 298-312; for those concerning the Teapot Dome leases, see pp. 313-28. David H. Stratton, "Albert B. Fall and the Teapot Dome Affair," 378 ff., contains an account of the "Oil Scandal in Court." The Fall Papers, University of New Mexico, contain some fifty bound-volumes of trial transcripts, court decisions, briefs, and other legal material gathered during the trials.

The federal courts in Cheyenne and Los Angeles each issued injunctions restraining further exploitation of Teapot Dome and Elk Hills. On March 13, in the Federal District Court in Cheyenne, Roberts and Pomerene filed suit against Sinclair's Mammoth Oil Company. They asked the court to set aside the Teapot Dome lease and contract because of fraud and conspiracy by Fall and Sinclair and because of Fall's lack of legal authority to lease the reserves. On March 17, in the Federal District Court in Los Angeles, they filed a similar suit against Doheny's Pan-American Petroleum and Transport Company, again charging fraud—by Fall and Doheny—and lack of legal authority by Fall to lease. Then on April 4, Chief Justice Walter I. McCoy of the District of Columbia Supreme Court signed an order directing the federal attorney for the district to call a grand jury to investigate alleged criminal features of the oil leases. The new jury began deliberations on April 25. Roberts and Pomerene assisted the district attorney in presentation of the case. They called, as witnesses, many of those who had testified before the Senate committee.[25]

Sinclair not only faced court charges in Cheyenne but also found himself indicted by a grand jury in Washington for contempt of the Senate. On March 23, he had appeared before the Teapot Dome committee to answer questions about his 1920 campaign donations. He refused to answer any questions. He did not, he said, "decline to answer . . . upon the ground that my answers may tend to incriminate me, because there is nothing [about] the lease of Teapot Dome which does or can incriminate me." Rather, Sinclair claimed that the committee was "without jurisdiction to question me further regarding the . . . lease." Ten times Sinclair, when questioned, refused to answer "on advice of counsel" on this "same ground." The next day, the Senate voted to ask for grand jury action against Sinclair for refusing to testify. On March 31, the grand jury indicted him for contempt of the Senate in refusing to answer ten questions. The indictment was the first of its kind in Washington in thirty years. Despite the distinction, Sinclair pleaded not guilty, and his lawyers began to prepare a defense.

[25] U. S. v. Pan-American Petroleum Company, 6 F.2d 43; U. S. v. Mammoth Oil Company, 5 F. 2d 330.

Sinclair gave the required bail of $1,000 and gained his freedom, pending the trial.[26]

Through the winter and spring of 1924, Teapot Dome had held the rapt attention of the legislative branch of government. Beginning in March, the judiciary had entered the story. The executive, from the beginning of the inquiry in October, 1923, had attempted to view from afar, if not with alarm. But Calvin Coolidge's administration had not neglected certain activity that contrasted forcefully with Harding's anti-conservation policy. On March 25, Coolidge, acting upon the advice of Secretary of the Navy Curtis Wilbur, appointed a special commission of notable experts to study the problem of conserving and providing storage facilities for the navy's oil reserves. The White House statement read, in part: "The purpose for which the naval oil lands were set aside was to provide reserves for the future. In order to do this in the best manner the oil should be, wherever possible, retained in the ground."[27]

Neither Coolidge nor anyone else could have determined, from the babel of testimony during the past months by geologists and experts before the Senate committee, what policy to adopt; the commission could perhaps, from its own studies, decide upon a program for the administration. Coolidge, however, had shown by his White House statement that he sympathized with the conservationists in their desire to leave the reserve oil below ground. And his appointment of the distinguished commission, whether stemming from conviction or from political expediency, was a sharp rebuff of Albert Fall's policy.

Calvin Coolidge, unlike Harding, would conserve the nation's oil resources; nevertheless, one may justly criticize his delay in

[26] *Leases upon Reserves* (1924), 3895-99; *Cong. Rec.*, 68 Cong., 1 Sess. (March 24, 1924), 4785 ff.; New York *Times*, April 1, 1924, p. 1; Busch, *Enemies of the State*, 116; Sinclair v. U. S., 279 U.S. 263. Sinclair claimed that the Public Lands Committee and Coolidge had made the "whole matter" of the investigation a judicial question, and that it now rested entirely within the courts to question him.

[27] Secretary of the Navy, *Annual Report of the Navy Department, 1924* (Washington, 1925), 55. Members of the commission were George Otis Smith, Director of the Geological Survey; Rear Admiral Hillary P. Jones, Commander in Chief of the U. S. Fleet; and R. D. Bush of the Bureau of Minerology of the state of California. See New York *Times*, March 26, 1924, pp. 1-2, for White House statement.

acting to finally preserve them, and question whether his support
for conservation was as much concern for natural resources as it
was for the welfare of business. A number of magazines and newspapers suggested during the spring of 1924 that the Teapot Dome
investigation would have a beneficial effect upon conservation
policy; since Fall had put anticonservationists on the defensive,
the conservationists had gained an incalculable amount of publicity for their views, and no administration, in the near future at
least, would dare to appoint a Secretary of the Interior who was
not friendly to conservation.[28]

On the other hand, Coolidge, worshipful of business as he was,
possibly had been advised by certain oil company officials that oil
conservation would be beneficial to them. Certainly one may in-
terpret Coolidge's actions later in 1924, when he established the
Federal Oil Conservation Board, as due in part to the rapid rise
in the oil supply and a consequent weakening in the price struc-
ture. Calvin Coolidge's conservation policy in the spring of 1924
may have been a shrewd synthesis of two calculated tactics—dis-
association from the besmirched policy of Albert B. Fall and support for the business interests with whom Coolidge exchanged
veneration.[29]

Early in April, Secretary Curtis D. Wilbur gave further clarification of the Coolidge administration's conservation policy. Coolidge named Wilbur to the navy post early in March. As with the

[28] See, for example, "Oil and Conservation," *The Outlook*, Feb. 13, 1924,
pp. 251-52. See *The Literary Digest*, LXXX (Feb. 9, 1924), 7-10, for a
summary of press reports and comments.

[29] For discussion of the motives behind oil company support for conservation and the work of the FOCB, see Roy C. Cook, *Control of the Petroleum Industry by Major Oil Companies* (Monograph No. 39, Temporary
National Economic Committee [Washington, 1941]), 14-15. Cook points out
that during periods of excess production and low prices, oil companies may
press for conservation "for the purpose of getting a system of production
restriction." As Harvey O'Connor suggests, "the very word 'conservation'
when applied to oil must be understood in a Pickwickian sense." *The Em-
pire of Oil* (New York, 1955), 62. See also Eugene V. Rostow, *A National
Policy for the Oil Industry* (New York, 1948), 27 ff.; Myron W. Watkins,
Oil: Stabilization or Conservation? (New York and London, 1937), 42, and
Charles G. Hagland, "New Conservation Movernment with Respect to
Petroleum and Natural Gas," *Kentucky Law Journal* XXII (May, 1934),
543-81. For comment on Coolidge's familiar reverence for business, see
James W. Prothro, *The Dollar Decade: Business Ideas in the 1920's* (Baton
Rouge, 1954), 89-90, 224-25.

new Attorney-General, Harlan Fiske Stone, who was Dean of
Columbia University Law School from 1910 until 1923, the Wilbur
appointment brought to the Cabinet a man in striking contrast to
his predecessor. Wilbur was a graduate of the Naval Academy
and a lawyer and judge for over thirty years in California. When
he accepted the navy job, he was Chief Justice of the California
State Supreme Court. Within a month of his appointment, Wilbur
sent a letter to Senator Frederick Hale, chairman of the Senate
Naval Committee, telling him that no leases or contracts would
hereafter be made without the personal approval of the Secretary
of the Navy. And unless they were "expressly authorized by Congress," or unless they were "absolutely esssential" to prevent drainage, no more leases would receive his approval.

One week after this announcement, Wilbur appointed Commander Nathan W. Wright as his "oil aide," to act for him in matters related to the oil reserves. Wright's friends classified him as
a conservationist; he had protested Harding's transfer of the reserves to Fall. Wilbur also established a Naval Petroleum Reserve
Office, under his immediate supervision, to study "the petroleum
situation" and to aid in restoring the naval reserves to the government. Finally, he assigned naval officers experienced in oil matters
as inspectors of the naval oil reserves.[30]

Given time, Calvin Coolidge usually acted where—in his view—
action was needed. But in April of 1924, it was still a debated
question whether such conservation policies as he and Wilbur had
inaugurated would improve their chances for four more years
in Washington. In February, Harold Ickes had told Pinchot: "My

[30] *Annual Report of the Navy Department, 1924,* p. 55; New York *Times,*
April 11, 1924, p. 6, and April 18, 1924, p. 33; Slattery, "From Roosevelt to
Roosevelt," 87; and Charles G. Hagland, "New Conservation Movement
with Respect to Petroleum and Natural Gas," *loc. cit.* The bulk of Hagland's essay is an extended discussion of state and federal laws concerning
oil conservation and the relation between those laws and oil production;
for brief comments on support for oil conservation by Secretary Wilbur and
by oil interests, see pp. 571-74.

A newspaper in Las Cruces, New Mexico, reporting Wilbur's new oil
policy, declared: "A new naval oil policy, designed to safeguard the government against any such leases as *those granted under former Secretary Denby*
has been announced [my italics]." The omission of any reference to Albert
Fall, not to mention the inaccurate reference to Denby, offers a commentary
on the southwest's attitude toward Fall. (Rio Grande *Farmer,* May 15,
1924)

own belief is that Coolidge has been slipping for some time and that his descent will be accelerated as it gathers momentum. I don't believe he will be nominated." Reporters from two Chicago newspapers and the Associated Press had recently gathered in Ickes's office; all of them, also, had agreed that Coolidge could not get the nomination. In March, Senator Borah had said that "the question is not so much whether the Republican Party will be defeated as whether it will survive." In late March, and again early in April, writing to Nebraska constituents, George W. Norris had denounced Coolidge in strong and moral language. Norris "would much rather someone else were the candidate than Mr. Coolidge. . . . He believes in machine politics. . . . He possesses no outstanding ability." Despite the shocking revelations of corruption in Washington and within the Republican party, Coolidge had, felt Norris, "not helped to uncover anything." He kept Daugherty "long after practically everybody urged and begged him to put him out . . . because he thought it was good politics and would help him to get the Republican nomination." He had sent his respects to Edward McLean, the man who had lived "a life of continual debauchery." Norris, at least, would not be offering his vote and prestige to Coolidge. William Howard Taft, however, saw more worth in the Coolidge name. Late in April, the Chief Justice informed Andrew Mellon that "the welfare of the country is critically dependent upon . . . Coolidge. The Republican party has no chance without him." Indeed, Taft could not remember "a case in which a party is so dependent on a man."[31]

Taft, more nearly than the others, was right. The winter just past had been a nightmare for the Republican party. Its leader in the White House, by outward appearances, had revealed little concern; yet, Calvin Coolidge had burned with an "inner wrath" over the political legacy left to him. If he had not overcome Teapot Dome, he had, thus far, survived it, remarkably free from its contamination. Coolidge had his critics—in abundance. They

[31] Ickes to Pinchot, Feb. 22, 1924, Box 248, Pinchot Papers; Borah, quoted by George Henry Payne, "The Political Drama of 1924," *The Forum*, LXXI (April, 1924), 504-508 (See also report of a public address by Borah, New York *Times*, April 7, 1924, p. 1.); Norris to Rev. W. L. Crom, April 7, 1924, Tray 2, Box 2, and Norris to Joseph Polcar, March 27, 1924, Tray 2, Box 1, Norris Papers; Taft to Mellon, March 28, 1924, cited in Pringle, *William Howard Taft*, II, 1060-61.

accused him of apathy, complacency, provincialism, short-sighted-
ness, and frequently of an undue concern for his party's interests.
But some of his bitterest critics agreed that he was honest, although, as one newspaper suggested, so were Mellon, Hoover,
Harding, and even Denby, and "while all these personally honest
men were in office an incredible assortment of dishonest things
were done."[32]

Yet, once Coolidge had accepted the enormity of the scandal
and had realized the need for action, he had moved with cautious
calculation. He had maintained a delicate balance between too
little concern and too much. He thus managed to achieve actions
beneficial to himself and to his party, while also conveying an
impression that the crime was not nearly so dastardly as his Democratic critics pretended.[33] A retrospective view in the spring of
1924 indicated that for a supposedly weak executive Coolidge had
in recent months acted with surprising vigor: he had rid himself
of Denby and Daugherty, replacing them with eminent men; he
had appointed special counsel, who already were carrying their

[32] White, *A Puritan in Babylon*, 277; New York *World*, editorial, reprinted
in Santa Fe *New Mexican*, Aug. 19, 1924. White notes that Coolidge "made
no protest to indicate his unhappy plight. . . . He wrote no letter easing his
inner wrath. When he snapped out 'let the guilty be punished' in his press
conference, he had spent his rage." Only once, in the privacy of his study,
did Coolidge suggest his feelings. To Herbert Hoover one day he "broke
out with this: 'Some people think they can escape purgatory. There are
three purgatories to which people can be assigned: to be damned by one's
fellows; to be damned by the courts; to be damned in the next world. I
want these men to get all three without probation.' And then having eased
the bowels of his wrath, he shut his mouth tightly in silence." *A Puritan
in Babylon*, 277.

[33] Despite his confession to Hoover, Coolidge preferred that the party
never confess, directly, its past errors. On April 3, 1924, Senator George W.
Pepper told a Portland, Maine political convention that the appointment of
Fall was a "terrible mistake" and that of Daugherty "a grave error in judgement." Days later, responding to a charge that he had served as the mouth-
piece of the administration, Pepper denied to the Senate that Coolidge even
knew that he was making the speech. In his memoirs, Pepper recalled: "I
was in favor of a frank admission of these party liabilities in the sure confidence that an operation is the effective way to stop the spread of infection. . . . Coolidge was alarmed by my frankness and let it be known that
he was not responsible for my utterance." New York *Times*, April 4, 1924,
p. 1, for the speech; *Cong. Rec.*, 68 Cong., 1 Sess. (April 8, 1924), 5813,
for the Senate comment and discussion on it; and Pepper, *Philadelphia
Lawyer*, 198, for final remark.

cases to court and gaining decisions; his administration, through Navy Secretary Wilbur, had shown disagreement with the Fall policy of exploiting the reserves and in its place had begun an oil conservation program that, however inadequate by certain standards, contrasted forcefully with that of his predecessor's. In such a fashion, Calvin Coolidge moved with his party through the treacherous days of the Teapot Dome revelations and set himself and the party on the road toward the June convention.

8

Teapot Dome
and the Election of 1924

The great impelling force behind the Teapot Dome investigation, once the hearings began, had been Walsh of Montana. He had grilled reluctant witnesses. He had fended off attack from members of the committee and from a partisan press. He had directed the committee while it probed for information, and he had prompted senators in debate, as they sought to legislate to meet the needs of the crisis. He had not labored alone, but he had to bear alone a wave of calumny that may or may not, in his own mind, have been offset by the many letters of praise that he received from time to time.[1]

[1] See Bates, "Senator Walsh of Montana," 320, 369-75. For a discussion of "powerful forces" which tried to discredit Walsh and the investigation, see Felix Frankfurter, "Hands Off the Investigation," *The New Republic*, XXXVIII (May 21, 1924), 329-31.

Given his essential role in the story of Teapot Dome, it was proper that Walsh should present, in a magazine of national circulation, an analysis of the committee's investigation. Editors of *The Outlook*, in acordance with their stated practice of "seeking . . . the strongest possible presentation of views opposed to our own," asked Walsh to write an article on Teapot Dome. Walsh gave them a summary of what he and the committee had discovered. The "outstanding item" to Walsh was Doheny's lease on Elk Hills, granted without competitive bidding at about the time he delivered $100,000 to Albert Fall, who only a short time before had admitted to being almost penniless. In addition to this was the discovery of Fall's sudden rise to wealth at the time he leased Teapot Dome to Sinclair. Not only had Fall profited, but the government had lost. The naval oil reserves had passed into private hands. The government, even under Fall's contract, would not get its rightful share of oil. Furthermore, artificial storage was more costly and less reliable than natural reservation in the earth.[2]

Walsh offered these and other points as "merely an outline." He elaborated details early in June, when he submitted his report to the Committee on Public Lands and Surveys. The committee, in turn, sent to the Senate on June 6 a majority report that was, according to Walsh, "in substantial conformity with" his own. The report was signed by Chairman Ladd and seven other members of the committee, all of them Democrats or progressive Republicans. Walsh thought this report was "an unimpassioned and impartial narrative of the proceedings before the committee and the disclosures made by the hearings."[3]

But Senator Spencer of Missouri presented a statement, signed by the five minority members, that they had been given insufficient time to read the Walsh report. The five, all of them Republi-

[2] Thomas J. Walsh, "What the Oil Inquiry Developed," *The Outlook*, May 21, 1924, pp. 96-98. The editors pointed out that their columnist Stanley Frost had not supported the "extreme claims" made by Walsh and others; hence the invitation to Walsh.

[3] *Cong. Rec.*, 68 Cong., 1 Sess. (June 6, 1924), 10937. Besides Ladd and Walsh, Senators Norbeck of South Dakota, Jones of Washington, Adams of Colorado, Kendrick of Wyoming, Dill of Washington, and Pittman of Nevada signed the majority report. Walsh said that the public interest shown in the hearings and in the committee's conclusions led the committee to ask the Senate to order 10,000 copies of the report printed. The Senate agreed.

can regulars, protested that it had been "physically impossible to examine . . . the report which attempts to pass judgment on disputed questions of law, and upon controverted facts. . . ." Nevertheless, to the minority, a "casual reading" had indicated "many mistakes and conclusions and inferences . . . which are unwarranted by the testimony." Walsh replied that Spencer had received a copy of the report "as soon as any other member of the committee had" and the entire committee had spent two days considering it. As Walsh suggested, Spencer would have every opportunity to draw up his own report. Spencer, in time, did submit a minority report, but for the moment he and the rest of the minority could only object to Walsh's interpretation.[4]

The Walsh majority report charged Fall with utter disregard for law and with an unwarranted assumption of authority. It denounced the transactions centering around the oil leases as "essentially corrupt," spelled out, with details from the hearings, the points that Walsh had listed in his *Outlook* article, and summarized other episodes of the investigation. Historian Joseph Schafer, writing in 1940, called Walsh's report "a masterly statement of the entire case, written in a judicial vein, without rancor and with scrupulous care not to overstep the evidence." Schafer wrote from the supposed perspective of the historian, but contemporary appraisals usually reflected the political loyalties of the assayer. The Boston *Evening Transcript*, for example, accused Walsh of assuming "the functions of the courts" in declaring the leases illegal and trying "to make party capital by attacking the administration of President Harding." The *Transcript* claimed these faults would greatly reduce the value of the report. Harry Slattery sent a copy of the report to William Kent, a former Congressman from California and a veteran conservationist. Slattery thought it was a "good, fair summary, with perhaps too kindly treatment of Denby and young Roosevelt. But it isn't the bitter type which falls of its own weight." To Navy Captain John Halligan, Slattery was more critical: "I must say that I have been disappointed in several phases of it, and particularly [in] what he

---

[4] *Cong. Rec.*, 68 Cong., 1 Sess. (June 6, 1924), 10937-38, 10949. Senators Spencer of Missouri, Smoot of Utah, Bursam of New Mexico, Cameron of Arizona, and Stanfield of Oregon signed the minority report.

says about [Denby], and also about certain phases of Fall's activities."[5]

Slattery's disappointment may have stemmed from Walsh's judicious conclusion to a story that had promised more reverberations than Walsh produced. As one editorialist suggested: "After the thunder and the earthquake, the still small voice. After the months of resounding inquiry . . . the report of Senator Walsh." The New York *Times*, succinctly summarizing the report, called Walsh a "stiff partisan," but a "good lawyer." He knew that the evidence had been inconclusive on many points. He had admitted that no proof existed of speculative profits from advance knowledge of the leases. He also had admitted failure to find evidence of an oil conspiracy at the 1920 Republican convention, and he had exonerated Denby and Theodore Roosevelt, Jr. A number of newspapers thought the report was a distinct letdown after the months of spectacular hearings. One commented: "If this is all that Senator Walsh had to recommend, we might as well not have undertaken the investigation at all." The *American Federationist*, suggesting that Prosecutor Walsh of the hearings had become Judge Walsh of the summation, stated: "The single, solemn truth is that the Walsh report is a flat fizzle. It doesn't sound like Walsh." The "fearful tempest" had lost its fury, "the heavy clouds their portents."[6]

[5] Senate Report No. 794, 68 Cong., 1 Sess., reprinted in *Cong. Rec.*, 68 Cong., 1 Sess. (June 6, 1924), 10938-49; Joseph Schafer, "Thomas James Walsh: A Wisconsin Gift to Montana," *Wisconsin Magazine of History*, XXIII (June, 1940), 448-73; Boston *Evening Transcript*, June 6, 1924; Slattery to Kent, June 16, 1924, Slattery Papers; Slattery to Halligan, June 16, 1924, *ibid*.

[6] New York *Times*, June 6, 1924, p. 16; *The Literary Digest*, LXXXI (June 21, 1924), 14-15, for the above quotation (from the *Journal of Commerce*); for other samples of press reactions to Walsh's report, Chester Wright, "Heading West," *American Federationist*, XXXI (July, 1924), 577-78. Walsh was quite sensitive about the public reaction. His private papers include a number of letters from him to newspapers, either thanking them for their approval, or dissenting from their criticism. To one editor in Hobson, Montana, he wrote: ". . . the comment made by you being distinctly censorious . . . , I am enclosing copies of editorials on my report from three leading republican papers of the country—the Philadelphia Inquirer, the Springfield Republican and the Washington Evening Star." Walsh asked the Hobson editor to print these, to show his readers that not all Republican editors agreed with him. Walsh to the Judith Basin *Star*, June 11, 1924, Box 374, Walsh Papers.

Joseph Schafer's evaluation of 1940 is valid; the Walsh report
was judicious and written without rancor. The chagrin of Democratic commentators bears witness to this. But Walsh may have
been politically wiser than his disappointed supporters imagined.
By remaining within the bounds of his evidence, Walsh had
avoided charges of undue partisanship. At the same time, he did
not erase, with such a report, the preceding months of publicity
and political jockying. As Daniels' *News and Observer* under-
stated: "Senator Walsh's work altered the entire political map of
the 1924 campaign and created an issue which will figure promin-
ently in the election."[7]

The forthcoming campaign did not, however, turn into a running debate over Teapot Dome alone. There were other issues of
varying importance. The magazine *Forum* ran a series of articles
from January through June of 1924, in which spokesmen for both
major parties discussed what the magazine editors considered
"campaign issues." Republican national chairman John T. Adams
and Democratic national chairman Cordell Hull led off with
articles on the tariff. Following them came discussions on transportation, taxation, agriculture, foreign policy, and prohibition.
True, the campaign rested partly upon all of these issues, but
obviously, voters would be influenced by countless other arguments, interests, and prejudices and not even the most partisan
Republican could, with reason, deny the campaign potential of
Teapot Dome. Nevertheless, the editors of *Forum*, consciously or
not, failed to list Teapot Dome among the issues.[8]

Democratic leaders were not so negligent. Cordell Hull recalled
that while chairman he "closely followed the Teapot Dome investigation . . . which, through exposing Harding's Secretary . . .
Fall, turned out to be a windfall for the Democratic Party." In
late May of 1924, in Washington, Josephus Daniels talked with
Hull about the Democrats' 1924 platform. They agreed, wrote
Daniels, "to try to get away from the old stereotyped platform
and appeal to the imagination and judgment of the country and
along new lines." Daniels suggested that they offer a plank labeled, "Thou Shalt Not Steal." Under this plank, Daniels would

[7] Raleigh *News and Observer,* June 6, 1924.
[8] *The Forum,* LXXI (January-June, 1924), 41-51, 198-206, 344-57, 492-
503, and 806-16.

—After Sullivan, *Our Times*, v. 6

"O We Ain' Gwine Steal No Mo"

list things not to be stolen; for example, "Thou shalt not steal the Naval Oil Reserves."[9] The platform that eventually emerged was less imaginative and more conventional than Daniels and Hull had proposed, but it contained, nonetheless, the essence of the eighth commandment.

[9] Hull, *Memoirs*, I, 115; Daniels to W. W. Ball, May 26, 1924, Ball Papers.

The *Democratic Campaign Book* also was to point out the Republicans' malefactions. Early in June, Hull and his assistant Gratten Kerans asked Walsh to write the chapter on the "Naval Oil Scandal" in the forthcoming book. They informed Walsh that they hoped to "present in 800 or 1000 words the most telling facts of Republican responsibility for the mismanagement and corruption which you and your Democratic associates have revealed. . . ." Walsh's "initiative and labors" in the investigation had been so vital and were so well known, that Hull and Kerans were "very eager" for Walsh to write the story. Walsh accepted the task readily and promised to "try to get it out within the next week or ten days."[10]

Other Democrats, meantime, were seeking to capitalize upon Walsh's reputation as the Teapot Dome prosecutor. Joseph P. Tumulty, once secretary to President Wilson, wanted to see Walsh made permanent chairman of the Democratic convention in 1924. Tumulty felt that if Walsh was "ignored and not 'played up,'" the Democrats would lose much of the credit that should be theirs "by reason of his prominence as the oil investigator." Tumulty, writing his sentiments to Arthur Krock of the New York *World*, wondered if the *World* "would be free to urge [Walsh's] selection?" Krock agreed with Tumulty "heartily," having, he replied, just urged Bernard Baruch "to lend his influence to this very thing." Krock agreed to take up the question with "the *World* council."[11]

Perhaps Tumulty's thought had been an obvious one, for soon after his correspondence with Krock, the New York *Times* reported "strong indications . . . in Democratic circles" that Walsh would be the permanent chairman. Some Democratic leaders in Congress said that it was "virtually settled." The reports were accurate. On June 25, in Madison Square Garden, New York City, Walsh took office as permanent chairman of the 1924 Democratic convention.[12]

[10] Kerans and Hull to Walsh, June 9, 1924, and Walsh to Hull, June 10, 1924, Box 374, Walsh Papers. For the results, see Walsh's "Review of Naval Oil Leases," *Democratic Campaign Book, 1924* (Washington, 1924), 135-38.

[11] Tumulty to Krock, May 29, 1924; Krock to Tumulty, May 31, 1924, Box 376, Walsh Papers.

[12] New York *Times*, June 5, 1924, p. 2; *Official Report of the Proceedings of the Democratic National Convention . . . 1924* (Indianapolis, 1924), 79;

Already Senator Pat Harrison, the temporary chairman, had set the indignant tone of the assemblage in his address on opening day. His first sentence flashed before the convention a reminder of enduring Republican corruption. In 1876, he told them, the hosts of Democracy had met in a St. Louis convention "to dedicate themselves to purging corruption from the public service. We meet today for a rededication to the same purpose. There was corruption then; there is a Saturnalia of corruption now." Harrison then flayed the opposition with orthodox fervor. His wit and his metaphors sparkled with references to oil and to numerous Republican shortcomings. When Walsh replaced Harrison in the chair the next day, he took up the arraignment. Teapot Dome did not monopolize his address, but it did dominate it. One newspaper believed that his speech confirmed "the general expectation" that the Democrats would campaign "mainly on the issue of honesty in government."[13]

After the chairman's address, and after other preliminaries, came the nominations. They produced a shattering experience for the convention and for the party. An acrid and exhausting struggle between William Gibbs McAdoo and Alfred E. Smith ended, after 29 sessions and 103 ballots, in the defeat of both, when the weary convention finally selected, from a host of nominees, John W. Davis of West Virginia.

McAdoo had entered the convention with about three hundred delegates pledged to him, 194 of them through presidential preliminaries. This support had helped him to remain in the race in the face of his Teapot Dome handicap, for the primaries had demonstrated his continued appeal in different parts of the coun-

---

hereinafter cited as *Proceedings of the Convention, 1924* (Democratic). Walsh carried out this role with distinction. He received numerous letters commending him for his work; he usually replied as he did to Clark Howell of the Atlanta *Constitution:* "I am more proud of having come away with [such] respect and esteem, than of any nomination the convention could have given me." Walsh to Howell, July 21, 1924, Box 374, Walsh Papers. Considering the marathon through which he, as chairman, passed, perhaps he was right.

[13] *Proceedings of the Convention, 1924* (Democratic), 7-25, 80-88; New York *Times,* June 26, 1924, p. 22.

try.[14] Whatever the basis of his continued support, McAdoo and
many of his followers had become more and more hopeful as convention-time neared. Breckenridge Long, on the eve of the convention, wrote: "McAdoo's strength is fast being translated into
delegates. West of the Mississippi River most of the states are for
him; and of the solid south he has a preponderating strength with
instructions from most of them; while in the n. e. country east of
the Miss. he has scattering votes. Even with the ⅔ rule he can
be nominated and it begins to look like he may." Senator William
H. King of Utah wrote to McAdoo in May: "I am glad to note the
growing strength of the movement in your behalf. I think your
stock has risen very much within the past six weeks." McAdoo
himself felt that his primary victories were a "foreshadowing [of]
certain success . . . if our friends do team work and our strategy
is right." It is also noteworthy that several major figures in the
McAdoo following, who had earlier deserted or expressed pes-
simism over his chances, had returned to McAdoo by convention
time. Breckenridge Long, assigned as floor manager of the Mc-
Adoo forces at the convention, held daily conferences with such
figures as Bernard Baruch and Thomas Chadbourne, financial
backers who had withdrawn support after Doheny's testimony.[15]

Preferential primaries aside, McAdoo derived much of his support from the Drys and—perhaps reluctantly on his part—from the
Ku Klux Klan, his strength thereby lying mainly in the South and
in the West. The Klan had been an issue in the McAdoo campaign almost from the beginning. In November, 1923, one official
in his organization wrote to McAdoo: "The effort to stick the KKK
on you is so absurd that it will correct itself in the course of time
if for no other reason than that you have an Irish secretary and
among your strongest supporters are . . . ardent Catholics and such
prominent Jews as [Bernard] Baruch." Whether McAdoo wel-

[14] Arthur W. Macmahon, "The United States: Domestic Politics," in Lindsay Rogers and Parker T. Moon (eds.), "Record of Political Events . . . ,"
Supplement to Political Science Quarterly, XL (March-Dec., 1925), 38. Lee
Allen, "The Democratic Primary in Texas in 1924," *loc. cit.*, 487-89, suggests that "the chief significance" of McAdoo's victory in the Texas primary
in May "was that it materially aided in the comeback of McAdoo following
the February crisis in his campaign." In Texas, the stigma of Teapot Dome
may have been offset by the support McAdoo gained from the Ku Klux Klan.
[15] Long Diary, May 29, 1924, and July 15, 1924; King to McAdoo, May
12, 1924, Box 305; McAdoo to W. A. Comstock, May 24, 1924, Box 304;
and David L. Rockwell to McAdoo, June 7, 1924, Box 305, McAdoo Papers.

comed it or not, however, Klan support came to him. In Texas, one supporter had "personal information from those in the inner councils" that unless McAdoo positively alienated the Klan "that vote in Texas" would go to him. Weeks before the convention opened, a Minnesota supporter informed McAdoo that "the Klan question is the only thing discussed in Minnesota," and he wrote McAdoo of "the absolute necessity of taking a stand in opposition to this organization . . . at once." However, McAdoo refused to denounce the Klan or to actively seek its support. As Breckenridge Long suggested at a strategy meeting in New York during the convention, "there was no sense in denouncing the Klan and entering upon the impossible task of competing with [Al] Smith for the Catholic vote, for that is just what it amounted to."[16]

Opposing McAdoo were several factions within the party: "Wets"; "business interests of the East," as Frank R. Kent called them; factions north and east of the Ohio River, who were reacting against the Klan's attacks on their racial origins and their Catholicism; and finally, those Democrats who saw Teapot Dome as a fatal burden for McAdoo or anyone else to carry.[17]

The man who profited most from such opposition was Al Smith, Governor of New York.[18] How much he profited, and how much

[16] G. F. Miller to McAdoo, Oct. 3, 1923, Box. 284; Herbert B. Swope to McAdoo, Oct. 25, 1923, and McAdoo to Swope, Oct. 29, 1923, Box 285; M. L. Fox to McAdoo, Nov. 1, 1923, and W. P. Hobb to McAdoo, Nov. 7, 1923, Box 285; Arthur F. Mullen to McAdoo, May 26, 1924, Box 305; and Long Diary, July 15, 1924, McAdoo Papers.

[17] Sexton Humphreys, "The Nomination of the Democratic Candidate in 1924," *Indiana Magazine of History*, XXXI (March, 1935), 1-9; Freidel, *The Ordeal*, 166 ff.; Frank R. Kent, *The Democratic Party: A History* (New York, 1928), 469 ff.; and Arthur Krock, "The Damn Fool Democrats," *The American Mercury*, IV (March, 1925), 257-62.

[18] Frank Freidel comments that Franklin D. Roosevelt (a Smith supporter) "was well aware that the strength Smith was gaining [as the convention neared] came not only from progressives, but in considerable part from conservatives opposed to McAdoo" (*The Ordeal*, 169). Sexton Humphreys claims that the Democratic factions opposed to McAdoo "rallied . . . around . . . Smith" (Humphreys, "Nomination of the Democratic Candidate in 1924," *loc. cit.*). Frank Kent believed that "the prime purpose of the forces behind Smith . . . was to beat McAdoo. . . . The nomination of Smith was incidental" (Kent, *The Democratic Party*, 469). Breckenridge Long believed that his supporters nominated Smith, "who never had a chance . . . , as the only available person behind whom could be [gathered] . . . the forces opposed to McAdoo under the guise of opposition to the Klan" (Long diary, Oct. 21, 1924, McAdoo Papers).

McAdoo lost, are intangible questions without clear solutions. But clearly race and religion were the prevalent issues in the grievous party strife that raged for twenty-nine sessions in Madison Square Garden. McAdoo had brought to this conflict his unfortunate association with Edward Doheny; insofar as it had injured him, it handicapped him from the first ballot.

On the first of April, Louis M. Howe had analyzed the situation for an acquaintance: The McAdoo leaders had "the good judgement to impress on their weak-kneed supporters the wisdom of standing by McAdoo even if he has no chance . . . so that they will be a part of a block so large that no one can be nominated without their consent." It looked to Howe "as if the McAdoo people would absolutely control the nomination, provided always they do not get into a factional fight among themselves." Howe made a "general guess" that after the leading candidates had demonstrated their inability to win the nomination, a back-room conference among "the leaders of the largest block of votes" would bring forth "some unguessable and perhaps unknown John Smith," who would then be chosen as the man they all really had wanted.[19]

As one authority points out, Howe made a "remarkably accurate prediction." Neither Smith nor McAdoo could or would agree to compromise. At one point, Smith offered to withdraw, if McAdoo would do the same, but McAdoo refused. Even the lesser candidates refused to withdraw, perhaps because Teapot Dome had aroused bright hopes for a Democratic victory, whoever the candidate. They intended not to budge until McAdoo and Smith eliminated each other; yet, short of compromise or exhaustion, the deadlock between these two could break only if votes shifted from one or more of the minor candidates.[20]

One of these, Governor Samuel M. Ralston of Indiana, appar-

[19] Howe to Thomas Mott Osborne, April 1, 1924, cited in Freidel, *The Ordeal,* 168-69.
[20] Freidel, *The Ordeal,* 169; Arthur W. Macmahon, "Record of Political Events," *loc. cit.;* Macmahon notes that even when McAdoo reached his high point of 530 votes on the sixty-ninth ballot, 233 votes went to the eleven lesser candidates (not including Smith); and when Smith reached his high point of 368 votes on the seventy-sixth ballot, 216 votes went to the minor candidates. James M. Cox, the 1920 Democratic nominee, thought that the Democratic confidence engendered by Teapot Dome "may have been responsible for the spirited . . . contest [in 1924]." *Journey Through My Years* (New York, 1946), 324.

ently could have had the nomination at one point, had he been willing to accept it. But he had protested even having his name proposed to the convention, and when told that he could win the nomination, he pleaded ill-health and rejected the offer. Ralston's rejection coincided with another major convention development—McAdoo's release of his delegates. Thereafter, his votes dropped swiftly, as did Smith's. Apparently, the groups which had sought to make Ralston the candidate turned to John W. Davis, who already had received 210 votes on the ninety-ninth ballot. When Oscar W. Underwood of Alabama, an economic conservative and a "Wet," began to profit from the newly released delegates, "votes in something of a panic" began swinging to Davis. On the one hundred third ballot, Davis received 839 votes and the nomination.[21]

For vice-president, Josephus Daniels suggested Charles W. Bryan, governor of Nebraska since 1922 and brother of William Jennings Bryan. Davis found him acceptable; only one ballot was necessary to choose him. Immediately after Davis—and before Bryan—won the nomination, Daniels had made a motion to adjourn, so that the delegates could consider their choice for vice-president. He was interrupted by "constant, persistent and innumerable cries, approaching unanimity and acclamation, of: 'Walsh,' 'Walsh,' 'Walsh.'" When an Illinois delegate rose to place Walsh in nomination, Chairman Walsh ruled him out of order. Later he specifically rejected, in a written statement to the convention, any possible nomination for the office.[22]

The fourteen-day spectacle of family bickering was a tragedy for the Democratic party. Either Smith or—despite Teapot Dome—McAdoo would have made a better candidate than Davis. Davis had great ability as a constitutional lawyer and was a man of integrity—a valuable commodity in 1924. But he also was wealthy and polished, and an economic conservative; his New York law firm was counsel for J. P. Morgan and Company. As one historian

21 Humphreys, "Nomination of the Democratic Candidate in 1924," *loc. cit.*; Macmahon, "Record of Political Events," *loc. cit.*; and *Proceedings of the Convention, 1924* (Democratic), pp. 963-73.

22 *Proceedings of the Convention, 1924* (Democratic), 972-73, 993-94, and 1026-38; Macmahon, "Record of Political Events," *loc. cit.* Walsh also had received 123 votes for presidential nominee as late as the one hundred second ballot.

summarized the Democratic handicap: Those happy under Republican prosperity had little reason to shift to a Democrat; dissatisfied farmers, union men, and others of the discontented would see little attraction in Davis, since even the more progressive McAdoo had been undesirable to them. Another historian of the period has suggested that corporation lawyer Davis was "a red flag to the Progressive bulls" and that Byran's nomination looked suspiciously contrived—"Wall Street and Bryan on the same ticket."[23]

A South Carolina newspaper editor commented on the convention: "I'm glad McAdoo was defeated and, though Davis is a fine figure . . . , lawyer, and Democrat, I fancy he has small chance of election." With McAdoo's nomination undesirable because of Teapot Dome, the convention should have chosen Walsh, "a wild man of the West, an able lawyer, radical labor man, millionaire, personally honest, McAdoo man, dry." Frank Hampton informed Senator Simmons that he was "not pleased with the nomination of Davis." McAdoo's defeat, of course, was a great disappointment, but the Davis choice would lose the Democrats three million votes to Senator La Follette, who was running on a third party ticket.[24]

The Republican convention was a peaceful contrast to the Democrats' brawl. Indeed, it was utterly humdrum. Coolidge had the nomination before the delegates formerly awarded it to him. William Allen White stated that between August, 1923, and June, 1924, Coolidge "remade the Republican party," taking it away from the Old Guard typified by such men as Henry Cabot Lodge. Preferential primaries and state conventions enabled Coolidge to enter the convention with 572 delegates pledged to support him. He won the nomination on the first ballot. The delegates chose Charles G. Dawes of Illinois as his running mate.[25]

Teapot Dome had not handicapped Coolidge; it had served him. His austere and taciturn character had become a rock of salvation

[23] Freidel, *The Ordeal*, 181; Leuchtenburg, *The Perils of Prosperity*, 134-35.

[24] W. W. Ball to Tom Miller, July 16, 1924, Ball Papers; Hampton to Simmons, July 17, 1924, Simmons Papers.

[25] White, *A Puritan in Babylon*, 296; John Garraty, *Henry Cabot Lodge*, (New York, 1953), 417; Arthur Macmahon, "Record of Political Events," *loc. cit.*

for Republicans swimming in the wake of the Harding legacy. His maneuverings during the party crisis of the previous winter undoubtedly had fortified his control over the party and suggested his ability to offset, if not entirely to nullify, the corruption issue in the campaign. With Davis as his Democratic opponent, Coolidge's chances looked favorable, despite the strident cries of corruption that were bound to arise from the Democratic campaigners.[26]

Coolidge and Davis were the two leading contestants, but at least one minor party candidate was their equal, even their superior, in ability and achievement. Republican Senator La Follette of Wisconsin received the presidential nomination on a Progressive party ticket from a heterogeneous movement centered in the Conference for Progressive Political Action.[27] Although he had profited by Doheny's implication of McAdoo, La Follette may well have won the nomination without it. In the campaign, he was to surpass the Democrats in stressing Republican corruption, and he and his supporters would carefully recall his role in the origins of the Teapot Dome investigation. Running with La Follette on the ticket was Burton K. Wheeler, Democratic Senator from Montana. He, also, was a bolter from his party and had encouraged the Senate inquiry into Teapot Dome. Both men could be expected to point with alarm toward the corruption.

Teapot Dome was significant, either by its prominence or by its absence, in the platform of the parties. The Democratic platform, not surprisingly, teemed with references to Fall's dishonor and to Republican mismanagement of the nation's resources. But while the Democrats emphasized Republican inefficiency and corruption, their platform also contained the expected planks on such issues as the tarriff, taxes, agriculture, and foreign affairs. Teapot Dome did not sustain their campaign, but it did nourish it. The

[26] Just after Harding's death, Breckenridge Long had pointed out: "Calvin Coolidge . . . is a different person than Warren Harding [and] we must make new plans. . . . We have to beat Coolidge—not Harding—and that is harder—maybe impossible. Harding was beaten. The only thing which could have prevented the certain election of a Democrat next year—or rendered it uncertain—was his death—and he died." Long Diary, Aug. 6, 1923, McAdoo Papers. But then after the winter of revelations, during which Coolidge caught a fair share of Democratic abuse, Long felt otherwise: "We want Coolidge nominated." Diary, March 16, 1924, *ibid.*

[27] McKay, *Progressive Movement of 1924;* La Follette, *Robert M. La Follette,* 1107 ff.

Republicans, in their platform, made no attempt to skirt clear of
Teapot Dome; they simply avoided mentioning it specifically.
They, too, recognized the need for "clean and honest government,"
but claimed that the recent congressional investigations had "exposed instances in both parties of men [willing to buy and sell
official favors]." They demanded a speedy prosecution of all
wrong-doers, but insisted that the innocent not be confused with
the guilty. The La Follette platform, meantime, pledged "a complete housecleaning" of the executive departments and a stringent
program of conservation.[28]

The Democrats' campaign book contained a chapter on the
"History of Naval Oil Scandals," in addition to Walsh's "Review
of Naval Oil Leases." The latter was by far the more restrained.
The Republicans, in their book, presented a chapter on "Public
Oil Lands," in which they stressed Walsh's support of the 1920
leasing bill, Daniels' desire for "autocratic power" while Secretary
of the Navy, and the "expeditious" actions of President Coolidge
in dealing with Teapot Dome. The La Follette campaign book,
The Facts, made a fierce assault upon Coolidge and his relations
with Edward McLean and upon his "weak, timid and vacillating"
role in the face of corruption. But to the Progressives, Davis and
the Democrats were no better: "Fraud, graft and corruption under
the last Democratic administration equalled in magnitude, if not
in venality, that of the administration now in power."[29]

Teapot Dome was the leitmotif of Davis' acceptance speech.
Standing in a driving rainstorm, before his hometown audience in
Clarksburg, West Virginia, Davis recounted the scandals of the
Republican administration. In graceful yet powerful language, he
indicted the Republican party for gross corruption and for complacency in the face of it. The Boston *Evening Transcript* called
the Davis speech a prosecutor's indictment, one that fell through
because it had charged too much. "There is no Teapot Dome in

---

[28] *Democratic Campaign Book, 1924*, pp. 3-46; *Republican Campaign
Textbook*, pp. 61-98; McKay, *Progressive Movement of 1924*, pp. 143-48.
One Progressive, as had Josephus Daniels, wanted the La Follette platform
to concentrate on "thou shalt not steal." Instead, the Progressives decided to
make monopoly their leading issue. McKay, *Progressive Movement of 1924*,
p. 148.
[29] *Democratic Campaign Book*, 135-50; *Republican Campaign Textbook*,
343-51; *La Follette-Wheeler Campaign Textbook* (Chicago, 1924), 41 ff.

the Administration as it is now constituted, and the country knows it."[30]

Coolidge, when he gave his own speech of acceptance three days later, acted as if the *Transcript* were right. He stressed the achievements of his and Harding's administration. He uttered not one aggressive tone and did not mention the Democratic party or Teapot Dome. In this speech, the *Transcript* saw "an extraordinary state paper." It was a privilege and a duty "to read, mark, learn and inwardly digest its every statement." The Raleigh *News and Observer* failed to see such qualities in it. In a three-column editorial, Daniels—or someone who wrote in his style—revealed the line of attack that Democrats would use in the campaign. Coolidge must, he said, accept responsibility for the conduct of "the thieves and plunderers who looted the oil reserves." As vice-president, Coolidge "must have been familiar with the slimy trail of oil, although, of course, he had no responsibility for the original corruption. His responsibility was in doing nothing on his own initiative to punish the plunderers." No man, concluded the editorial, had ever "so hemmed and hawed and dallied while brave men uncovered crime under his very nose. It will be impossible . . . to cast the odium on Harding and put a halo on Coolidge."[31]

If the Democratic tactic was to maximize Coolidge's implication in the scandal, the Republican national committee's response was to deny that Teapot Dome, as an issue, even existed. On July 18, Republican national chairman William M. Butler stated: "I read about Teapot Dome in the newspapers many weeks ago, but I have not heard anything about it since. It is not much of an issue. It is purely ephemeral. . . ." One newspaper commented that "too

[30] *Proceedings of the Convention, 1924* (Democratic), 1052-67; New York *Times*, Aug. 12, 1924, p. 1; and Boston *Evening Transcript*, Aug. 12, 1924. Harry Slattery had sent Davis some material "with especial reference to oil." Later, he supplied Davis with information on forestry and conservation. Slattery sent a copy of the oil material to Pinchot, a Republican, if a Progressive one, and commented: "When you have looked this over, I assume you will want to return it—as probably it would be wiser not to have this Democratic 'help' in your files, even on conservation." Slattery to Pinchot, July 28, 1924, Slattery Papers.

[31] Boston *Evening Transcript*, Aug. 15, 1924; Raleigh *News and Observer*, Aug. 15, 1924. This editorial, of course, appeared during the campaign, but it remains one of the better statements by Daniels' paper on the entire Teapot Dome story to that point.

many Republicans" were taking this attitude and that Butler "led all the rest in callous indifference" to Teapot Dome. The *American Federationist*, speaking presumably for much of the labor vote, described Butler's statement as a "typical ward politician announcement" and "about as hard-boiled as anything that has yet been said in this campaign." Labor, said the journal, had no desire to present Teapot Dome as a partisan issue, since the "oil buzzards" had gone after the oil reserves "not because they were Republicans [or] Democrats, but because they were buzzards." Butler, however, by speaking as he had, came "very close to pinning his own party label on the specter." At the same time, the American Federation of Labor saw more than Teapot Dome as an issue. The La Follette-Wheeler platform had pledged definite action in support of labor. The executive council of the AFL had approved the platform and would attempt to elect La Follette and Wheeler.[32]

Although monopoly was their supreme issue, La Follette and Wheeler made effective use of Teapot Dome. Wheeler even devised a standard technique: during his speech, he placed a chair before him and demanded that Coolidge, the "strong, calm man," take the stand. He then directed at the chair a barrage of questions on the scandals; whereupon he concluded that "the usual silence emanates from the strong, calm man in the White House" and motioned for the witness to withdraw. La Follette, on the other hand, retained his customary earnest and dedicated manner. In Minneapolis, he charged that Coolidge, as vice-president, had known about the leases. In Brooklyn, he said that oil ruled the State Department. This noble old warrior, his life running out, was in a hopeless race, but he still retained, as he had for over four decades, his crusading ardor for political regeneration.[33]

Davis waited until September 11, in Denver, to mention Albert

[32] New York *Times*, July 19, 1924, p. 2; Aug. 3, 1924, Sec. 2, p. 4; *American Federationist*, XXXI (Sept., 1924), 705 ff., 741-48. Later, the *Federationist* would associate Davis with Teapot Dome by suggesting that since he was an attorney for Standard Oil, which itself had received one of the richest sections of the naval oil reserve in California, he must have sat in on the decision by Standard Oil to seek the reserve. *Ibid.*, XXXI (Nov. 1924), 910.

[33] La Follette, *Robert M. La Follette*, II, 1127-46; New York *Times*, Sept. 25, 1924, p. 2. Oswald Garrison Villard, after a week of traveling with Wheeler, wrote to La Follette that Wheeler was "doing extremely good

Fall for the first time in a campaign speech. He referred to the Republicans' platform statement that the nation's conservation policy had originated with the Republican Theodore Roosevelt and that the party held it a privilege to build a memorial to him. "Shades of the mighty dead!" exclaimed Davis; "it will be a sorry memorial if adorned, when erected, with a statuette of Albert B. Fall." After this opening sally, Davis, in succeeding speeches, began to display wit as well as scorn over Fall and the corruption associated with his name.[34]

Other Democrats joined him. On October 1, in Washington, Daniels attacked Coolidge and the Republican "conspiracy of silence" over Teapot Dome. On the fourth, in Schenectady, New York, Governor Al Smith (accepting renomination for governor) denounced Teapot Dome before an enthusiastic throng. On October 25, in a special radio broadcast from Washington, Senator Pat Harrison repeated the charge that Coolidge knew about the "scandal" before the investigation began. Said Harrison: "If he had not possessed eyes to see nor ears to hear, he could have smelled it, because everybody else in the country at that time was smelling [it]." On November 2, a reporter interviewed Franklin D. Roosevelt, who said that Coolidge's "early silence" about Teapot Dome was "understandable" and that it was "not fair" to make an issue of it. When Coolidge failed to protest, said Roosevelt, "he was carrying out what our Republican friends . . . describe as Mr. Coolidge's belief in attending to his own business." However, his activity after he became President could not be condoned, claimed Roosevelt. He should then have "immediately repudiated" the leases. He should have acted, for as President he had the authority, and the crime had been committed. His failure to act came "pretty close to making him a participant in the crime."[35]

Coolidge greeted all such attacks with complete silence. He made few speeches on any subject. In early October, William H. Taft called on him and found him "very cheerful" and "quite con-

work, quiet, modest and unassuming yet dramatic to a remarkable degree by his simple straightforward narrative of Teapot Dome and the Daugherty scandals. I have never seen audiences more fascinated" (La Follette, *Robert M. La Follette,* 1139).

[34] New York *Times,* Sept. 12, 1924, p. 1.

[35] *Ibid.,* Oct. 2, 1924, p. 2; Oct. 5, 1924, p. 1; Oct. 26, 1924, p. 16; Nov. 3, 1924, p. 4.

fident of election." On October 23, Coolidge wrote to his father: "The outlook appears to be promising, but as I have often told you, elections are very uncertain." *The Literary Digest* showed Coolidge far in the lead almost from the beginning of the campaign, and its final report on November 1, 1924, showed Coolidge receiving more votes than all of his opponents combined.[36]

Coolidge carried thirty-five states, receiving a total of 382 electoral votes. Davis carried eleven states earning 136 votes. La Follette won Wisconsin and 13 electoral votes. Explanations of the results are about as involved and intelligible as such expositions usually are. But it seems clear that Teapot Dome, despite Democatic exertions, was only one, and perhaps even a relatively minor, influence in the election.[37]

In Albert Fall's New Mexico, Teapot Dome was not a major issue. Fall never lacked friends in New Mexico, even after the scandal had made a villain of him elsewhere. Also, as a western state, New Mexico had its share of anti-conservationists, who were sympathetic to the policies Fall had followed while Secretary of the Interior. In 1924, a few editorial voices did arise in opposition to the Republican ticket in the state, charging it to be a Fall ticket. But the objection was more to Albert Fall, the old state political boss, than to Fall, the discredited Interior secretary. In September, at the state Democratic convention in Santa Fe, the keynoter declared: "New Mexico bows her head in humiliation over the fact that Albert B. Fall . . . claims this state as his home." On the other hand, when the convention drew up resolutions supporting or opposing various items, it neither directly nor indirectly mentioned Teapot Dome. During the gubernatorial campaign, Democratic nominee Sam G. Bratton did mention Fall and claimed that New Mexico would "be a hundred years living down the disgrace he brought down on the state." The Santa Fe *New Mexican*

[36] Claude Fuess, *Calvin Coolidge*, 353-54; *The Literary Digest,* LXXXIII (Nov. 1, 1924), 5-8. At the same time, the *Digest's* poll also showed La Follette running ahead of Davis. The *Digest* was remarkably accurate in predicting the state by state vote for Coolidge; it guessed correctly in forty-six states.

[37] For an able discussion of this problem, see J. Leonard Bates, "The Teapot Dome Scandal and the Election of 1924," *American Historical Review,* LX (Jan. 1955), 303-22. See McKay, *Progressive Movement of 1924,* pp. 274-77, for a breakdown and a distribution map of the vote in 1924.

delivered at least one indignant editorial in condemnation of the Coolidge administration's "monumental and shocking" scandals. But state and local questions were paramont in the race in New Mexico, and after Coolidge carried the state in November, the *New Mexican* delivered the post-mortem: "The voters refused to take Fall, Daugherty, Denby and Forbes as the issue."[38]

The Democratic party in 1924, insofar as it had any issues, made honesty in government the bedrock of the national campaign. But there were no real issues, no burning questions to influence great blocs of voters. Without issues, the candidates themselves increased in importance. A real weakness of the Democrats was their candidate, as well as the way in which they chose him. Teapot Dome had helped to eliminate McAdoo, one of their most attractive candidates, although quite possibly he would have been killed off anyway in the Democratic convention fiasco.

Several shrewd Democrats, analyzing their defeat, saw it rooted in the loss of McAdoo and in the selection of Davis. The historian William E. Dodd wrote to Walsh that "the greatest calamity" in the Teapot Dome story was Doheny's implication of McAdoo. If McAdoo had "told Doheny where he must cease his operations, we should have . . . a different history to read," wrote Dodd. "There would have been no Coolidge, except as one of the least of vice presidents." Furnifold Simmons wrote to McAdoo of "the monumental and fatal blunder committed by our party, when it failed to nominate [you] the only man who . . . could have won." Josephus Daniels, however, saw in McAdoo a strong but a losing candidate, Although Daniels supported McAdoo in the 1924 convention, in 1927 he wrote to Franklin D. Roosevelt: "I believe that [if McAdoo] had been nominated in 1924 before the bitter feeling of Madison Square [Garden], that he would have pulled the labor vote and . . . have won the party many of the dissatisfied farmers in the West, but I do not think he could have been elected." William Kent, conservationist and former congressman from California, wrote to Gifford Pinchot: "Looking back over the whole situation the only good that could have been accomplished would have been the nomination of McAdoo and the backing he would

<hr />

[38] Santa Fe *New Mexican,* Sept. 15, 17, and 30, Oct. 13 and 28, and Nov. 5, 1924. Cf. New York *Times,* Oct. 28, 1924, Sec. 3, p. 3, reporting Albert Fall to be "a big issue in New Mexico."

have received." Kent thought that the Democrats "committed suicide in the convention. . . . Davis would have been a real leader and a great President, but he had no party back of him." Walsh, without expressing himself on McAdoo, saw a plain explanation for the defeat. He thought it "strange how many theories are advanced by our people to account for the result, when it must be perfectly obvious that the . . . party cannot win with a candidate taken from the environment from which Mr. Davis came." McAdoo himself thought that the "tragedy . . . in 1924" stemmed from the New York convention fight.[39]

Contemporary newspapers and magazine analyses, too, often blamed the defeat upon what the Philadelphia *Record* called "the bitterness of the convention fight" and the "unreasoning prejudice never entirely wiped out." According to *The Literary Digest*'s survey, "scores of Democratic papers" believed that the Democrats had "committed slow suicide at Madison Square Garden."[40]

Davis, trying to re-unite a shattered party and overcome his political handicaps, was a weak candidate. Many weeks before the election, Breckenridge Long had begun to view the Davis campaign as "hopeless." "From the first," he wrote, "Davis has allowed himself to be surrounded by incompetents, has received and acted upon bad advise, has no organization, has no equipment for a campaign—save his own great ability and his own remarkable

[39] Dodd to Walsh, June 5, 1924, Box 376, Walsh Papers (Dodd evidently meant that Coolidge, even while serving out Harding's term, was only a succeeding vice-president and would never have been elected in his own right, in a contest against McAdoo. Dodd thought that McAdoo had been shown "in a compromising, not worse, position."); Simmons to McAdoo, Jan. 31, 1925, Simmons Papers; Daniels to Richard Lloyd Jones, May 26, 1924, Box 304, McAdoo Papers; Daniels to Roosevelt, July 19, 1927, Box 15, Daniels Papers (Daniels also was "quite sure Smith could not have been elected. Perhaps nobody [in the Democratic party] could."); Kent to Pinchot, Nov. 10, 1924, Box 249, Pinchot Papers; Walsh to McAdoo, Dec. 4, 1924, Box 375, Walsh Papers; McAdoo to Simmons, Feb. 12, 1925, Simmons Papers. See also McAdoo to Walsh, Nov. 15, 1924, Box 375, Walsh Papers, and numerous letters from McAdoo to individuals throughout the country, Box 306, McAdoo Papers, similar to his remarks to one correspondent: "The election verified my worst fears. The Democratic Party has received one of the worst defeats in its history. Nothing else, however, could have been expected after the action of the New York convention" (McAdoo to Thomas L. Chadbourne, Nov. 13, 1924).

[40] *The Literary Digest,* LXXXIII (Nov. 22, 1924), 12-13.

personality. But they are not sufficient. . . . His untimely and un-
necessary denunciation of the Ku Klux Klan has lost him strength
in states where it was needed and has added nothing in states he
could not possibly carry." Long might also have noted another
fundamental fact: the Democratic party was numerically weaker
than the Republican. Since 1896, it had defeated the Republican
party only twice and had never polled 50 per cent of the vote in
any one election. In every election since 1896, except for the war-
time election of 1916, the Republican party had polled over 50 per
cent of the vote.[41]

Calvin Coolidge, silent, relatively untarnished by scandal, and
in control of the majority party, was a strong candidate. Harding,
his record tainted, had died through what many grateful Republicans called an act of God—grateful for the succession as much as
for the removal. For, as William Allen White so aptly suggested,
a Puritan then came to reign in Babylon. Thereafter, the Ohio
gang "vanished like dead leaves before an east wind."[42] Coolidge
began to restore a measure of public faith in the presidency and
to gather within his hands the control of the Republican party.
In June of 1924, he dominated his party in its convention. In
November, the vote reflected his popularity, since his victory was
as much a personal as a party one. The Republicans gained in
both houses of Congress, but not in proportion to Coolidge's own
popular vote. At the same time, the actual increase in Republican

[41] Long diary, Sept. 19, 1924, and Oct. 16, 1924, McAdoo Papers; Hugh
L. Keenleyside, "The American Political Revolution of 1924," *Current History*, XXI (March, 1925), 833-40; Samuel Lubell, *The Future of American
Politics* (Rev. ed.; New York, 1956), 36. Lubell shows a Republican plurality of 1,252,000 in 1924. As he suggests, this plurality already was beginning to decline in the face of a rising tide of new Democratic voters,
but the shift would not be decisive until 1932.

[42] Claude M. Fuess, "Calvin Coolidge—Twenty Years After," *Proceedings
of the American Antiquarian Society*, LXIII, Part 2 (Oct. 21, 1953), 351-69.
White's term "Puritan" had, of course, little direct reference to religion in
seventeenth-century New England. Rather, he used it as Gamaliel Bradford
did: contrasting "the mad, hurrying, chattering, extravagant, self-indulgent
harlotry of twentieth-century America and the grave, silent, stern, narrow,
uncomprehending New England Puritanism of Calvin Coolidge." In 1927,
Walter Lippmann also called Coolidge a Puritan in the same figurative way.
White, *A Puritan in Babylon*, 258 (quoting Bradford); Walter Lippmann,
Men of Destiny (New York, 1927), 10-18.

congressional strength suggests that, whatever caused the Republican victory, Teapot Dome had not indicted the party any more than it had the party leader.[43]

Democrats had tried to soil Coolidge with Teapot Dome. Republicans had tried to absolve him. Coolidge himself had remained, for the most part, silent, and in this perhaps he was wisest of all. It is likely that the great inarticulate body that voted on election day, insofar as corruption influenced their decision, not only trusted him to clean up corruption, but also were sickened by the noise and the fury of accusations, and voted for the candidate who had not continually reminded them of their own government's ills. As Walter Lippmann suggested, the people liked Calvin Coolidge. In a time of luxury and pleasure, Americans installed in the White House "a frugal little man who in his personal life is the very antithesis of the flamboyant ideal that everybody is frantically pursuing. . . . At a time when Puritanism as a way of life is at its lowest ebb among the people, the people are delighted with a Puritan as their national symbol." From California William Kent wrote to Gifford Pinchot: The election was "what I expected but it certainly is sickening to see the tired and sordid way that our people voted. They wanted to believe in the myth of 'Cool Cal,' they wanted to be let alone and resented the idea of things being stirred up."[44]

If the voters were apathetic over Teapot Dome—and that is the conventional interpretation[45]—they may have voted not against

[43] A highly suggestive if inconclusive point is Gifford Pinchot's support—however mild—of Coolidge in the campaign. Pinchot was a veteran progressive, and he had great appreciation for what he called La Follette's "magnificent work" in conservation; of this he told Harold L. Ickes: "I don't propose to forget it." But Pinchot accepted Coolidge in 1924, although he had little enthusiasm for him as a president. Pinchot to Ickes, Sept. 26, 1924, Box 248, Pinchot Papers; McGeary, *Gifford Pinchot*, 314.

[44] Kent to Pinchot, Nov. 10, 1924, Box 249, Pinchot Papers; Lippmann, *Men of Destiny*, 10-18. Lippmann, as does Gamaliel Bradford, "The Genius of the Average: Calvin Coolidge," *Atlantic Monthly*, CXLV (Jan., 1930), 1-13, offers an acute analysis of Coolidge's political shrewdness and his capacity to blunt issues and to appeal to the American public.

[45] Walsh, trying to explain the election results, complained of a "woefully low discrimination and moral vigor in the electorate." Walsh to George W. Anderson, Nov. 25, 1924, Box 373, Walsh Papers. Election figures reveal nonparticipation, although not necessarily apathy, among the voters. Barely 50 per cent of those eligible to vote did so. Even with the excitement of an important third nominee and the efforts by several partisan

corruption but for the continued status quo, for the glut of "Coolidge prosperity," and for the Coolidge concern for dollars and cents and American business, after the years of war and heady but disturbing Wilsonian idealism. If Harding's huge 1920 vote indicated a desire for "normalcy," four years had hardly satiated that yearning. Scandals notwithstanding, 1924 may have been a repetition of 1920. The La Follette ticket alone, of course, made a difference in the two elections, but La Follette's candidacy helped Coolidge, if it helped either major candidate.[46]

If the voter was disturbed over Teapot Dome, Coolidge could have been even more attractive because of it. He was relatively free from the corruption, although he had sat among the corrupted. He had reformed his Cabinet, had appointed counsel to prosecute Teapot Dome's accused, and had begun an oil conservation program.[47] In November of 1924, such tangible actions may have

---

and non-partisan groups to bring out the vote, only about 30,000,000 voted out of nearly 57,000,000 who were registered. See Hugh Keenleyside, "The American Political Revolution of 1924," *Current History* XXI (March, 1925), 833-40. But see also Bates, "The Teapot Dome Scandal and the Election of 1924," *loc. cit.*, for a discussion of the subject.

[46] Magnetic in attraction for a small but enduring category of progressives, La Follette held them and influenced others. Many Republicans, not predisposed for any candidate, undoubtedly made the same analysis that Harold L. Ickes made: "It looks to me as if I would be forced into the La Follette camp before long. But where else is there for a chap like me to go?" Ickes to Gifford Pinchot, Sept. 22, 1924, Box 248, Pinchot Papers. McKay estimates, however, that La Follette won Republican votes mostly "in those sections where the result was already a foregone conclusion, as in the South. The Democrats, on the other hand, lost valuable 'pivotal' votes to the Progressives in those parts of the country where (like New York and California) it is imperative that the Democrats [hold them in order to win the election]" (McKay, *Progressive Movement of 1924*, p. 223). Davis himself was sure that the La Follette ticket helped the Republicans; Friedel states that the people Davis frightened away from La Follette, by denouncing him as a radical menace, "went not toward himself but toward Coolidge" (Friedel, *The Ordeal*, 181).

[47] On June 30, 1924, a grand jury had indicted Fall and Sinclair for conspiracy; Fall and Doheny for conspiracy; and Fall, Doheny, and Edward Doheny, Jr., for bribery. Their trials did not open until after the election, but the indictments were as likely to point up the Coolidge administration's prosecution of crime, as they were to emphasize the corruption of Republican Fall and his friends. An exchange of letters in mid-summer between Congressman John J. Rogers of Massachusetts and Attorney-General Harlan F. Stone suggests Republican thinking on this subject. Rogers reported to Stone "a general impression that . . . men like Fall" were not behind bars because they were "men of influence with the Republican administration."

loomed up in the voter's mind in place of the hysteria and the headlines of the past winter, when Democrats were jubilant and Republicans were in dark despondency. Rather than destroying the Republican party, Teapot Dome, through Calvin Coolidge, may have helped it to prevail.

To Rogers, this was "having an extremely bad effect," and he thought Stone should issue a statement "evidencing exactly what is being done" about prosecution of the accused men. Stone, the day after the grand jury indicted Fall, Sinclair, and the Dohenys, replied that since special counsel was handling Teapot Dome, "there would perhaps be some impropriety" in his making any statement. Fortunately, however, "the papers this morning have announced the indictments, which will satisfy the public interest for the present." Rogers to Stone, June 30, 1924, and Stone to Rogers, July 2, 1924, Records of Naval Oil Reserve Investigation, General Records of Justice Dept., Box 107, National Archives.

9

Interlude

After the 1924 election, Teapot Dome, as a political issue, remained largely somnolent for three years. Between the Coolidge triumph and January of 1928, Teapot Dome found its sustenance in court trials and conservation policies. Now and then, however, political voices broke forth in the old familiar tones. On January 20, 1925, the Senate adopted the Walsh majority report on the Public Lands Committee's investigation. At the time, this action apparently concluded the activity that La Follette had instigated in April of 1922; afterwards, it proved to have marked only an interlude.

Senator Spencer of Missouri had submitted to the Senate on January 15 a minority report on the investigation. The report defended Fall's leases yet cast responsibility upon the Wilson administration for inaugurating a leasing policy. Denouncing the majority of the Public Lands Committee for a devotion to "rumors" and an abuse of the Senate's investigating functions, it defended Denby and upheld Harding's executive order of 1921 transferring the reserves to Interior. It did condemn Fall for accepting the Doheny loan, but Walsh hardly exaggerated when he said that Spencer's report was "fantastic in its distortions." The report was, he charged, "a fly-specking affair, a straining after something to criticize for the sake of criticism." The Senate rejected Spencer's report.[1]

Even before this tacit Senate condemnation of Albert Fall, the renewed Coolidge administration began to reverse the policy he had established while Secretary of the Interior. During the remainder of his term, Coolidge elaborated an oil conservation program, one in keeping with his cautious and frugal nature. With every elaboration, the shadow of Albert Fall on the naval oil reserves grew more and more dim.

In his annual report, released December 1, 1924, Secretary of Interior Hubert Work recommended the creation of a permanent federal commission to promote oil conservation; members would include the secretaries of war, army, interior, and commerce.[2] On December 19, Coolidge carried out Work's suggestion. To the

[1] For Spencer's report, see *Cong. Rec.*, 68 Cong., 2 Sess. (Jan 15, 1925), 1870 ff.; also New York *Times*, Jan. 16, 1925, Sec. 6, p. 2, and Jan. 21, 1925, p. 1. Besides Spencer, the signers of the minority report included Senators Smoot, Stanfield, Bursum, and Cameron, the same ones who had protested the Walsh report to the Senate in June, 1924. The Senate vote against Spencer was forty-two to twenty-eight; the vote in favor of Walsh's report was forty to thirty. Not a single Democrat voted for the Spencer report, and every vote against the Walsh report was Republican. The votes against Spencer and for Walsh came from Democrats and a small group of Republicans usually classified as progressives. For the debate and the vote on the two reports, see *Cong. Rec.*, 68 Cong., 2 Sess. (Jan. 15, 1925), 2133 ff. The remarks by Walsh, quoted above, are in *Cong. Rec.*, 69 Cong., 1 Sess. (March 17, 1925), 312 ff.; Walsh injected this belated criticism in an itemized refutation of Spencer's report, lest, he said, "some incautious historian might accept as reliable [Spencer's] strictures upon [the majority] report" (*ibid*). For a severe criticism of Spencer, see an editorial from the *Journal of Commerce and Commercial Bulletin*, Jan. 17, 1925, reprinted in *Cong. Rec.*, 68 Cong., 2 Sess. (Jan. 20, 1925), 2134.

[2] Secretary of Interior, *Annual Report* (Washington, 1924), 8. Coolidge had retained Work from the same position in his previous Cabinet. Despite Work's gestures toward conservation, Gifford Pinchot—predictably—had a low opinion of him. Pinchot to Henry L. Stimson, Dec. 1924, Box 254, Pinchot Papers.

four secretaries that Work had named, he wrote letters appointing them to a Federal Oil Conservation Board. They were to "enlist the full cooperation of representatives of the oil industry" in an investigation of the best methods for conserving the government's oil supply. In July, 1925, Coolidge transferred supervision of the naval oil reserves from the Bureau of Mines to a new "conservation branch" of the Geological Survey. By the end of the year, Secretary Work was writing of the "new policy of conservation" that had been "conceived during the past year under . . . Coolidge." The Secretary claimed that the "working slogan of this administration is efficiency, which, applied to our natural resources, means their wise use as well as preservation for future needs." He claimed that creation of the new conservation board in the Geological Survey was "for the purpose of placing every possible safeguard around the leasing of the Nation's estate."[3] Finally, on March 17, 1927, Coolidge tried to erase another blot on the Republican record: he revoked Harding's executive order that had transferred the oil reserves to the Interior Department. On August 1, 1927, the Secretary of the Navy formally took over the reserves from the Secretary of the Interior; thus they returned to the department from which Albert Fall had received them five years earlier.[4]

While the Coolidge reforms in oil conservation from 1924 to 1928 worked a partial restitution, the court trials during the same period also restored property to its previous caretakers. The trials were tiresome affairs, but they produced spectacular evidence. The ways of justice were fraught with delays and concealment.

[3] Coolidge to the secretaries of war, navy, interior, and commerce, reprinted in *Federal Oil Conservation Board Hearings, February 10 and 11, 1925* (Washington, 1925), viii-ix (Coolidge informed the board that the commission he had appointed in March of 1924, to advise him on oil policy, would continue to function "in its limited field and might to advantage sit with the Conservation Board in its conferences."); Hubert Work, *The Department of the Interior: A Review for 1925* (Washington, 1925), 2-3; Secretary of Interior, *Annual Report* (Washington, 1925), 31; New York *Times*, July 2, 1925, p. 2.

[4] Secretary of the Navy, *Annual Report 1927*, (Washington, 1928), 63; New York *Times*, April 3, 1927, p. 22. The State Department issued the revocation in routine fashion, along with its publication of other executive orders. The White House announced later that Coolidge had issued the order in keeping with the Supreme Court decision revoking the leases and contracts on the Elk Hills reserve (see p. 183).

Clever counsel, repeated appeals to higher courts, and once a mistrial created exasperating barriers for the government's prosecutors to overcome.

In September, 1924, Owen Roberts and Atlee Pomerene set in motion an investigation that, in time, added fresh dimensions to the Teapot Dome scandal and provided the basis for its re-entry into the political mainstream in 1928. Government agents working for Roberts and Pomerene discovered the existence of a corporation named the Continental Trading Company, one that seemed to have a significant connection with Teapot Dome. During preparations for the civil suit at Cheyenne, the agents, in looking over records of banks in which Fall had accounts in the West, found a reference to 3.5 per cent Liberty bonds, along with a list of their numbers. Through the Treasury, they traced the bonds to stockholders in the Continental Trading Company, Ltd., a Canadian corporation; whereupon Roberts and Pomerene filed an affidavit in a Toronto, Ontario court, requesting authorization to take deposition from the president of Continental, H. S. Osler, who lived in Ontario.[5]

The affidavit claimed that the Continental company had been organized in November, 1921, at a meeting in the Vanderbilt Hotel in New York City. The men at this meeting included what Francis Busch has described as "combined interests [who] represented a large share of the oil, above and below ground, in the Western Hemisphere"—Osler; Colonel A. E. Humphreys of Humphreys Mexia and Humphreys Texas Oil Company; H. M. Blackmer, chairman of the board of Midwest Refining Company; James E. O'Neil, president of the Prairie Oil and Gas Company; Harry Sinclair, head of Sinclair Consolidated Oil Corporation; and R. W. Stewart, president of Standard Oil of Indiana. This group, as private individuals and not as representatives of their companies,

[5] Walter S. Bowen and Harry Edward Neal, *The United States Secret Service* (Philadelphia and New York, 1960), 93-104; M. R. Werner and John Starr, *Teapot Dome* (New York, 1959), *passim; Cong. Rec.*, 70 Cong., 1 Sess. (May 29, 1928), 10519 ff.; New York *Times*, Sept. 26, 1924, Sec. 4, p. 4, and Oct. 1, 1924, p. 1. Carl Taeusch, *Policy and Ethics in Business* (New York and London, 1931), 197-221, contains a discussion of the Continental Trading Company, along with generous extracts from testimony by company officials before the Senate investigating committee (see pp. 189 ff.).

had asked for and received incorporation in Canada as the Continental Trading Company, Ltd.

On November 17, 1921, Continental contracted with Humphreys Texas Company and Humphreys Mexia Company for the purchase of 33,333,333 barrels of crude oil at $1.50 a barrel. On the same day, Continental sold this contract to the Sinclair Crude Oil Purchasing Company and the Prairie Oil and Gas Company, jointly, at an increase of $.25 a barrel. The Sinclair and Prairie Oil Companies took delivery of the oil directly from Humphreys, but paid for it through Continental. Between January 1, 1922, and May 26, 1923, over 8,700,000 barrels of oil exchanged hands under this agreement, and the Continental Trading Company thereby netted a profit of more than $2,000,000. The Continental owners invested this profit in Liberty bonds, buying them through a New York agency of the Dominion Bank of Canada. Osler, the Continental president, then distributed these bonds to Continental's shareholders.

Roberts and Pomerene were anxious to question Osler and other witnesses in Canada, hoping to learn who owned Continental stock and thus received the bonds. When Continental went out of business in February, 1924, it had destroyed all books and papers. But the government had the numbers of the bonds, and the secret service agents already had traced $90,000 worth of them to Albert B. Fall. The skullduggery of Continental thus was relevant to that of Teapot Dome, and Roberts and Pomerene had legitimate claim to investigate Continental's activities.[6]

The Ontario Supreme Court directed Osler to appear in Toronto before the United States counsel there and answer questions. But Osler was in the African interior, presumably hunting elephants; the court's judgments said nothing about his immediate return. Sinclair already was under indictment for the Teapot Dome lease, and thus he could refuse to testify about Continental. Two more of the company's organizers were living abroad, Blackmer near Paris, and O'Neil near Cannes, France. Neither of them showed any disposition to return home soon. When summoned before a special State Department representative in Paris, on February 24,

[6] Busch, *Enemies of the State*, 119; 56 *Ontario Law Reports*, 307-18, 635-52; New York *Times*, Oct. 1, 1924, p. 1; and Taeusch, *Policy and Ethics in Business*, 197-200.

1925, both men refused to testify and affirmed they had nothing to do with Teapot Dome. In Chicago, early in March, a Federal marshall trying to serve a subpoena on R. W. Stewart could not locate him. Stewart turned up within a month, but O'Neil and Blackmer disappeared for some time.[7]

Roberts and Pomerene found more immediate success in their civil cases in California. After a protracted trial, Judge Paul J. McCormick of the United States District Court in Los Angeles, on May 28, 1925, held that Doheny's $100,000 loan to Fall was a bribe that had induced Fall to grant Doheny the lease on the Elk Hills reserve. According to the court, Fall and Doheny were guilty of fraud and conspiracy; and while Harding had exceeded his presidential powers in making the transfer of the reserves to Fall's jurisdiction, Denby's role in the transaction was "passive." Judge McCormick voided the contract between the government and Doheny's Pan-American Petroleum Company; he did not judge the wisdom of the contract, only its validity. He said that "if it were not for the fraud and the conspiracy of . . . Fall and . . . Doheny and the unlawful delegation of power in the agreements, the contracts and leases in suit would be authorized." He charged Pan-American for the oil it had extracted, but directed the government to pay for the work Doheny had done under the contract for building tanks at Pearl Harbor. Doheny at once appealed McCormick's decision.[8]

At Cheyenne, the government lost a decision. On June 19, 1925, Judge T. Blake Kennedy of the Wyoming District Court upheld Sinclair's lease on Teapot Dome. He found against the government on every point that Roberts and Pomerene had raised. He

[7] 56 *Ontario Law Reports,* 635-52; New York *Times,* Dec. 14, 1924, p. 1; March 7, 1925, p. 1; and March 8, 1925, p. 1, Walsh thought that if Treasury agents had been more prompt, they "might have caught" O'Neil and Blackmer before they left the United States. O'Neil died in France in 1932; he had never returned home. Blackmer came home in 1949; eighty years old, he had spent some twenty-five years in exile. He paid the government $3,671,065 in back taxes and $60,000 in penalties. His years abroad, according to one account, were "lightened by a second marriage and some high living in France." Walsh to Lewis Gannett, June 9, 1928, Box 163, Walsh Papers; *Labor,* August, 1931; "Henry Blackmer's Return," *Life,* XXVII (Oct. 10 ,1949), 59-61.

[8] U.S. v. Pan-Am., 6 F.2d 43-89 (1925). See also Hagland, "The Naval Reserve Leases," *loc. cit.,* 293-328, for comment on this and other cases.

upheld the authority of Fall and Denby to make the lease, and of Harding to transfer the reserves. Despite the adverse decision, Roberts and Pomerene managed to establish the fraudulent character of the Continental Trading Company and to demonstrate that Fall—or he and his business associates—had received a total of at least $233,000 in Liberty bonds from the Continental profits. Judge Kennedy allowed oral and documentary evidence for this to remain in the record, but he dismissed as unproved the charge of collusion between Sinclair and Fall; the government had been unable to offer direct proof that Fall had received any Continental bonds from Sinclair. Kennedy, in contrast to McCormick at Los Angeles, delivered a positive opinion on the value of the contract: "It is not only possible, but very probable, that . . . if the contracts are fairly and honestly carried out, [they] will actually conserve oil which would otherwise have been lost." Despite the court's opinion, Roberts and Pomerene appealed its decision.[9]

The government won both on Doheny's appeal from the Elk Hills decision and on their own from the Teapot Dome decision. The United States Circuit Court of Appeals in San Francisco upheld Judge McCormick's decision against Doheny; the Circuit Court of Appeals in St. Louis reversed Judge Kennedy's decision against the government and ordered his court to cancel Sinclair's lease on Teapot Dome. Doheny and Sinclair appealed to the United States Supreme Court.[10]

On February 28, 1927, the Supreme Court in unanimity cancelled Doheny's lease upon Elk Hills and returned the reserve to the government; it refused to order repayment by the government of any money Doheny and his company had expended on Elk Hills or at Pearl Harbor. The Court remarked that Secretary Edwin Denby "is presumed to have had knowledge of what he signed. . . . But the evidence sustains the finding that he took no active part in the negotiations, and that Fall, acting collusively with Doheny, dominated the making of the contracts and leases." On October 10, 1927, in another unanimous decision, the Court restored Teapot Dome to complete ownership and control of the federal government. It declared the lease to be the culmination of

[9] U.S. v. Mammoth Oil Co., *et al.*, 5 F.2d 330-54 (1925).
[10] Pan-Am v. U.S., 9 F.2d 761-73 (1926); U.S. v. Mammoth Oil Co., *et al.*, 14 F.2d 705-33 (1927).

TEMPLE OF JUSTICE

—Harding in the Brooklyn *Eagle*

SAMSON?

a conspiracy between Fall and Sinclair, the purpose of which was "to circumvent the law and to defeat public policy." From the beginning, Fall was "keen to control the leasing" and "eager" to administer the reserves. The Court found that Denby "intended to be passive and let Fall dominate." It also assailed the drainage argument that Fall had expounded. These two decisions ended the civil trials in the legal history of Teapot Dome.[11]

The first of the criminal trials in the story opened on November 22, 1926, when Doheny and Fall came before the Supreme Court of the District of Columbia to answer to a charge of conspiracy. Veterans of the Teapot Dome investigation appeared as witnesses,

[11] Pan-Am. v. U.S., 273 U.S. 456-510; and Mammoth Oil Co., *et al.* v. U.S. 275 U.S. 13-15.

among them Thomas Walsh, Josephus Daniels, Harry Daugherty, Edward McLean, and Irvine Lenroot. Fall himself did not testify, but Doheny was on the stand for over two hours. He was a good witness for himself, although he admitted—before his counsel could interpose— that quite recently he had loaned Fall $5,000. On December 16, the jury acquitted Fall and Doheny of conspiracy.[12]

Sinclair was also on trail at this time; and on March 17, 1927, in the Criminal Branch of the District of Columbia Supreme Court, a jury found him guilty of contempt of the Senate. His counsel immediately announced an appeal to the United States Supreme Court. Ultimately, on October 17, in the same court, Sinclair and Fall went on trial for conspiracy. For two weeks the trial proceeded, as witneses appeared, some of them to tell of the Continental Trading Company. Then suddenly Pomerene moved for a mistrial, charging a "close, intimate, objectionable and improper surveillence" of the jury by agents of the Burns Detective Agency. The agents had been hired by Harry Sinclair. Justice Frederick J. Siddons ordered a mistrial and discharged the jury.[13]

For this latest action, Sinclair drew another contempt verdict in February, 1928. This time he was sentenced to six months in jail. He also appealed this decision. On April 8, 1929, the United States Supreme Court affirmed his three-month sentence for contempt of the Senate Public Lands Committee. On June 4, 1929,

[12] See Busch, *Enemies of the State*, 123-56, for a detailed description of the trial; also New York *Times,* Dec. 11, 1926, Sec. 1, p. 8, and Dec. 17, 1926, Sec. 1, p. 7.

[13] Sinclair v. U.S., 279 U.S. 263 and 749; New York *Times,* Nov. 22, 1927, p. 1. Gifford Pinchot first informed Owen Roberts of the Burns agents. On October 24, he sent Roberts a "partial list" of the Burns employees who were covering the jurymen "with the hope of seeing that their verdict is satisfactory to your opponents." An informant, whom he did not then identify, had come to Pinchot with the list and the details of the affair. As Pinchot told Roberts: "The information . . . is not of the kind that becomes valueless if its origins cannot be quoted." Pinchot to Roberts, Oct. 24, 1927, copy in Slattery Papers. For awhile after the story broke, a Washington reporter received credit for discovering the shadowers, but eventually the source of the revelations came out. One of the Burns Agency's operatives, William J. McMullin, for some reason, went to Pinchot and told him the story. Possibly because his home state was Pennsylvania, McMullin chose Pinchot, who was at the time in Washington. See *International Labor News Service,* Nov. 19, 1927.

it affirmed his six-month sentence for criminal contempt of court. On May 6, 1929, he went to jail.[14]

Soon after Justice Siddons declared the mistrial, Roberts and Pomerene sought a retrial of the conspiracy charges against Fall and Sinclair. Fall was quite ill at his home in El Paso and gained a delay. On April 9, 1928, the new conspiracy trial began, with Sinclair alone standing before the court. By then, Teapot Dome, in the attire of the Continental Trading Company, had once more burst onto the national political scene. Significant though it was, Sinclair's trial had to find its place amidst a new complex of Senate revelations and party accusations.

On January 24, 1928, the Senate had begun a second—although briefer—inquiry into Teapot Dome. The new inquiry grew immediately out of a Senate resolution by George Norris. Prompting Norris was Paul Y. Anderson, a reporter for the St. Louis *Post-Dispatch*. In the fall of 1927, the editor of the *Post-Dispatch*, O. K. Bovard, assigned Anderson to find out whether or not the government intended to pursue further its investigation of the Continental Trading Company. Fall presumably had $230,000 worth of the original $3,000,000 investment, which did not account for $2,770,000. The Supreme Court had declared that Continental was organized "for no legitimate purpose." Bovard thought that the investigation should continue.[15]

Anderson went to see Owen Roberts and suggested that Roberts trace the bonds. But Roberts feared that he would be charged with usurpation of his authority for going beyond his duty as special counsel. Anderson then went to the Treasury Department, and again he got no encouragement. He went to Attorney-General

[14] Sinclair insisted that he had done nothing illegal in hiring the agents, that he had neither tried to influence nor to intimidate the jurors. He only wanted, he said, to see that they were not improperly approached by other parties. The court felt otherwise; the surveillance was an obstruction of justice, since, if nothing more, it had produced a mistrial. William J. Burns himself and several other principals also drew short sentences or fines. Sinclair v. U.S., 279 U.S. 263 and 749.

[15] James W. Markham, *Bovard of the Post-Dispatch* (Baton Rouge, 1954), 100 ff.; George Norris to Bovard, Jan. 9, 1929, Tray 7, Box 7, Norris Papers. Norris, telling Bovard in detail of the part Anderson played in bringing about the Continental inquiry, wrote that Anderson "first conceived the importance and the necessity of re-opening this investigation and carrying it to its logical end. The country owes Anderson a debt of gratitude." See also Norris, *Fighting Liberal*, 225-33.

John G. Sargeant, who evidently saw no reason for action by the Department of Justice. After these futile inquiries, Anderson wrote a story, "Who Got the Bonds?", in the *Post-Dispatch* of November 12, 1927, in which he discussed the question and described his interview with Sargeant.[16]

As his next move, Anderson asked Norris to introduce a Senate resolution directing the Public Lands Committee to investigate, and quickly, since the statute of limitations was about to run out on some of the transactions. Norris was "thoroughly convinced . . . Anderson was right, not only in the necessity for a further investigation, but also in his conclusion that [without] a Senate Resolution, the chances were that it never would be undertaken." With La Follette dead, Norris suggested that Walsh should introduce the resolution. But Anderson already had seen Walsh, who had declined the opportunity. Walsh reportedly was "tired of having his motives criticized" and felt that if he introduced the resolution, he would be accused of aspiring for the 1928 presidential nomination. Norris finally decided to introduce the resolution himself at the next session of Congress.[17]

But since Congress would not convene for some weeks, Norris thought that if he and Anderson should publicize the need for an investigation, Coolidge would order the Justice Department to take on the job, even before Congress convened. Anderson published in the *Post-Dispatch* his interview with Norris and argued the need for an investigation. Next, Norris declared that he would bring the question before the Senate if Coolidge failed to act. Coolidge did nothing. A few days before Congress convened, Anderson called on Norris, who was now willing to prepare and introduce the necessary resolution.[18]

[16] Sargeant replaced Harlan F. Stone in 1925, when Coolidge named Stone to the U.S. Supreme Court. According to Norris, Anderson's article "created a great deal of comment and was very widely circulated and discussed. It is impossible to tell just how much good it did [or] how many . . . Senators . . . were . . . influenced by it toward further investigation." But Norris believed that Anderson "had more to do with resurrecting the matter and causing an additional investigation . . . than any other one person." Norris to Bovard, Jan. 25, 1929, Tray 7, Box 7, Norris Papers.

[17] Norris to Bovard, Jan. 9, 1929, Tray 7, Box 7, Norris Papers; Markham, *Bovard of the Post-Dispatch*, 102.

[18] Markham, *Bovard of the Post-Distpatch*, 102; and Norris to Bovard, Jan. 9, 1929, Tray 7, Box 7, Norris Papers. Norris thought that since, ac-

—Cassel in the New York *Evening World*

"Whiter Than Snow"

Norris, at this point, was no new critic of Teapot Dome.
Throughout its history, he had been consistently critical of the
scandal and its Republican principals. In private correspondence
and in the Senate, he had revealed his feeling on the subject often;
and in November, 1927, when the Brooklyn *Eagle* asked him to
write for publication a letter to the editor discussing the recent
court decisions on Teapot Dome, the Senator complied with a
long discussion of the great sums used by "oil" in fighting the

cording to rumors, some of the bonds had paid off the Republican campaign debt in 1920, and since Coolidge had been in that campaign, "there
was a particular reason why [the President] should want to have the facts
cleaned up." Norris should have remembered that his own political—and
moral—standards were higher than Coolidge's.

cases. He stated that "it seems to be an impossibility, in our criminal courts, to convict a hundred million dollars and the ordinary person is beginning to be impressed with the idea that a different rule is applied to the millionaire than . . . to the ordinary citizen." Norris' letter and its phrase about a million dollars received wide publicity after the *Eagle* published it. Then on January 4, 1928, he proposed to the Senate a resolution ordering an investigation into "the transactions and activities of . . . the Continental Trading Company." The Senate should "trace all the Government bonds held and dealt in by said corporation [in order to learn] the beneficiaries of all the illegal transactions connected with the fraudulent and dishonest sale or leasing of the . . . naval oil reserves." On January 9, the Senate passed the resolution.[19]

As Norris once told O. K. Bovard, before Paul Anderson went to work, "it was generally believed throughout the country that the Teapot Dome investigation was ended and that no further attempt would be made to pursue the subject."[20] But Norris and Anderson—in a manner reminiscent of La Follette and Slattery—initiated a new investigation, one that now rested, as once before, with the Public Lands Committee. The committee swung Teapot Dome back into the glare of their scrutiny and into the midst of national politics. Twice in six years a Republican-controlled Senate had approved a Republican Senator's resolution to investigate an affair involving high Republican officials. In neither case did the party thereby commit suicide.

On January 24, 1928, the committee began hearings in the same room where Walsh had labored so strenuously during the first investigation. Its members were a mixture of veterans and newcomers. The chairman was Gerald P. Nye, Republican of North Dakota. The prosecutor once again was Walsh, who immediately seized command. The hesitancy he had shown to Paul Anderson now suddenly disappeared. Hours after the hearings began, he placed in the record a copy of the contract between the Humphreys Company and the Continental Trading Company, as well as extensive transcripts of testimony on the subject given at the

[19] Norris to Brooklyn *Eagle* editor, Nov. 12, 1927, Tray 7, Box 7, Norris Papers; New York *Times*, Nov. 15, 1927, p. 20; *Cong. Rec.*, 70 Cong., 1 Sess. (Jan. 9, 1928), 934, 1185.

[20] Norris to Bovard, Jan. 25, 1929, Tray 7, Box 7, Norris Papers.

civil trials in Cheyenne. His first witness was M. T. Everhart, son-in-law of Albert Fall.[21]

Everhart appeared only in response to a subpoena, and he insisted that the subpoena be placed in the record to show that he did not volunteer to appear and that he gave testimony only under the force of the subpoena. Still, Everhart gave the committee information that the courts had tried to get for the past four years. He admitted that in May, 1922, in Washington and in New York City, Sinclair delivered to him $233,000 worth of Liberty bonds—all of which went to Fall. In addition, Sinclair later loaned Fall an additional $36,000. According to Everhart, a large portion of the Liberty bonds were used to pay off notes which Fall, Everhart, and their Three Rivers Cattle Company had assumed. The transactions revealed by Everhart, added to the amounts already uncovered by the Senate committee, made Sinclair's contributions to Fall total $304,000. The $100,000 loan from Doheny and the $5,000 loan that Doheny had revealed at his trial meant that Fall had received at least $409,000 from the two oil men. Everhart appeared quite free of any complicity in the Continental transactions; he had been merely the messenger carrying money from Sinclair to Fall. As he left the witness stand, he remarked to a friend that he had been "through hell" and now felt more at ease than he had in years. Senator Kendrick, an old friend, shook his hand and so did Walsh.[22]

Witnesses following Everhart to the committee room offered less evidence, and some refused to offer anything at all. On February 2, R. W. Stewart, one of Continental's organizers, refused to tell anything about the disposition of Continental's $3,000,000 profit. He declared only that he got none of it and that he had nothing to do with its distribution. He could not say whether or not Fall received any of the profits. Other oil men during the succeeding days displayed to the committee memories as dim as Stewart's.[23]

[21] Senate Committee on Public Lands and Surveys (70 Cong., 1 Sess.), *Leases upon Naval Oil Reserves* (Washington, 1928), 3-49. To distinguish these hearings from those held in 1923-24, all references hereinafter cited as *Leases upon Reserves* (1928).

[22] *Leases upon Reserves* (1928), 48-68; New York *Times,* Jan. 25, 1928, p. 1.

[23] *Leases upon Reserves* (1928), 164-98.

Then, on February 11, some of the pressure from Continental's
organizers shifted to Republican party leaders: that day the Public
Lands Committee received a report claiming that $24,000 of the
Continental profits had helped to wipe out part of the Republican
campaign deficit in 1920. At once, the committee veered off into
this newer channel even though Will Hays, the 1920 Republican
national chairman, immediately denied having any knowledge of
the Continental Trading Company during his tenure. John T.
Adams, the Republican chairman from 1921 to 1924, was aboard
the S.S. *Conte Biancamano* in the North Atlantic, bound for Italy.
In reply to a wire from the New York *Times*, Adams claimed that
he knew "absolutely nothing of any Continental . . . bonds having
been received by the Republican National Committee."[24]

Impressed or not by these Republican pleas of innocence, the
Public Lands Committee cast reflections also toward the Democratic party. Chairman Nye announced that the committee would
summon prominent Democratic leaders, in an effort to learn the
source of some $400,000 used to pay off part of the Democratic
deficit assumed in 1920. At the close of the 1920 campaign, the
Democrats owed about $600,000; by 1924, they owed $200,000.
There was no public record of the source of the $400,000 that had
been paid. In 1923, however, Sinclair had testified that he contributed in 1922 to the campaign fund of both parties; and, according to Nye, the committee believed that if "this oil money"
of Sinclair's went to one party it was "quite apt to have gone to
the other, too." Cordell Hull, Democratic national chairman, acted
as promptly as had Hays and Adams. Nye's "libel" that Continental bonds helped to liquidate any part of the 1920 Democratic
deficit was, said Hull, "as false and foul as [any] ever perpetrated." On February 23, Hull appeared as a volunteer witness
before the Senate committee and testified that he had "never met
any of those gentlemen" who founded Continental and "had no
contributions from any of [them]." With Hull to the committee
room came Major Oliver D. Newman, assistant director of finance
for the Democratic national committee from 1922 to 1924. He,
too, felt "positive" that none of the Continental Liberty bonds had

[24] Washington *News*, Feb. 11, 1928; New York *Times*, Feb. 12, 1928, p.
1 and 26.

come to the party during the two years he had worked with it.[25]

At last, during the final days of February, the committee learned the destination of some of Continental's bonds. On February 16, two New York brokers testified that they had traced $26,000 worth of them to the Republican national committee. On February 23, K. C. Schuyler, an attorney for Henry Blackmer, admitted that he had placed $750,000 worth of the Liberty bonds belonging to Blackmer in a bank box in New York City. On the same day, several bank employees brought before the committee an assortment of bank books, ledger sheets, and cancelled checks. None of this evidence showed that Continental profits helped to cancel the Republican deficit, but it did show that about $300,000 was deposited to the credit of the Republican national committee, mostly in Chase National Bank, in November and December of 1923.[26]

The committee's excursion into high finance came down to hard political earth on the first of March, when Will Hays testified. He admitted that Sinclair had given him $260,000 for the Republican campaign fund. Of this amount, $100,000 later went back to Sinclair. When Walsh asked Hays why he had not admitted these contributions in his 1924 testimony, Hays replied, "I was not asked about them."[27]

Hays's testimony was politically incriminating as it stood. On March 10, two Republicans worsened it. In a letter to Walsh, Secretary of the Treasury Andrew Mellon said that late in the fall of 1923, he had received $50,000 in Liberty bonds from Hays, who had accepted them from Sinclair. Mellon could keep the bonds, Hays told him, and turn an equal amount of money over to the Republican national committee. Mellon returned the bonds to Hays and later made a $50,000 contribution of his "own funds" to the Republican deficit. On March 13, Mellon testified before the committee and repeated his story, with elaborations. On the same day, William M. Butler, the current chairman of the Republican national committee, also testified. He volunteered the

[25] Washington *Post*, Feb. 14, 1928; New York *Times*, Feb. 14, 1928, p. 1, and Feb. 19, 1928, p. 1; and *Leases upon Reserves* (1928), 398-99.
[26] *Leases upon Reserves* (1928), 357-416, *passim.*
[27] *Ibid.,* 459-481.

statement that in 1923 Hays called him to a conference in the Biltmore Hotel in New York City and there offered him a package supposedly containing $25,000 in bonds. In return, Butler was to make a subscription of equal value to the Republican national committee. Butler "declined to do it," he recalled; whereupon Hays "took the package and went away."[28]

This spate of denials, admissions, and implications did not blind the critical eye of many Democrats, or one powerful Republican. Senator William E. Borah of Idaho repudiated the Continental-Sinclair money. On March 5, he appealed to national chairman Butler to purge the party of the "stigma" of "oil money" by returning to Sinclair all the money that he had given to the party. Borah wrote to Butler: "The investigation . . . has now disclosed beyond peradventure that the Republican Party received large sums of money, or securities, from Mr. Sinclair, which the Republican party cannot in honor and decency keep. . . ." To Borah, "the whole transaction . . . had in view an ulterior and sinister purpose," and he felt that the money "should be returned to the source from which it came." He himself would hold no party responsible for the sins of its individual members, but once the Continental transaction stood revealed, the Republican party did become responsible if it failed to repudiate that transaction. This Republican leader believed "that there are plenty of Republicans who will be glad to contribute from one dollar up to any reasonable sum to clear their party of this humiliating stigma. . . ." In reply, Butler pleaded innocence: "Whatever the transactions were, they were done and completed long before my election as Chairman. . . . As I see it, the obligation, if any, for repudiation is upon those who conducted the transactions." In any event, the hearings had not ended and Butler did not care "to prejudge the case." If Borah's

[28] *Ibid.*, 549-54, and 575 ff. See p. 560 for a copy of Mellon's letter to Walsh. A reference to Mellon in the testimony before the committee on March 10 apparently prompted the Secretary to send Walsh the information about the bonds. The committee had subpoenaed all appropriate memoranda left by the late John T. Pratt, who had helped to clear the Republican deficit of 1920. The memoranda included a slip of paper with the names "Andy," "Weeks," "Butler," and "Du Pont" written on it. See *Leases upon Reserves* (1928), 545; also the exchange of letters between Mellon and Walsh, reprinted *ibid.*, 554-560.

conclusion was "borne out by the finding of the committee," Butler would "give sympathetic attention" to the proposal.[29]

Individual Republicans reacted to Borah's plan at once and in varied ways. William Allen White wrote candidly to him: "You are on the right line. . . . The louder you talk the better it will be for the party. We can't go into the campaign of 1928 with the blight upon us of tainted money in '20 and '24."[30] White, as did Borah, saw wisdom in admitting the taint in order to repudiate it. Not enough Republicans agreed with them, however, to contribute the necessary amount to Sinclair, and Democrats scorned the idea as a show of sanctimony.

Borah received hundreds of letters and as many small contributions. One contributer sent $1000, saying: "Unless our party gets out of this terrible and only too justified reputation, it may well be said that Sinclair and Hays caused its downfall." Senator Guy D. Goff, Republican of West Virginia, offered to be "one of one hundred and sixty to contribute one thousand dollars or one of thirty-two to give five thousand dollars to make possible the return of this most revolting oil donation." By March 30, Borah had collected $6,184. Thereafter, the influx dwindled to a halt at about $8,000.[31]

Theodore Roosevelt, Jr., who donated $100, told Borah, "of course you're right." But the Republican majority, if it had any opinion at all, must have felt as Gerald P. Nye did, who thought the scheme "the most foolish step Senator Borah ever took." Borah's motives were "the best," said Nye, but Borah was "unfair to

[29] Borah to Butler, March 5, 1928, and Butler to Borah, March 7, 1928, Box 763, Borah Papers. Borah wrote the letter on March 5 and released it to the press on March 11; see New York *Times*, March 12, 1928, p. 1, and March 13, 1928, p. 1. Borah felt that although the hearings had not ended, "enough has been disclosed to fix the responsibility. . . . There is not a particle of doubt, not the slightest, but that this money was received and used by the organization for the benefit of the party." Borah to Butler, March 8, 1928, Box 763, Borah Papers.

[30] White to Borah, March 13, 1928, *ibid.*

[31] S. O. Levinson to Borah, March 16, 1928 (Levinson sent $100 with this letter; he later sent $900 more); Goff to Borah, March 16, 1928; Borah to Goff, March 17, 1928; and Goff to Borah, March 21, 1928, Box 703, Borah Papers. As the money came in, Borah deposited it in the Riggs National Bank in Washington. For lists of the contributors, the amounts they gave, and other records kept by Borah, including his bank deposit book, see "Sinclair Fund," Borah Papers.

the people." The "poor devil who can't afford it" would put up his
$1.00 to $10.00 contribution and to no avail. In any case, Nye
could see little difference in the campaign contributions of both
political parties. Perhaps newspaperman Frank Knox better summarized the general Republican attitude. After his wife had contributed $25.00, Knox told Borah that she was "terribly shocked
at my cynicism . . . because I declined to match her contribution;
but I, being a hard-boiled newspaper man, loved you for your
idealism but clearly foresaw the blind alley you were traveling. . . ."[32]

By mid-April, Borah had reached the end of that blind alley
and had given up hope of repaying Sinclair. He began to return
the money to those who had contributed. As late as August of
1928, he still showed a desire to enter the upcoming campaign free
of Sinclair's money, but as Senator Bronson Cutting of New Mexico suggested to him: "It seems evident that those in charge of the
party affairs are not sufficiently interested . . . to make it worth
while to continue your efforts." Borah, however, continued to see
potential danger in a corruption issue for 1928. In April, he told
a Chicago audience: "The world will judge the Republican Party
not by what took place prior to the . . . exposures, but by the
course and conduct of the party after the exposures." Corruption,
he said, would "undoubtedly be one of the issues of this campaign.
We cannot . . . and . . . should not avoid it."[33]

Democrats agreed with him. Joseph Robinson of Arkansas,
Democratic floor leader in the Senate, found a basis for perjury in
Will Hays's testimony before the public lands committee in 1924.
At that time, said Robinson, Hays "deliberately concealed [his]
use . . . of the bonds obtained from Mr. Sinclair, and in that sense
subjected himself to a possible charge of perjury." Political ad-
vantage aside, Robinson's criticism had substance. Not only had
Hays skirted near to perjury; he had blundered as political leader.
As one newspaper expressed it: "Hays has done his party a great
and aggravated disservice." He concealed the truth about Sin-

[32] Roosevelt to Borah, March 16, 1928, Box 703, Borah Papers; Nye
speech in Baltimore, reported in New York *Times*, March 19, 1928, p. 1;
Knox to Borah, Dec. 21, 1928, Box 703, Borah Papers.

[33] Borah to S. O. Levinson, Aug. 16, 1928; Cutting to Borah, Aug. 20,
1928, Box 703, Borah Papers; New York *Times*, April 29, 1928, p. 1.

clair's donations, only to have "the ugliness of the situation come out at this late date [and so] a bad matter has been made far worse." Then on March 14, Senator Caraway returned to his 1924 role and let loose a verbal volley at Will Hays. At best, he said, Hays was "a fence," who "knew that certain goods were stolen goods and he was trying to help the thief find a market for them. . . ." Mellon, although declining to assist in the marketing of the goods, failed to reveal their nature, said Caraway, and "handed them back so that the fence could find somebody else."[34] Meanwhile, from the newspaper press came a predictable chorus of Democratic accusations. The Houston *Chronicle* saw the trail of political corruption traced at last "to the very holy of holies of the Republican party—the National Executive Committee." The Charleston *News and Courier* believed that if the American electorate could fasten attention on the implications of the Continental revelations, "election of a Democratic President in November would follow as a matter of course." The Norfolk *Virginian-Pilot* raised the uncomfortable question: "[If Sinclair's contribution] was the pure thing that Mr. Hays and other Republican leaders represent it to be, why . . . these elaborate precautions . . . to hide its source from the public gaze?" Republican editorials, on the other hand, sometimes offered frank confessions in the manner of Senator Borah. The St. Paul *Pioneer Press* saw "no excuse, save a desire for concealment, for the devices and secretive methods employed to cover the slimy trail of Sinclair's oil-soaked bonds." The Columbus *Ohio State Journal* thought that "the honor of the Republican party insistently demands the return of this dirty money and the public repudiation of favors received from interests which debauched the Government. . . ."[35]

Despite such reactions from press and politician, the Continental inquiry never reached the fevered intensity of the 1924 investigation. The sums of money at stake were spectacular, the revelations were often exciting, and the individuals implicated were notable either in politics or in the oil industry. But the Continental revelations were, by comparison, pale replicas of the outpourings

[34] *Cong. Rec.*, 70 Cong., 1 Sess. (March 12, 1928), 4519, 4673; Philadelphia *Public Ledger*, March 14, 1928.

[35] See *The Literary Digest*, XCVI (March 24, 1928), 7-8, for these and other press comments.

of 1924. Nevertheless, as the Continental inquiry sped to its conclusion, new and fuller evidence of Teapot Dome's torturous history appeared. By the last of April, the Senate committee had
determined that $769,000 of Continental's profits went to Harry
Blackmer and about $800,000 to James O'Neil. Will Hays got
$160,000 to help pay off the Republican deficit. Albert Fall had
received at least $233,0000. On May 1, Sinclair admitted to the
committee that he had received from Harry Blackmer $757,000
in Liberty bonds; $233,000 worth of these he paid to Fall, although
Sinclair claimed not to know, at the time he paid them, that Continental's profits had bought them. He told the committee that
during the past ten days he had turned over his share of the Continental money to Sinclair Crude Oil Purchasing Company, along
with $142,000 interest.[36]

Sinclair, testifying on May 1 and 2, was the last important witness to appear in the Continental investigation. On May 14, Walsh
informed a correspondent that "the committee is about winding
up its inquiry into the Teapot Dome matters and I feel that it has
got to the bottom of the affair." Already in adjournment since
May 2, the committee met briefly on May 31 for the last time. At
the end of that session, except for an investigation into certain
leases of oil lands in the Salt Creek fields in Wyoming, the Senate
had ended its official investigation of Teapot Dome.[37]

Two days before the Public Lands Committee adjourned, Walsh
and Nye submitted to the Senate separate reports on the Continental inquiry. Walsh stated that his was "the unanimous report

[36] *Leases upon Reserves* (1928), 1073 ff. Sinclair stated that he delivered
to Fall's son-in-law, M. T. Everhart, the $233,000 for a third interest in
Fall's Three Rivers Cattle Company.
[37] Walsh to Effie Gourley, May 14, 1928, Box 163, Walsh Papers. On
April 19, 1928, Senator Norris introduced a resolution calling for a Senate
investigation of Fall's leases of the Salt Creek Oil field to Sinclair. Fall, on
January 1, 1923, had drawn up a contract with Sinclair whereby the Sinclair Crude Oil Purchasing Company, should, for a stipulated price, receive
the government's royalty oil from the field for the next five years. The contract gave Sinclair an option to renew it on the same terms at the end of
five years. On February 20, 1928, Sinclair renewed it. For the Senate investigation (approved April 30, 1928), see U. S. Senate, *Salt Creek Oil
Field, Wyoming* (Hearings Before the Committee on Public Lands and
Surveys, 70 Cong., 1 and 2 Sess. [Washington, 1928-29]). During the spring
of 1928, Salt Creek was an aberration of the Teapot Dome story, and never
was it much more than that.

of the Senators present at the time it was under consideration."
Walsh wrote into his report a terse summary of the Continental
Trading Company's history. He minced no words in criticizing the
company's organizers, and his remarks about Will Hays, Andrew
Mellon, and Harry Sinclair were acrid. The investigation, he contended, had revealed the Continental Trading Company as "a
contemptible private steal, the speculations of trusted officers of
great industrial houses, pilfering from their own companies, robbing their own stockholders, the share of the boodle coming to
one of the free-booters serving in part as the price of the perfidy
of a member of the President's cabinet." Walsh concluded with
an effective tabulation: "The expense of the inquiry, . . . which
has resulted in the recovery for the Government of slightly in excess of $2,000,000, with the prospect of getting as much more, has
been [to date] $14,165."[38]

Nye claimed that his own report was "in no wise at odds with
the [Walsh] report . . . but is in addition [to it]." But Nye, rather
than adding to Walsh's report, transcended it. He made a flamboyant attack on the Continental Trading Company, and Fall and
his oil friends. The "sum and substance of the real story of the
looting of the naval oil reserves and the formation and operation
of the Continental Trading Company" was expressed in a single
sentence: "Conceived in darkness and selfishness and dedicated
to the proposition that the cause of privilege and the privileged
must be served." For the Senate investigation had "uncovered
the slimiest of slimy trails beaten by privilege. . . . The trail is
one of dishonesty, greed, violation of law, secrecy, concealment,
evasion, falsehood, and cunning."

Yet, consciously or not, Republican Senator Nye made the indirect point that Teapot Dome and its ramifications went beyond

[38] *Cong. Rec.,* 70 Cong., 1 Sess. (May 29, 1928), 10519; Senate Report
No. 1326, Part I, *Cong. Rec.,* 70 Cong., 1 Sess. (May 29, 1928), 10519-
523. This report also appears in *Leases upon Reserves* (1928), 1171-83.
Secretary of the Treasury Mellon, on May 23, 1928, sent to Senator Nye a
statement that Continental's owners had made payments of about $2,000,000
to the Treasury for back taxes, jeopardy assessments, penalties, and interests.
Mellon remarked: "We are unable to say that the payments . . . are wholly
the result of disclosures made before the . . . committee, but as a result of
these disclosures and of the department's own investigations, these payments have been made." *Cong. Rec.,* 70 Cong., 1 Sess. (May 25, 1928),
9842-43.

Republican party lines. In 1924, Cooidge had suggested that "men are involved who belong to both political parties." Nye, in 1928, stated that "contributions are not made because of enthusiasm for any one party, but for the sake of such returns as might be won through the winning party"—witness Doheny and Sinclair, who gave to both parties. "All in all," he said, "we are confronted with the picture of a most unhealthy influence upon our life as a nation and upon our democracy through campaign contributions."

The Senator's dialectic then veered off in still another direction, as he began to suggest positive "benefits" growing out of the investigation. The oil industry would now reform itself, political parties would be cautious in the use of campaign contributions, the people would take care of their natural resources, and the government would profit from millions of dollars in back taxes. "But the greatest benefit," perorated Nye, "has been that confidence restored to people in government by the manner in which conspirators against the Government have been made to respond."[39]

The reader who groped through Nye's now purple and now pedestrian prose must have wondered whether Teapot Dome, by the spring of 1928, had become a national curse or a national blessing. The 1928 presidential campaign would produce claimants for both conclusions.

---

[39] Senate Report No. 1326, Part II, *Cong. Rec.*, 70 Cong., 1 Sess. (May 29, 1928), 10529-531.

10

The Residue
of Teapot Dome

Early in April of 1928, while the Continental inquiry neared its climax, Harry Sinclair went on trial for conspiracy before the District of Columbia Supreme Court. Too ill to travel to Washington, Fall did not stand trial with him. But already he had given a private deposition at his home in El Paso. He told Atlee Pomerene that he did not receive a penny from Sinclair for the Teapot Dome oil leases.[1]

Fall's deposition may have affected the jury at Sinclair's trial. Beginning on April 10, the trial lasted less than two weeks. During that time, the government dismissed its bribery indictment

[1] Fall's deposition required a total of sixteen hours, divided over four days. It ran into thousands of words; Fall, as usual, was loquacious. See New York *Times*, April 1, 1928, p. 26, and March 30, 1928, p. 1, and April 2, p. 2, for accounts of the deposition.

against Edward Doheny, Jr., in order to bring him to the stand as a witness. There he told of his trip to Fall's office in 1922 with the now infamous "black bag" full of his father's money. Whatever relevance this incident had to the charges against Sinclair, the government lost its case; the jury acquitted Sinclair of conspiracy to defraud the government. The United States Supreme Court had nullified the Teapot Dome lease and condemned it as the culmination of a conspiracy between Sinclair and Fall. Now a jury had acquitted Sinclair of any conspiracy with Fall. In the words of one report, the acquittal "was the greatest surprise Washington had had in years." Roberts and Pomerene "appeared dumbfounded" at the decision and sat in silence. Sinclair, "ashen pale" when the jury filed in, smiled at the verdict. Senator Nye, who had once spoken of public confidence being restored, remarked, "this is emphatic evidence that you can't convict a million dollars in the United States."[2]

The jury's acquittal of Sinclair, a pallid conclusion to a garish affair, harmonized with much of Teapot Dome's history in 1928. The Senate investigation of the Continental Trading Company never reached the heights scaled by the 1924 inquiry; although the Democrats once again viewed Republican corruption with customary alarm, Teapot Dome had even less influence in the 1928 election than it had in 1924, and it did not materially affect the selection of either presidential candidate.

For a while, thrust forward partly by Teapot Dome, Walsh did contend for the Democratic nomination. Claude Bowers, at the time an editorial writer for the New York *Evening World*, surveyed the field of potential candidates in August of 1927. He felt that Al Smith could not be nominated because of his "Tammany affiliations," his residence in New York City, and "his wet ideas." Joseph T. Robinson of Arkansas was "too far South," Carter Glass of Virginia was "too old," Walter George of Georgia was a "protectionist," and William G. McAdoo "would make it hard to keep down the factions." Bowers wrote to Walsh, "if I had [control of] the nomination, you would be the nominee." He was a poor prophet,

---

[2] *Ibid.*, April 22, 1928, p. 1; and see Hagland, "The Naval Reserve Leases," *loc. cit.*, 327, for an opinion that the government lacked sufficient evidence to convict Sinclair.

but his argument for supporting Walsh reflected the view of many Walsh supporters.[3]

McAdoo and Smith, despite the 1924 fiasco, remained the two outstanding candidates.[4] Yet each man represented certain irreconcilable forces, and if the party was to avoid another convention suicide, either McAdoo or Smith must give way, or a third candidate must replace them. To many Democrats, Walsh seemed to be a likely compromise: Teapot Dome had made him a national figure; he held an eminent position within his party; he was a dry, as was McAdoo, but was a Catholic, as was Smith; he was identified neither with the urban Northeast nor the rural South. The 1924 convention had proved his popularity with the party workers. Bishop James Cannon, Jr., who helped to swing five Southern states to Herbert Hoover (and away from Al Smith) in the 1928 election, thought that Walsh was "the ablest, best qualified dry man in the Democratic party." He was "thoroughly incorruptible and a sincere dry," and at the same time he was "an outspoken but not fanatical or priest-ridden Roman Catholic." Cannon told reporters that he would "gladly support Senator Walsh for President."[5]

[3] Bowers to Walsh, Aug. 8, 1927, Box 179, Walsh Papers; see "Campaign of 1928," Walsh Papers, for numerous letters to Walsh, in which the correspondents, favoring him as the Democratic nominee in 1928, gave as their reasons his work in the Teapot Dome investigations.

[4] Perhaps anticipating Smith's nomination, more than one Republican had tried as early as March, 1928, to associate Smith with Harry Sinclair. Senator Arthur Robinson, Republican of Indiana, several times during March assailed Smith from the Senate floor. He recalled that eight years earlier, while governor of New York, Smith had named Sinclair as a member of the New York Racing Commission. Robinson implied also that Sinclair had been influential in the Smith administration. Gerald P. Nye added the observation that he understood Sinclair had been a liberal contributor to Smith's 1920 gubernatorial campaign, and that following the election, Smith named him to the racing commission. Smith denied that Sinclair had contributed, and a heated exchange of letters and comments between Smith and Nye followed. *Cong. Rec.,* 70 Cong., 1 Sess. (March 21, 1928), 5095 ff.

[5] See Richard V. Oulahan's story, New York *Times,* March 5, 1928, p. 3, for discussion of Walsh's qualifications and appeal; also Roy V. Peel and Thomas C. Donnelly, *The 1928 Campaign: An Analysis* (New York, 1931), 10; Freidel, *The Ordeal,* 229-33; and Edmund A. Moore, *A Catholic Runs for President: The Campaign of 1928* (New York, 1956), 92-100, for discussion of the 1928 campaign. Cannon's remarks are in James Cannon, Jr., *Bishop Cannon's Own Story,* ed. Richard L. Watson, Jr. (Durham, 1955), 395-96.

In early February, 1928, Walsh disclaimed any hopes for the nomination. But in March, when the McAdoo forces in California put Walsh forward as their candidate, he filed in the state primary in opposition to Smith. McAdoo, in September of 1927, had issued a statement that he would not actively seek the nomination himself. Instead, he placed his energies and hopes with Walsh, the man most likely to defeat Smith. Walsh, however, denied that he entered the race only to stop Smith; he was running, he said, because his friends had insisted that corruption would be the principal issue in the campaign, thus making him the logical candidate.[6]

Whatever motivated him, Walsh soon began a positive search for support. But his campaign never got off the ground. In the California primary, he ran a poor third behind Al Smith and James A. Reed. In primaries in Michigan, Wisconsin, Illinois, Massachusetts, and Ohio, Smith overwhelmed him. Only in Oregon did Walsh make a respectable showing. On May 4, he withdrew from the race. He wrote to an acquaintance that he felt "no keen disappointment or any great regret" over the defeat, but he did believe that the work he had done "for the party and the country seems to be so little appreciated by the rank and file. Obviously, there is a multitude who put booze above every other question. . . ." Teapot Dome, in company with his Catholicism and his dry sentiments, helped to make Walsh a candidate. Evidently this was not enough. Whatever influenced the primary results, Teapot Dome had not attracted much support for its great prosecutor.[7]

[6] Walsh to James D. Phelan, Feb. 4, 1928; Peel and Donnelly, *The 1928 Campaign*, 10. That corruption would have been his emphasis in a campaign is suggested by a letter from Walsh to a California supporter. A week before the primary there, Walsh wrote to him: "I am deeply sensible of the honor implied in my selection . . . as the most logical candidate to lead in a campaign in which above every other issue will be stressed the dire need of a general housecleaning. . . . It cannot be overlooked that to this good day no word has ever been uttered by any [responsible Republican] in denunciation of the debauchery for which [the Republican party] is responsible." Walsh to John P. Carter, April 26, 1928; Box 179, Walsh Papers. For the report that Walsh was being used to stop Smith, and for Walsh's disclaimer, see New York *Times*, March 4, 1928, p. 1, and April 5, 1928, p. 2.

[7] Walsh to Claude Bowers, April 16, 1928; Walsh to John P. Carter, April 26, 1928; Walsh to I. M. Brandjord, May 11, 1928; and Walsh to J. T. Carroll, May 10, 1928, Box 179, Walsh Papers; Peel and Donnelly, *The*

With the McAdoo withdrawal and the Walsh defeat, Al Smith's nomination followed inevitably. In late June at the Houston, Texas convention, Franklin D. Roosevelt nominated him in an eloquent address. He won on the first ballot. Senator Joseph T. Robinson of Arkansas received the nomination for the vice-presidency.[8]

The Republicans, at their Kansas City convention earlier in the month, had nominated Herbert Hoover, and for vice-president, Senator Charles Curtis of Kansas. During the preconvention campaign, while the public wondered whether or not Coolidge intended to run, Hoover's candidacy had gained strength steadily. When Coolidge made no open gesture toward the nomination, Hoover became the only real contender. By convention-time, he claimed 673 pledged delegates; on the first ballot he received 837 votes and the nomination.[9]

In the campaign, Smith, as one authority has put it, "tried to make prosperity the main issue—to outdo the Republicans in his conservative appeal." But eventually, the campaign evolved into an abusive discussion of liquor and religion. The Republicans ignored Teapot Dome with studied ease. The Democrats, evidently undiscouraged by their 1924 experience, quarried the scandal as an old mother lode not yet exhausted. A week before the Democratic convention in Houston, Josephus Daniels told Franklin D. Roosevelt: "The Democratic Party would not only be defeated,

---

1928 Campaign, 175-76, for a chart of the 1928 primary votes. In Michigan, for example, Smith polled 77,276 votes, while Walsh received 1,034. The California vote was 134,471 for Smith, and 46,770 for Walsh. Worst of all for Walsh was Massachusetts, where he polled 254 votes to Smith's 93,874.

[8] Peel and Donnelly, *The 1928 Campaign*, 12; *Official Report of the Proceedings of the Democratic National Convention . . . 1928* (Indianapolis, 1928), 98-104, 205-218, and 244-52; Freidel, *The Ordeal*, 241-44. On the eve of the convention, Smith's supporters claimed 703 pledged delegates out of a total of 1,100. He received 849 2/3 votes on the first and only ballot.

[9] *Official Report of the Proceedings of the Nineteenth Republican National Convention . . . 1928* (New York, 1928), 220 and 250; Peel and Donnelly, *The 1928 Campaign*, 18. After the convention, Senator Norris spoke of "the big Hoover steam roller" and of Hoover dominating the convention "not only while it was in actual operation, but for weeks before hand." Portion of Norris' statement to press, June 16, 1928, copy in Tray 1, Box 5, Norris Papers.

but humiliated if the prohibition issue is paramounted. It seems to me that we have a great opportunity if we can make the big issue privilege and its twin brother, corruption. They always go together."[10]

In muggy Houston, on the opening evening of the Democratic convention, Claude Bowers delivered a dazzling keynote address, one that crackled with denunciations of shameless Republican debauchery. Democrats must, said Bowers, "battle for the honor of the nation, besmirched and bedraggled by the most brazen and shameless carnival of corruption that ever blackened the reputation of a decent and self-respecting people." The "brilliant record" of the Wilson administration was "as a splotch of glorious sunshine against the smutty background of eight years of privilege and crime. . . . Privilege and pillage are the Gold Dust twins of normalcy. The Wilson administration is a green spot bounded on one side by the Mulhall mess and on the other by an oil tanker flying a pirate's flag."[11]

To such Democratic clamor over Teapot Dome, Republicans thrust forth Smith's association with Tammany Hall or else spoke not of scandal at all. The platform that the Republicans assembled for Hoover to stand upon was silent on Teapot Dome, although it stressed Coolidge's Oil Conservation Board, "which is now conducting an inquiry . . . in the effort to devise a national policy for the conservation and proper utilization of our oil resources." And in a familiar refrain, the platform deplored the fact that "certain American citizens of both parties have traffic [ed] in national in-

[10] Freidel, The Ordeal, 245; Peel and Donnelly, The 1928 Campaign, 49. Gilbert C. Fite, "The Agricultural Issue in the Presidential Campaign of 1928," Mississippi Valley Historical Review, XXXVII (March, 1951), 653-72, points out that the farm problem was not without influence, but emphasizes that liquor and religion were the chief issues in the campaign. But cf. Lubell, The Future of American Politics, 42-43, for ramifications beyond simply religious division; see also Moore, A Catholic Runs for President, 145-200, for a running account of the campaign. See Daniels to Roosevelt, June 18, 1928, Box 15, Daniels Papers, for the quotation above.

[11] Proceedings of the Convention, 1928 (Democratic), 8-21. As a keynote address in the classic mold, this speech by Bowers was brilliant. Flambouyant, and teeming with distortions though it was, it contained matchless phrases and imagery. Will Rogers, who claimed to have suggested Bowers for the job, warned beforehand: "You haven't heard the Republicans called anything till you hear this fellow." Rogers in New York Times, June 26, 1928, p. 27.

terests for private gain." George Norris found the platform "a sad
disappointment to every progressive citizen." It was silent, among
other things, "on the disgraceful and unpatriotic disclosures . . .
of the naval oil leases." Yet Norris did not find this surprising,
since "the same men who controlled the convention have fought
every . . . step to uncover any of these disgraceful and treasonable
frauds."[12]

In his acceptance speech, Hoover, as had the platform committee, avoided Teapot Dome. When the Democrats made what
he called "much ado" about corruption, Hoover found it "hard to
bear, especially coming from Tammany Hall." Hoover later recalled that he "answered" these charges on August 11, in a speech
at Stanford University, where he spoke to 70,000 listeners before
him and to millions more by radio. His remarks on corruption
were fleeting. "In the past years," he said late in his speech, "there
has been corruption participated in by individual[s] . . . of both
political parties." This dishonesty in government was "treason
to the state" and "destructive of self-government." He concluded
his one paragraph on corruption by stating that "there must be no
place for cynicism in the creed of America."[13]

Hoover's tactics did not, however, soften the Democratic tirades.
The Democratic platform bristled with the charge of "sordid corruption and unabashed rascality [by] cabinet ministers . . . , vul-
gar grafters, [and] givers and receivers of stolen funds." In Helena, Montana, the home of Senator Walsh, Smith told an audience
of 3,500 that the oil deals were "treason." He attacked Hoover's
silence, he contrasted the state of the public domain under Josephus Daniels and under the Republicans, and he made the pertinent observation that the Supreme Court had condemned the
leases. Although Teapot Dome was only one of about eight de-
finable issues in the campaign, the Smith headquarters still sought
expert advice for exploiting it. Late in the summer of 1928, Senator Robert Wagner, Democrat of New York, asked Harry Slattery to go to Albany and talk to Smith. Slattery met with the
governor and agreed to prepare material for him on conservation

[12] Republican National Committee, *Republican Campaign Textbook* (Chicago, 1928), 80, 112; George Norris' statement to press, June 16, 1928,
copy in Tray 1, Box 5, Norris Papers.

[13] Hoover, *Memoirs*, II, 207; New York *Times*, Aug. 12, 1928, p. 3; *Proceedings of the Convention, 1928* (Republican), 292-93.

and Teapot Dome. Over a period of several weeks, he supplied Smith with an extensive account of the entire Teapot Dome story. The Smith headquarters printed some of this material, and Smith took portions of it along on his western tour in September.[14]

For a while during the Continental investigation, the behavior of Republicans such as Senator Borah had suggested that the party would offer a new defense against Teapot Dome in the 1928 campaign. Borah had proposed repentance and reform, rather than denials of Republican responsibility and attempts to implicate Democrats. But the party's platform and its candidate chose to follow the Coolidge formula—admit nothing and say nothing of scandal. As the campaign neared its end, individual Republicans showed varying reactions to the corruption issue. George Norris, perennial party maverick and Teapot Dome critic, issued a plea for all "Progressives" to support Smith: "When I think of the oil scandals and the debauchery and the crime . . . in high places, . . . I think of [the past] seven years with a sense of humiliation and shame, and I feel like condemning myself when I remember that . . . I did my mite toward putting the Harding Administration in power." The men who had defended Fall and his associates, he asserted, now were backing Hoover, and Hoover himself, during the committee's "weary grind toward the facts," had sat in the cabinet in daily touch with the conspirators. Norris did not accuse Hoover of participation in the debauchery, but he did charge him with remaining "as silent as a sphinx," while knowing of the crimes. The Nebraska Progressive backed Smith for more reasons than Teapot Dome alone, but it did add weight to his choice.[15]

---

[14] *Proceedings of the Convention, 1928* (Republican), 187; New York *Times,* Sept. 25, 1928, p. 2; Peel and Donnelly, *The 1928 Campaign,* 52; Slattery to Robert Moses, Sept. 10, 11, and 14, 1928, and Nov. 2, 1928, Slattery Papers; Robert Moses to Slattery, Sept. 18, 1928, *ibid.* Peel and Donnelly say that "judged by the frequency of their employment, their effectiveness, and their importance," prosperity, prohibition, graft, religion, water power, agriculture, government economy and reorganization, and foreign affairs were the 1928 issues. One result of Slattery's work for Smith was his 113-page manuscript, "The Story of the Teapot Dome Oil Scandal," which he subtitled, "The Fight to Save the Naval Oil Reserves, and its Political Aspects." Copy in Slattery Papers.

[15] New York *Times,* Oct. 28, 1928, p. 28. In July, Norris told Gifford Pinchot: "My sympathies are all with the movement in favor of an independent candidate for President, who would be right on what, to my mind, is the fundamental and the greatest issue in the present campaign, . . . the

Gifford Pinchot's decision for Hoover rested not on Teapot Dome but on liquor. He had no enthusiasm for either candidate and saw "nothing to do . . . but to let the wet and dry issue decide" his stand. Teapot Dome had not forced Pinchot out of his party in 1924, and as a crusading prohibitionist, his decision to remain loyal in 1928 came readily to him.

William Allen White, faced on election day with Tammany and Teapot Dome, found the first more enduring and thus more unpalatable. To one correspondent, he wrote: "I do not apologize for Teapot Dome, nor Sinclair, nor Doheny, nor the little house on K Street. They were rotten. . . . But [they] were sporadic. Tammany is always in scandal." To another he replied: "Everyone must admit that Smith had no more hand personally in the corruption of Tammany than Hoover had in the corruption of the Harding administration," but Tammany was a system, and it was the system, not "the sewer . . . or milk scandals" that made Tammany "a menace." Al Smith had never complained against Tammany; Hoover, on the other hand, had not yet said that Sinclair, Doheny, Fall, and Daugherty were "all right."[16]

Charles Evans Hughes represented still another Republican viewpoint. The New York *Evening World,* bringing forth an old issue, had called Hughes "the biggest legal light in the regime under which the oil lands were turned over to Sinclair" and had recalled that he was "in the Cabinet meeting when the transfer was decided upon." On November 1, Hughes delivered a public address at Kismet Temple in Brooklyn. He called the *Evening World*'s charges "absolutely false" and said that "none of these leases was decided upon in any Cabinet meeting [or] ever brought before the Cabinet." He suggested that "the mud-slingers besmatter themselves" in trying to "besmirch" Coolidge and Hoover. When the *Evening World* repeated its charges, Hughes replied

---

Power Trust." Norris finally decided to back Smith because he had "risen far above Tammany" and because his position on water power was "practically the same as that of the Progressives." Norris to Pinchot, July 2, 1928, Tray 1, Box 5; July 14, 1928, and Sept. 8, 1928, Tray 1, Box 6; and Norris to W. T. Rawleigh, Nov. 9, 1928, Tray 1, Box 5, Norris Papers.

16 Pinchot to Norris, July 23, 1928, and Sept. 14, 1928, Tray 1, Box 6, Norris Papers; White to Edward J. Woodhouse, July 20, 1928, and White to Myron S. Blumenthal, Oct. 18, 1928, in *Selected Letters of William Allen White,* ed. Walter Johnson (New York, 1947), 284-85.

once more in a speech that closed out the Republican campaign. From the library of his apartment in New York City, between eleven-thirty and midnight on November 5, he spoke to a nation-wide radio audience. He repeated his denials; and as he closed his speech, the clock in his library, sounding clear over the network, struck twelve. It marked the end of the campaign—and the end of Teapot Dome as an issue in national politics.[17]

Hoover won the election by a comfortable margin in the popular vote and a decisive one in the electoral column. Teapot Dome had no real effect upon this outcome. William Allen White said that with the overwhelming Republican vote of 1924, "the oil scandal as an issue was wiped out of American politics." Numerous Democrats at the time chose to think otherwise. After 1928, even the most persistent of them probably accepted the political inefficacy of Teapot Dome, although as a synonym for corruption and Republican misrule, it continued to survive, especially in the Democratic lexicon.[18]

During the presidential campaign, Hoover had stepped with circumspection around Teapot Dome. Once in office, he inaugurated immediately a policy that undoubtedly swept Teapot Dome beyond all possible recall as a campaign issue. Eight days after he entered the White House, the new President announced a new oil conservation policy. During his administration, he stated, there would be "no leases or disposal of government oil lands, no matter what category they may lie in; of government holdings or government control, except those which may be made mandatory by Congress. . . . In other words there will be complete conservation of government oil in this administration." Two days later, on March 15, he announced that the Secretary of the Interior would review the 20,000 existing leases, in order to determine whether the holders had been complying with the law.

[17] Statements by Hughes and the *Evening World* in Henry C. Beerits, "Memorandum on 'The Fall Oil Scandals,'" Folder 45, Box 173, Hughes Papers.

[18] Peel and Donnelly, *The 1928 Campaign*, ix; and White, *A Puritan in Babylon*, 307. Hoover received 21,392,190 popular votes, good for 444 electoral votes; Smith received 15,016,443 poular votes and 87 electoral votes. See Stratton, "Behind Teapot Dome: Some Personal Insights," *loc. cit.*, 385-402, for discussion of Teapot Dome's place in "American political folklore."

Hoover had several reasons for making this new move. Apart from a likely desire to erase Teapot Dome from his party's record, he was aware of a growing concern over oil shortages. The Federal Oil Conservation Board had discovered extravagant waste, depletion, and overproduction of oil. Hoover's program was, in part, an answer to this need for new controls. Also, as a former member of the board, the President had decided that the FOCB was not as "vigorous as . . . it should be in conserving oil areas on public lands," which were "open to oil operators under a system of permits which had been greatly abused."[19]

Two years after inauguration of Hoover's policy, Secretary of the Interior Ray L. Wilbur reported that no prospecting permits on oil lands had been issued "except where equities demanded it," that new drilling had been discouraged, and that producers had been encouraged to hold their oil in the ground. Meanwhile, over 12,000 permits had been cancelled for noncompliance with the law[20]

While the Interior Department executed these belated reforms, Albert Fall stood his trial, received a guilty sentence, and entered prison in Santa Fe, New Mexico. On October 7, 1929, he finally had appeared before the District of Columbia Supreme Court to face the charge of accepting a bribe from Edward Doheny. On October 25, the jury found him guilty and recommended mercy. Already he was fragile in health and emaciated in appearance. The trial drained more life from him. In consideration of his physical condition, Justice William Hitz sentenced him to a year in prison and fined him $100,000. Fall appealed to the District of Columbia Appellate Court, which upheld the sentence. The United States Supreme Court refused to review the case. Hope of a presidential pardon dimmed when, in a speech at Marion, Ohio, dedicating a Harding memorial, Hoover praised Harding and denounced the men who had betrayed "not alone the friendship and trust of their staunch and loyal friend, but . . . their country."

[19] New York *Times*, March 13, 1929, p. 1; and March 16, 1929, p. 7; Ray L. Wilbur, *Two Years of the Department of the Interior, 1929-31* (Washington, 1931), 1; Hoover, *Memoirs*, II, 237 ff.; and Ray Lyman Wilbur, *The Memoirs of Ray Lyman Wilbur*, eds. Edgar Eugene Robinson and Paul Carroll Edwards (Stanford, 1960), 559. For discussion of Hoover's conservation policies, see Peffer, *Closing of the Public Domain*, 203 ff.
[20] Wilbur, *Two Years of the Department of the Interior*, 7.

Since he suffered from chronic tuberculosis, Fall was allowed to serve his term in the agreeable climate at New Mexico state prison, in the high country near Santa Fe. On July 20, 1931, he entered the prison.[21]

The jury convicted Fall for accepting a bribe from Doheny, but Doheny himself went free on the bribery charge. After a brief trial in March, 1930, a jury in the District of Columbia Supreme Court found him not guilty of bribing Fall. Senator George W. Norris had earlier suggested that it was impossible to convict a hundred million dollars in the United States. Millionaire oil man that he was, the businessman-as-hero image of the 1920's may have helped to save Doheny from a conviction—although his trial took place five months after the stock market crash of 1929. There is a very real possibility that, at least technically, Doheny was innocent of the charges against him. Under the United States criminal code, the offer of a bribe was a separate and distinct offence from the acceptance of one. In each case, the intent of the transaction, as it existed in the mind of the defendant, determined or refuted the guilt. Doheny took the stand at his trial, denied his guilt, and made a good witness for himself. Fall, in his own trial, did not testify at all. Also, Fall had been involved with Sinclair, while Doheny had not. Finally, Fall's letter declaring McLean as the source of his $100,000 loan was an admitted lie and was presented in his trial; this letter did not enter the Doheny trial.[22] Nevertheless, in the face of Sinclair and Doheny's acquittals, Fall's conviction smacked of injustice at worst, of irony at best. But irony was no stranger to Teapot Dome.

Not only did a jury of his peers find Fall guilty, but editorialists throughout the country indignantly denounced him. His party all but excommunicated him. His health and his aggressive spirit broken, his money and his land lost through payment of debts and lawyers' fees, Albert Fall paid a drastic penalty. His legal conviction is a matter of record—as is his social ostracism. But Fall

---

[21] 49 F.2d 506 (1931); 283 U.S. 867, 51 S. Ct. 657; New York *Times*, Oct. 9, 1929, Sec. 1, p. 6; Oct. 12, 1929, p. 1; Oct. 26, 1929, p. 1 and 8; and June 17, 1931, p. 2.

[22] See article New York *Times*, March 30, 1930, Sec. 3, p. 7, edited by Current Events Committee of American Association of Legal Authors, for these points; see also Hagland, "The Naval Reserve Leases," *loc. cit.*, 327, for similar suggestions as to why Doheny went free.

—Page in the Louisville *Courier-Journal*

THE LONG, LONG TRAIL

had many supporters who challenged the conviction and who
never ostracized him. In their opinion, he had made some egre-
gious errors in judgment (notably the McLean lie), but he had
also made an honest attempt to act upon his convictions about development of the country's natural resources. One old New Mexico friend in later years recalled: "I found it difficult to believe
Fall guilty of having accepted a bribe. . . . Even now, after the
passing years have permitted cool consideration of all the evidence, . . . it remains my belief that Fall was guilty of bad judgement rather than acceptance of a bribe." Another old acquaintance once wrote: "I am very weary of Herbert Hoover. That he
allows Judge Fall to go to the pen—knowing that he was not
guilty—of his own first-hand knowledge—is not to be forgiven."
And in 1935, another New Mexican said: "Nobody around here
believes Judge Fall ever did anything wrong. They know him

too well. And even if he had, they would still be for him. Mr. Fall
built up this country."[23]

Fall's biographer, David Stratton, notes that Fall became a
scapegoat for the Republican party, that "all of the transgressions
associated with the oil scandal, and to a certain extent all of the
iniquity of the Harding administration were imputed to him." If,
writes Stratton, Fall had wanted to sell the oil leases for personal
gain, "it seems unreasonable that he would have taken $400,000
. . . when in all probability the price of bribery for such valuable
government oil properties should have been at least $2,000,000."
There is much truth in Stratton's observation, for Fall's leasing
policy was not simply a response to bribery. He brought to Washington with him a westerner's antipathy for conservation and a
belief in the unrestrained development and use of natural resources. His lease of the reserves was an expression of that policy.
The money from Doheny and Sinclair was—for a while—a munifi-
cent correlative. But this very correlation was his nemesis; after
he confessed to telling a lie in December, 1923, when he stated
that Edward McLean had loaned him $100,000, all his other ac-
tions became suspect. Walsh, the courts, and the press produced
the judgment of guilt that Fall still bears. And Fall went to prison
—while the two oil millionaires, who participated in whatever
crimes he committed, went free.[24]

Teapot Dome's legal history ended with the Fall and Doheny
verdicts. Thereafter, Albert Fall, the scandal's essential figure,
withered and brooded for thirteen years. On May 9, 1932, he left
the Santa Fe prison, after serving nine months and nineteen days
of his sentence, most of it in the prison hospital. He had not paid,
he would never pay, his $100,000 fine. Agents of the Justice De-
partment, investigating Fall's financial status, found him quite

[23] Stratton, "Albert B. Fall," 363; Curry, An Autobiography, 300; Hutchinson, Bar-Cross Man, 304; El Paso Herald Post, Aug. 15, 1935, quoted in
Sonnichsen, Tularosa, 267. The Fall Papers in Albuquerque contain numerous letters from supporters of Fall, declaring their faith in his innocence.
[24] Stratton, "Albert B. Fall," 511-13; see also Stratton, "Behind Teapot
Dome," loc. cit., 392-94. In 1928, a Washington newspaper quoted an
"informant" as saying: "The poor old fellow [Fall] realizes what a victim of
blunders he has been made by himself and others. He admits that his statement about McLean having loaned him the money . . . was 'a damn fool
thing for me to do' and can only explain it by that same phrase." Washington Herald, March 30, 1928.

unable to pay it. His funds exhausted by the expenses of litigation through the mid-twenties, Fall was virtually penniless by the
time he entered prison. Since he had won time off for good behavior, the Justice Department petitioned the sentencing court to
amend his commitment and allow him freedom without paying
the $100,000.[25]

Three years after his release, a reporter visited him and found
Fall "a pathetic, broken old man." In 1925, through foreclosure,
he had lost his great ranch at Three Rivers. Doheny's oil company, holding a mortgage on the property, had sold the ranch and
forced Fall to give up even the one-hundred acre tract surrounding his home, although Fall insisted that the tract and the home
were not included in the original foreclosure. Fall claimed that
Mrs. Doheny was responsible for the order to move; he and Edward Doheny were "still friends." Doheny himself was ill, perhaps a little insane over the death of his only son, and he evidently never knew of Fall's destitution.[26]

After Fall's release from prison, Mrs. Fall—described as his
"staunchest champion" and a "fighter for him every inch of every
battle"—earned money in various modest ways: by operating a
store in Three Rivers, and a restaurant in El Paso, and by home
canning of fruits and vegetables. When she and Fall were evicted
from Three Rivers, an El Paso home remained to them. Once a
handsome villa, it soon turned shabby. In time, Fall became
permanently hospitalized, first at William Beaumont Hospital in
El Paso, then at the Veterans' Hospital in Albuquerque, and finally in El Paso again, at the Catholic Hotel Dieu. At Three Rivers,
he had watched the sky and the Sierra Blancas and had read about
the past—histories, biographies, and novels. At Hotel Dieu, he

[25] Stratton, "Albert B. Fall," 447, 493; New York *Times*, May 4, 1932,
p. 2, and May 10, 1932, p. 1. The government eventually dropped its conspiracy indictment against Fall, as well as against Sinclair, Doheny, and
Edward Doheny, Jr.

[26] Baltimore *Sun*, Sept. 9, 1935, reprint from dispatch in the Milwaukee
Journal; "Fall Ill: Fights to Save Home," *The Literary Digest*, CXX (Aug.
24, 1935), 7; Stratton, "Albert B. Fall," 495-510. Fall's friend George Curry
recalled that Doheny had once declared, "Fall will never want for anything." Curry had "no doubt that had Doheny retained control of his affairs he would have carried out his pledge" (*An Autobiography*, 304-305).

read only newspapers. He was reading when his heart stopped; Mrs. Fall already had died in a room across the hall.[27]

Two years before Emma Fall died, Harry Slattery became administrator of the Rural Electrification Administration; upon his appointment, two Wasington newspaper columnists recalled that "it was Slattery who first unearthed the Teapot Dome scandal and forced a Senate investigation." Several days later, Slattery received a letter from Mrs. Fall. She had read the column. She told Slattery, "I can't but believe you will feel a little conscience stricken when you see published for the benefit of thousands who have never ceased to love and honor Albert B. Fall . . . the material I had knowledge of to start with, and have gathered during these intervening years." Her concluding remark expressed a fervent hope: "Vindication for Fall, as sure as retribution for his traducers." But she never published a vindication. Neither did Fall. During his last years, as he lay dying in El Paso, Fall thought often of the scandal that wrecked him and scarred a decade of American politics. As he remembered his catalytic role, he no doubt wished it might have been different.[28]

[27] Santa Fe *New Mexican*, Dec. 1, 1944; Washington *Herald*, March 30, 1928; Sonnichsen, *Tularosa*, 267-69; Las Cruces (N.M.) *Sun-News*, Dec. 1, 1944.

[28] Drew Pearson and Robert Allen, "Washington Daily Merry-Go-Round," Washington *Times Herald*, Dec. 30, 1939; Mrs. Albert (Emma) Fall to Harry Slattery, Jan. 15, 1940, Slattery Papers.

Bibliographical Note

PRIMARY SOURCES

Historical studies of politics in the 1920's are scarce, as are studies of the decade's great political scandal. In light of Teapot Dome's impact upon American politics in the 1920's, this is a little perplexing. But as Henry F. May's illuminating study, "Shifting Perspectives on the 1920's," *Mississippi Valley Historical Review* (December, 1956), has indicated, American historians have long tended to view these years as a deplorable period; and Teapot Dome unquestionably has contributed to this impression. The New Deal following the decade and Progressivism preceding it have been much more enticing and somehow more worthy of study to historians.

An unfortunate result is too much cliché-ridden condemnation of the 1920's, along with—paradoxically—a certain nostalgia for the very insouciance and frivolity that, in the conventional view,

explain the decade's shortcomings. A villainous Albert Fall, bath-
tub gin and immorality, rebellious collegians with Menckenian
American Mercury in hand, and emancipated Fitzgerald flappers
are some of the prevailing images of the decade. Part of this is
due to Frederick Lewis Allen's *Only Yesterday* (New York, 1931).
Thirty years after its appearance, Allen's book remains the most
provocative account of the decade. Brilliant in its evocation of
much that was true about the twenties, Allen's book (along with
its imitators) has unduly shaped historical recall of these years.
Those who write about the decade have rarely disturbed Allen's
portrayal, and those who only read about the decade usually do
not want to. American historians have done little to challenge or
to verify existing knowledge and opinion about the twenties; they
are, however, beginning to take a closer look. Arthur S. Link, in
"What Happened to the Progressive Movement in the 1920's?"
The American Historical Review (July, 1959), has recently shown
that "historians young and old, but mostly young, have . . . discovered that the period of the 1920's is the exciting new frontier
of American historical research and that its opportunities are almost limitless."

I have attempted to probe this frontier at one point, by explor-
ing the decade's big political scandal. Beyond this, someone might
write a large book on nothing more than the trials and other legal
issues that Teapot Dome produced. The social historian can find
in the scandal numerous inferences about the morals and manners
of the American people and their government during the decade.
A study of Teapot Dome's relationship to American intellectual
life in the 1920's would be not only valuable but also fashionable,
as historiographical currents are flowing just now. Nevertheless,
some old-fashioned political history is, I believe, a prerequisite to
these other approaches to the scandal and to the 1920's. In
"Echoes of the Jazz Age," *Scribner's* (November, 1931), his su-
perb recall of the decade that claimed him, F. Scott Fitzgerald believed it a "characteristic of the Jazz Age that it had no interest
in politics at all." However much he may sympathize with Fitzgerald's political alienation, it is high time for the historian of the
1920's to study the subject that supposedly interested Fitzgerald's
Age not at all.

MANUSCRIPTS

Source materials on politics in the 1920's—and on Teapot Dome—
are abundant. In the Library of Congress, the papers of William
E. Borah, Josephus Daniels, Charles Evans Hughes, William
Gibbs McAdoo, George W. Norris, Gifford Pinchot, Thomas J.
Walsh, and William Allen White, to name only eight collections,
are voluminous. All of them are rich sources for political studies
of the twenties. Most of them are invaluable for a study of Teapot
Dome. The Walsh papers are indispensable for any approach to
the scandal. The Pinchot, Norris, and Daniels papers (as well as
Walsh's) are important for any study of the scandal that goes beyond the immediate Senate investigation. The Hughes papers are
only incidentally helpful for Teapot Dome, and, surprisingly,
William Allen White's papers seem to have very little of practical
value on the scandal. The papers of Calvin Coolidge in the Library of Congress are most disappointing, partly because of the
man's taciturn style on paper as well as in person and partly because the collection is meager (again, perhaps, reflecting their
subject). The McAdoo papers, only recently opened for use, offer
the proverbial storehouse of information.

The Harry A. Slattery papers in Duke University Library are
indispensable for the early history of Teapot Dome and also for
any study of conservation in the United States from 1910 to 1946.
Portions of Albert B. Fall's papers are available for use at Albuquerque; their value may be suggested by reference to Barbara
Anthes, compiler, *List of the Albert B. Fall Papers in the Library
of the University of New Mexico* (1957).

GOVERNMENT RECORDS

The National Archives contain a large body of material collected by the Justice Department and by Coolidge's special counsel, Owen Roberts and Atlee Pomerene, during their investigation
and subsequent prosecution of Fall, Doheny, and Sinclair. Any
study of Teapot Dome's legal history requires use of this large
collection; the student of Teapot Dome's political history can find
it helpful, but not especially rewarding. The Fall papers in Albuquerque contain some fifty bound volumes of trial transcripts,

court decisions, briefs, and other legal material gathered during the trials.

Among published government documents, the essential item on Teapot Dome is the record of the Senate's investigation of the oil leases. These hearings (1923-24 and 1928) total about 5,000 pages. They are often verbose and tedious reading, but without them there would hardly be a story to tell. Furthermore, they provide much besides testimony before the committee; parts 5 and 6 of the 1928 hearings, for example, contain an excellent collection of photostats, transcripts, and other material used by the Senate committee. An obvious source of great value is the *Congressional Record*; not so obvious is some of the material that turns up during a methodical search through its pages. *Cong. Rec.*, 70 Cong., 1 Sess. (May 29, 1928), for instance, contains a "Chronology of Events in the History of the Naval Petroleum Reserve, No. 3, Teapot Dome," prepared by Rita Dielmann of the Legislative Reference Bureau, and a "Chronology of the Oil Scandal as Disclosed to the Public Up to April 9, 1928," compiled by Edwin E. Witte of the Wisconsin Legislative Reference Library. The same issue contains a "History of the Continental Trading Co. (Ltd.) of Canada," offered by Senator Nye, whose data came from the Senate hearings and which provides a convenient summary of the Continental investigation's findings. Max W. Ball, *Petroleum Withdrawals and Restorations Affecting the Public Domain* (U. S. Geological Survey, Bulletin 623 [Washington, 1916]), offers a brief historical account of oil-land law and oil withdrawals, 1897-1914, and some 400 pages of related documentary material. See also Attorney-General, *Withdrawn Oil Lands of the United States*, a Supplement to the Annual Report for 1915 (Washington, 1916).

NEWSPAPERS AND JOURNALS

Any student of American politics in the 1920's quickly acquires a debt to the New York *Times*—which needs listing here only to acknowledge and to emphasize the debt. The Harry A. Slattery papers contain thousands of usable clippings from many metropolitan newspapers, especially from New York, Philadelphia, and Washington. Slattery collected news stories on a bewildering variety of subjects, but conservation, Teapot Dome, and politics

were his primary interest. For information on Albert Fall, the
Santa Fe *New Mexican* is the best newspaper source in the Southwest. Josephus Daniels' Raleigh *News and Observer* is an excellent Democratic newspaper for the 1920's. If one is seeking a
counter-weight, the Boston *Evening Transcript* is unexcelled in
partisanship for Coolidge.

No single periodical published during the twenties is notable
for information on Teapot Dome. A half dozen are generally informative on politics, with *The Outlook* perhaps most so, if only
for its articles by Stanley Frost. See, in particular, "That Teapot
Dome Alarm Clock," "Oil, Mud, and Tom-Toms," and "The G.
O. P. at the Bar," in March, 1924, issues. Senator Walsh himself
wrote several articles, the most useful being "The True History
of Teapot Dome," *The Forum* (July, 1924). Two useful contemporary accounts of the 1924 election are Hugh Keenleyside, "The
American Political Revolution of 1924," *Current History* (March,
1925), and Arthur Macmahon, "The United States: Domestic
Politics," *Political Science Quarterly* Supplement (March-Decem-
ber, 1925). A penetrating appraisal is Gamaliel Bradford, "The
Genius of the Average: Calvin Coolidge," *Atlantic Monthly* (January, 1930). Preston Slosson, at the end of the decade, wrote
acute analyses of Harding and Coolidge for *Current History* (Oct.,
Nov., 1930). His estimate of Harding is an incisive essay, transcending the spate of memoirs and banal reminiscences of Harding. The analysis of Coolidge is equally provocative and is more
judicious than Coolidge, in the midst of the depression, had reason
to hope for. Both articles offer comment upon Teapot Dome and
its role in each President's life.

POLITICAL MEMOIRS AND AUTOBIOGRAPHIES

Political memoirs and autobiographies covering the twenties
are practically useless for a study of Teapot Dome, although some
of them have definite value otherwise for the politics of the period.
Most rewarding is *The Autobiography of William Allen White*
(New York, 1946). Any time White touched pen to paper, he
wrote entertainingly and with illumination. His intimate association with politicos during the twenties gives his book value. Harry
Daugherty's *Inside Story of the Harding Tragedy* (New York,

1932) is partly autobiography, partly an attempt at exoneration
from the misfortunes of the administration he helped to create.
It is an outstanding example of the trivia that political historians
of the decade encounter. Herbert Hoover has shown more willingness, in his *Memoirs*, especially vol. II (New York, 1952), to
talk about Teapot Dome than have some of his Republican contemporaries—for example, Walter E. Edge, *A Jerseyman's Journal*
(Princeton, 1948). Edge, once a Republican congressman from
New Jersey, discusses Harding's nomination, the Coolidge and
Hoover administrations, and various congressional debates of the
1920's, but never once mentions Teapot Dome. Hoover, by contrast, writes with scorn of the Harding administration's scandals
and of the legacy that Coolidge derived therefrom. But his mem-
oir is still meager in its discussion of Teapot Dome. Cordell Hull
is one of the few prominent Democrats of the period who has
published *Memoirs* (New York, 1949). He says little on Teapot
Dome, although he offers an occasional remark that is informative
on Democratic tactics at the time.

None of these volumes—although White's comes closest—is a
major and enduring contribution on the twenties. The decade
may have produced its novelist in Fitzgerald and its dramatist in
O'Neill. Its political diarist or its autobiographer, in the tradition
of John Quincy Adams or his grandson Henry, has never appeared.

SECONDARY SOURCES

Among secondary studies of the twenties, the best single book
on the Democratic party is *Franklin D. Roosevelt: The Ordeal*
(Boston, 1954), Frank Freidel's second volume in his biography of
Franklin D. Roosevelt. Since Roosevelt had no connection with
Teapot Dome, Freidel has little on the scandal itself; however, his
accounts of the 1924 and 1928 campaigns are of great value. Frederick Paxson, *Postwar Years: Normalcy, 1918-1923* (Berkeley,
1948) contains a judicious summary and evaluation of the Harding administration. Kenneth McKay, *The Progressive Movement
of 1924* (New York, 1947) illuminates a political faction and its
efforts before and during the 1924 election. Roy Peel and Thomas
Donnelly, *The 1928 Campaign: An Analysis* (New York, 1931),
is an early post-mortem that is still one of the most useful. Ed-

mund Moore, *A Catholic Runs for President: The Campaign of
1928* (New York, 1956) is authoritative on the Smith campaign in
1928. Both William Leuchtenburg, *The Perils of Prosperity, 1914-
32* (Chicago, 1958), and John D. Hicks, *Republican Ascendancy,
1921-1933* (New York, 1960), the latest syntheses of the twenties,
contain useful chapters on politics. Their treatment of Teapot
Dome is, of necessity, minimal.

BIOGRAPHIES

A handful of biographies touch upon the twenties, with few
of them offering much upon Teapot Dome. Claude Fuess, *Calvin
Coolidge: The Man From Vermont* (Boston, 1940) and William
Allen White, *A Puritan in Babylon* (New York, 1938) devote considerable space to Coolidge's presidency, but neither book is a
profound study of the twenties, of the President, or of the scandal
that threatened to overcome him. The Fuess book is sober and
informative, but lacks depth or analysis; and even a hint of scandal rarely clutters the sedate pages. White's book glitters with
sometimes shrewd, sometimes dubious analyses of character and
of politics but lacks dependable documentation. White had in-
sight and an enormous fund of personal memories, but he used
his rich imagination and the memories of his contemporaries to
the neglect of written primary sources. Coolidge awaits a biographer who will encompass the virtues of Fuess and White, while
transcending both of them. Harding awaits a respectable biographer of any kind. The only published study that in any way resembles a life of Harding is Samuel Hopkins Adams, *The Incredible Era* (New York, 1939). Adams worked well with what he
had, which was very little documentary material and a vast store
of secondary trivia and contemporary impressions. As did numerous others who have interpreted the twenties, he allowed the gloss
and the frivolity of the times to intrude too much upon his work.
Fola and Belle C. La Follette, *Robert M. La Follette* (New York,
1953) contains an invaluable chapter on Teapot Dome. Volume
two of William T. Hutchinson, *Lowden of Illinois* (Chicago,
1957), contains a masterful discussion of the 1920 Republican
convention and of the political events and campaigns leading up
to it.

GENERAL STUDIES

For conservation during the twenties, there are two basic books: John Ise, *The United States Oil Policy* (New Haven, 1926), and E. Louise Peffer, *The Closing of the Public Domain* (Stanford, 1951). Both volumes cover more than the twenties but both contain extensive material on the decade. Ise has an entire chapter on Teapot Dome; his account is that of an ardent conservationist, angered by the then recent revelations, and is totally unsympathetic to Fall and the Republican administrations. Despite its open bias, this has long been the best single narrative account of Teapot Dome in print, although the book went to press before the investigation ended.

There are innumerable sketches and summaries of the scandal, as, for example, a lengthy chapter in Mark Sullivan, *Our Times: The Twenties* (New York, 1935), and an even longer chapter in M. R. Werner, *Privileged Characters* (New York, 1935). Both of these flow with journalistic ease, and Sullivan's contains excellent cartoons and pictures; but each of them is little more than a summary of the material found in the daily press and the Senate Committee hearings. M. E. Ravage, *The Story of Teapot Dome* (New York, 1924) merely summarizes the investigation through the 1924 hearings and was outdated almost as soon as it appeared. M. R. Werner and John Starr, *Teapot Dome* (New York, 1959) is a recent account, done in the Allen-Sullivan tradition. A vivid narrative, it ably synthesizes most of the conventional lore—and perpetuates the simple stereotypes of good men opposing conspiracies by bad men. The most extensive account of Teapot Dome's legal history is in Francis X. Busch, *Enemies of the State* (New York, 1954), which contains a 79-page summary of the civil and criminal trials. For a legalist's analysis of the cases, see Charles G. Hagland, "The Naval Reserve Leases," *Georgetown Law Journal* (March, 1932).

PERIODICALS

Among secondary studies on the twenties and on Teapot Dome, periodical articles are more useful than are book-length studies. Some valuable letters revealing Daugherty's role in Harding's nomination are in Randolph C. Downes, editor, "President Making: The Influence of Newton H. Fairbanks and Harry M. Daugherty on the Nomination of Warren G. Harding for the Presidency," *Northwest Ohio Quarterly* (Fall, 1959). See this quarterly also for Charles Elsworth Hard, "The Man Who Did Not Want To Become President" (Summer, 1959). A friendly sketch of Harding, bordering on sympathy, is Finley Peter Dunne, "A Look at Harding from the Sidelines," *Saturday Evening Post* (September, 1936). Historians of the 1920's have scarcely gone beyond the early interpretations of Harding offered by Frederick Lewis Allen. Judging from production to date, Harding and his administration appear destined for an enduring condescension in American historiography; there may be justice in this, but even Harding needs more historical appraisal, if only to confirm the prevailing stereotypes. A good account of the 1920 Republican Convention—and one that challenges the conventional wisdom—is Wesley Bagby, "The 'Smoke-Filled Room' and the Nomination of Warren G. Harding," *Mississippi Valley Historical Review* (March, 1955). Bagby raises a good deal of skepticism about the supposed dictation of Harding's nomination by any predatory group, oil or otherwise. Coolidge is never likely to enjoy (and hardly deserves) a revisionist biography; however, a latter-day article that shades on veneration is Claude Fuess, "Calvin Coolidge—Twenty Years After," *Proceedings of the American Antiquarian Society* (October 1953).

For the 1924 campaign, useful historical studies include Lee N. Allen, "The Democratic Presidential Primary Election of 1924 in Texas," *The Southwestern Historical Quarterly* (April, 1958); James H. Shideler, "The La Follette Progressive Party Campaign of 1924," *Wisconsin Magazine of History* (June, 1950); Shideler, "The Disintegration of the Progressive Party Movement of 1924," *Historian* (Spring, 1951); and Sexson E. Humphreys, "The Nomination of the Democratic Candidate in 1924," *Indiana Magazine of History* (March, 1935). Most commendable is J. Leonard Bates, "The Teapot Dome Scandal and the Election of 1924," *American Historical Review* (January, 1955). Bates effectively describes the complex political situation in 1924 and concludes that "there is no way of knowing" how much the corruption issue influenced voters. He does suggest that Democratic implication in the scandal prevented Democrats from making successful use of Teapot Dome in the election. Two other articles by Bates that merit attention are "The Midwest Decision, 1915," *Pacific Northwest Quarterly* (January, 1960), and "Josephus Daniels and the Naval Oil Reserves," *U. S. Naval Institute Proceedings* (February, 1953); and on the conservation background to the Fall-Pinchot conflict, see Bates, "Fulfilling American Democracy: The Conservation Movement, 1907 to 1921," *Mississippi Valley Historical Review* (June, 1957). (For conservation in the West, a significant study is *The Politics of Conservation: Crusades and Controversies, 1897-1913*, by Elmo R. Richardson [Stanford University Press, 1962]). Two valuable articles by David H. Stratton are "New Mexican Machiavellian?", *Montana Magazine of Western History* (October, 1957), and "Behind Teapot Dome: Some Personal Insights," *Business History Review* (Winter, 1957).

UNPUBLISHED MATERIALS

Stratton is at work on a full-scale biography of Fall; meanwhile, his "Albert B. Fall and the Teapot Dome Affair" (University of Colorado Ph.D., 1955), is available on microfilm (University Microfilms, Ann Arbor). Two other valuable doctoral dissertations are Harold T. Pinkett, "Gifford Pinchot and the Early Conservation Movement in the United States" (American University, 1953), and J. Leonard Bates, "Senator Walsh of Montana, 1918-1924: A Liberal Under Pressure" (University of North Carolina, 1952). A brief but able master's thesis is Robert Alfred Waller, "Business Reactions to the Teapot Dome Affair: 1922 to 1925" (University of Illinois, 1958); portions of this thesis will appear in an early issue of *Business History Review*.

Index

Adams, John T., 118, 125, 143, 156, 191; defends Daugherty, 118, 125

American Federation of Labor, 46; supports La Follette, 168

American Federationist, 155, 168

American Forestry, and press campaign against Fall, 27

Anderson, Paul Y., investigation of Continental Trading Company by, 186, 187, 187 n. 16, 189

Ashurst, Henry F., 106

Augusta *Chronicle* (Georgia), 61

Ballinger-Pinchot Affair, 39, 73; effect of on Pinchot, 7, 21; compared to Teapot Dome, 85

Baltimore *Sun*, 87, 94, 103

Baruch, Bernard M., and McAdoo campaign, 104, 114 n. 30, 137, 158, 160

Beveridge, Albert J., 108; criticizes Republican party, 122-23

Blackmer, H. M., and Continental Trading Company, 180, 181, 182, 192; in exile, 182 n. 7

Blackstone Hotel, "smoke-filled room" conference at, 3

Blivin, Bruce, 110

Bone, Scott, 22 n. 18

Borah, William E., 34, 118, 149; and "Sinclair Fund," 193-95

Boston *Evening Transcript*, 80, 117, 133, 154, 166, 167; as Coolidge's "court paper," 75

Bovard, O. K., and Continental Trading Company investigation, 186, 189

Bowers, Claude, 201; 1928 keynote address of, 205

Bratton, Sam G., and New Mexico gubernatorial campaign, 170

Brock, Walter E., and McAdoo
  campaign, 104, 137-38, 140
Brooklyn *Eagle*, 136; letter of
  George W. Norris in, 188-89
Brotherhood of Locomotive Fire-
  men and Enginemen, 104
Bryan, Charles W., nomination of,
  163
Bryan, William Jennings, 60, 99
Bryant, R. C., 8, 26
Burns Detective Agency, jury
  shadowing of, 185
Busch, Francis X., 180
Butler, William M., 91, 167-68;
  testimony of, 192-93
Byrnes, James F., 94
Byrns, Joseph W., 93

Cannon, James, Jr., opinion of
  Walsh, 202
Caraway, Thaddeus, 55, 134, 196;
  attacks Fall, 75-76; attacks
  Denby, 83-84, 97
Catron, Thomas, 10
Chadbourne, Thomas, and McAdoo
  campaign, 114 n., 160
Chapman, H. H., 31
Charleston *News and Courier*, 196
Chicago *Tribune*, 12, 25, 89, 107
Christian Advocate, 111
Clackamus County (Oregon),
  aluminum teapots in, 98
Cobb, John N., 24
Columbus *Ohio State Journal*, 196
Conference for Progressive Political
  Action, meeting of in St. Louis,
  103; and La Follette, 165
Continental Trading Company,
  organization of, 180, 181; Senate
  investigation of, 189-93, 196-99;
  and 1920 Democratic campaign
  fund, 191; and 1920 Republican
  campaign fund, 191, 192; and
  Senate Committee findings on,
  197
Coolidge, Calvin, nomination of
  for vice-president, 2; and conservation, 4; becomes president,
  59, 59 n. 27; moves into White
  House, 61-62; directs Daugherty
  to attend hearings, 80, 81; talks
  with Slattery, 86; and *Mayflower*

conference, 90, 91-92; selects
  special counsel, 97; and resignation of Denby, 109, 117; and
  resignation of Daugherty, 118,
  124, 125, 125 n. 47, 126-28; and
  McLean telegrams, 131-36; appoints oil commission, 146, 147;
  estimate of, 149-51; nomination
  of in 1924, p. 164; in 1924 campaign, 169, 170, 173, 174; election of in 1924, pp. 170, 173-75;
  appoints Federal Oil Conservation Board, 178-79
Copeland, Royal S., 105
Cox, James M., 59-60
Creel, George, opinion of Doheny,
  103 n. 11
Curtis, Charles, nomination of, 204
Cutting, Bronson, 107 n. 18, 195

Daniels, Josephus, 60, 61, 94, 96,
  112, 166, 171, 204; and oil reserves, 17, 34; and Senate investigation, 35; oil policy of
  criticized, 118-19; and 1924
  Democratic platform, 156-57
Daugherty, Harry M., 54, 92, 93,
  106, 142; and Harding campaign, 3; directed to attend hearings, 80, 81; offers to aid Roberts
  and Pomerene, 116; resignation
  of, 118, 124, 128, 129
Davis, John W., 136; nomination
  of, 163, 164
Dawes, Charles G., nomination of,
  164
Democratic Campaign Book, 158
Democratic Convention of 1924,
  pp. 158-64, 171-72
Democratic National Committee,
  and Teapot Dome, 78
Denby, Edwin, named Secretary
  of Navy, 13; leases reserves, 18;
  demand for resignation of, 97,
  105, 109; resignation of, 116-17
Dial, Nathaniel D., 112
Dill, C. C., 115
Dodd, William E., and McAdoo
  campaign, 111, 171
Doheny, Edward L., 30; testimony
  of, 69, 85; lends Fall $100,000,
  pp. 74, 85, 100, 101; McAdoo as

lawyer of, 100; trial for conspiracy of, 184-85; freed of bribery
charge, 211. *See also* Pan-
American Petroleum and Transport Company
Doheny, Edward L., Jr., and "the
little black bag," 75, 85; at Sinclair trial, 200, 201

Edge, Walter, on Harding's cabinet
appointments, 12 n. 29
Election of 1924, vote in, 170; and
indictment of Fall, Sinclair, and
Doheny, 175 n. 47, 176. *See
also* Teapot Dome
Elk Hills. *See* Pan-American Pe-
troleum and Transport Company
Erwin, John, 67
Everhart, M. T., testimony of, 190

Fall, Albert B., visit to Harding of,
8, 11, 12; before 1920, pp. 8-11,
106; personality of, 10, 11;
named Secretary of Interior, 12,
12 n. 29; opposed by Pinchot
and Slattery, 13; and Alaska, 22,
23; and Forest Service, 20, 23,
23 n. 19, 28; conference with
Pinchot of, 24; rumors of resignation of, 29; leases California
reserves, 31, 35, 36; response to
Senate resolution of, 47, 48, 48
n. 8; resignation of, 51-52,
52 n. 16, 53-55; testimony of,
65; names McLean as source of
loan, 70; admits to lying, 72;
explains lie, 74, 74 n. 18; effect
of lie upon, 75; denies receiving
money from Sinclair, 79, 200;
visit to Woodrow Wilson of,
107 n. 18; refuses to testify, 108;
as issue in New Mexico in 1924,
pp. 170-71; and Continental
Trading Company, 183, 190;
trial for conspiracy of, 184-85;
sentenced to prison, 210-11; last
years of, 211-15
Fall, Mrs. Albert (Emma), 214,
215
Federal Oil Conservation Board,
147, 179, 205, 210
Finney, Edward C., announces
leasing of Teapot Dome, 38

Fletcher, Duncan, 105
Forbes, Charles R., 56
Forest Service. *See* U.S. Forest
Service
Forum, 1924 campaign issues dis-
cussed in, 156
Frazier, Frank, letter of on Mc-
Adoo, 137-39
Frelinghuysen, Joseph S., 12
Frost, Stanley, 120-21, 136

Garfield, James R., 8
Garret, Finis J., 94 n. 41
George, Walter F., 201
Glass, Carter, 201
Goff, Guy D., and Borah "Sinclair
Fund," 194
Gompers, Samuel, and Teapot
Dome investigation, 45, 46 n. 5
Greeley, William B., 7 n. 13, 14, 27
Greene, William C., 9
Gregory, Thomas W., 100; nomi-
nated as special counsel, 97;
withdraws nomination, 108
Griffin, Robert S., 35, 39

Hale, Frederick, 148
Halligan, John, 35, 39, 154
Hamon, Clara Smith, 142
Hamon, Jake, 142, 143
Hampton, Frank, and McAdoo
campaign, 99, 100, 138, 164
Hardin, John Wesley, 10
Harding, Warren G., nomination
of, 1; and conservation, 4; elec-
tion of, 7; chooses cabinet, 12;
approves of leases, 47; western
tour of, 55, 56, 56 n. 23, 57;
estimate of, 56 n. 23, 58, 58
n. 25, 59; death of, 57, 58, 58
n. 25, 173
Harrison, Pat, 76, 134, 169; 1924
keynote address of, 159
Harvey, George, 109
Heflin, J. Thomas, 89, 90, 91, 97,
106, 119, 120, 132, 134; exchange of with Lodge, 122 n. 42
Hicks, John D., 58
Hitchcock, Gilbert M., 41, 107
n. 18
Hitz, William, sentences Fall, 210
Holland, Rush, 91

Hoover, Herbert, 53, 58, 83, 210;
and Denby's resignation, 117;
and Daugherty's resignation,
124, 127; nomination of, 204; in
1928 campaign, 205, 206; election of, 209; and conservation,
209, 210
House, E. M., 101
Houston *Chronicle,* 196
Howe, Louis M., 162
Hughes, Charles Evans, 83; and
oil reserve transfer, 34; and
Daugherty's resignation, 127;
and 1928 campaign, 208, 209
Hull, Cordell, 136; and Senate inquiry, 66, 67; denies donations
from Sinclair, 68; and Teapot
Dome, 90; and 1924 campaign,
156, 157, 158; testimony of, 191
Humphreys, A. E., and Continental
Trading Company, 180, 181

Ickes, Harold L., 5; opinion of
Pinchot, 21, 21 n. 16, 22; opinion of Coolidge, 77-78, 148-49

Jennings, Al, testimony of, 142, 143
Johnson, Hiram W., 34, 76
Johnson, J. T., testimony of, 69
Johnston, William H., 103, 104

Kendrick, John B., 44, 46; and oil
leases, 36, 37, 50
Kennedy, T. Blake, upholds Sin-
clair's lease, 182-83
Kent, Frank, 108; on Coolidge ad-
ministration, 87-88; on McAdoo,
99-100, 103, 161
Kent, William, 154, 156, 171-72,
174
Kerans, Grattan, 67, 68, 158
King, Judson, 29
King, William H., 26, 160
Knox, Frank, 108; on Borah "Sin-
clair Fund," 195
Krock, Arthur, 158
Ku Klux Klan, and McAdoo, 160,
161, 173

Labor, 66
Ladd, Edwin E., 43, 44, 66; chairman of Public Lands Committee, 120

La Follette, Robert M., 17; relationship of with Slattery, 20;
prepares for investigation, 33,
34, 34 n. 5; resolution of to investigate leases, 39, 40, 41, 42;
asks Walsh to lead inquiry, 46;
investigates gasoline prices, 49,
50; and 1924 campaign, 103,
104, 165, 168, 175, 175 n. 46
Lane, Franklin K., 5, 17, 100
Lathrop, John, 35 n. 9, 39, 45, 46
Leasing Law of 1920, pp. 17, 18,
18 n. 8
Lenroot, Irvine, 43, 45, 66, 69, 71,
74, 93, 98, 100, 115; at 1920
convention, 2; and Wardman
Park conference, 119-20; resigns
as committee chairman, 120
Lippmann, Walter, 174
Literary Digest, The, 111, 172;
predicts 1924 election results,
170
Lockwood, George, 128; advice to
Coolidge, 123-24, 125-26
Lodge, Henry Cabot, 41, 118, 127,
134, 164; exchange of with Heflin, 122 n. 42; defends Coolidge,
132
Long, Breckenridge, on McAdoo
campaign, 101, 104, 105, 113,
137; at Democratic convention,
160; on Coolidge, 165 n. 26; on
1924 Democratic campaign,
172-73
Longworth, Nicholas, 93, 94
Love, Thomas, 104
Lowden, Frank O., 1

McAdoo, William G., 136, 137,
139, 140, 141; campaign for
presidency by, 59, 60, 60 n. 30,
61; counsel for Doheny, 61; support for nomination of, 99; reaction of supporters of to
Doheny testimony, 101; asks to
testify, 105; testimony of, 110-
12; Chicago conference of,
112-14; defeats Underwood,
138; and 1924 convention, 159-
64; contemporary estimates of
defeat of, 171-72; and 1928
campaign of, 201, 202, 203

McCamant, Wallace, 2
McCormick, Paul J., voids Doheny
    contract, 182, 183
McCoy, Walter I., 145
McGee, W J, 4
McKellar, Kenneth, 49, 84
McLean, Edward, offers to testify,
    71; questioned by Walsh in
    Palm Beach, 72; telegrams of to
    Washington, 131-32; testimony
    of, 132
Magee, Carl, testimony of, 68, 69
Mammoth Oil Company, lease on
    Teapot Dome by, 38; contract
    of with government upheld by
    courts, 182-83; lease of on Tea-
    pot Dome cancelled, 183. *See
    also* Sinclair, Harry F.; Naval
    Oil Reserves
Massachusetts Forestry Association,
    26
Mellon, Andrew W., testimony of,
    192, 193 n. 28
Moses, George H., 105-106

Nashville *Tennessean*, 67
Nation, The, 107, 135
National Association of Oil Pro-
    ducers, 46
National Conservation Association,
    5
National Republican, The, 88
Naval Affairs Committee, 17, 43
Naval Oil Reserves, establishment
    of, 16; control of given to Sec-
    retary of Navy, 17, 18, 18 n. 8;
    Denby leases drilling rights in,
    18; transferred to Interior De-
    partment, 18, 19; investigation
    of proposed, 39-42; Senate com-
    mittee hearings on begin, 64;
    returned to Navy Department,
    179. *See also* Teapot Dome;
    Mammoth Oil Company; Pan-
    American Petroleum and Trans-
    port Company
Navy News, 18
New, Harry S., 26
Newell, Frederick H., 24
Newlands, Francis, 4
Newman, Oliver D., 191-92
New Republic, The, 107, 110

New York *Evening World,* 201,
    208
New York *Herald Tribune,* 122
New York *Times,* 20, 29, 45, 65,
    80, 102, 107, 111-12, 118, 133,
    143, 155, 191
New York *World,* 39, 45, 56, 67,
    75, 78, 90, 102, 112, 134, 135,
    158
Norbeck, Peter, 43, 44, 66
Norfolk *Virginian-Pilot,* 196
Norris, George W., 43, 44, 66, 98,
    115; criticizes Coolidge, 88, 89,
    149; criticizes McLean, 135;
    and investigation of Continental
    Trading Company, 187-88;
    letter of to Brooklyn *Eagle,* 188-
    89; and 1928 campaign, 206, 207
Nye, Gerald P., 189, 191, 194-95,
    201; report of on Continental
    Trading Company, 197-99

Oil and Gas Journal, The, 38
Olmsted, Frederick E., 25
O'Neil, James E., and Continental
    Trading Company, 180-81; exile
    of, 182 n. 7
Osler, H. S., and Continental
    Trading Company, 180, 181
Oulahan, Richard V., 136
Outlook, The, 153, 154

Palmer, A. Mitchell, 71
Pan-American Petroleum and
    Transport Company, leases of
    on California oil reserve, 38;
    lease of on Elk Hills reserve, 51;
    contract of with government
    voided by courts, 182; lease of
    on Elk Hills cancelled, 183. *See
    also* Doheny, Edward L.; Naval
    Oil Reserves
Payne, George H., 76, 77
Pepper, George W., confers with
    Coolidge, 91; supports Roberts
    as special counsel, 114, 115; on
    Daugherty's resignation, 127,
    150 n. 33
Pinchot, Gifford, supports Harding,
    4, 4 n. 7; meets with Harding,
    6, 8; before 1920, pp. 6-7; op-
    poses Fall and Denby, 13; letter

Pinchot, Gifford (con'd.)
of to Theodore Roosevelt, Jr.,
18, 19; opinion of Interior Department, 20, 21; campaign of
against Fall, 22, 25, 26-28, 29;
conference of with Fall, 24, 25;
as governor, 31, 50; on Fall's
retirement, 54; on Harding, 57;
on Coolidge's chances, 78; opposes Roberts, 114, 115; and
1928 campaign, 208
Pittman, Key, 115
Pomerene, Atlee, as special counsel, 108, 115; files for injunction, 144; files suit against Sinclair and Doheny, 145; and
Continental Trading Company
investigation, 180
Public Lands and Surveys Committee, requested to investigate
reserves, 43; begins investigation, 63, 64; adjourns, 144;
Walsh majority report of, 153-
56; Spencer minority report of,
153-55; majority report of
adopted, 177; minority report
of rejected, 178

Raleigh News and Observer, 40,
76, 78, 94, 117, 156
Ralston, Samuel M., 104, 136;
and 1924 convention, 162-63
Reed, James A., 101, 203; and
testimony of Doheny, 100
Republican national convention of
1920, pp. 1-3
Republican national convention of
1924, p. 164
Republican presidential campaign
of 1920, investigation of in
1924, pp. 141-43, 192
Rhodes, Eugene Manlove, 53
Roberts, Owen J., as special counsel, 114, 115; files for injunction,
144; files suit against Sinclair
and Doheny, 145; and Continental Trading Company investigation, 180
Robinson, Joseph T., 50, 118, 201;
and resignation of Denby, 97,
105; criticizes Will Hays, 195-96
Rockwell, David, 138-40
Roe, Gilbert, 49

Roosevelt, Archie, testimony of,
79-80
Roosevelt, Franklin D., 169, 204
Roosevelt, Theodore, Jr., and trans-
fer of reserves, 19, 20, 194
Roper, Daniel C., 60, 61, 105 n. 14
Rugg, Arthur P., 91

St. Louis Post-Dispatch, 186, 187
St. Paul Pioneer Press, 196
Salt Creek Oil Field, Wyoming,
investigation of leases in, 197,
197 n. 37
Santa Fe New Mexican, 11, 45, 73,
107, 170-71
Sargeant, John G., 187
Schafer, Joseph, estimate of Walsh,
154
Schuyler, K. C., 192
Seymour, Augustus T., 91
Sherman, E. A., 25
Siddons, Frederick J., 185, 186
Simmons, Furnifold M., and Mc-
Adoo campaign, 60, 99, 164, 171
Sinclair, Harry F., leases Teapot
Dome, 36, 36 n. 9; testimony of,
68, 69, 70; indicted for contempt, 145; and Continental
Trading Company, 180-81; trial
for conspiracy of, 185, 186, 200,
201; trial for contempt of, 185;
acquitted of conspiracy, 201.
See also Mammoth Oil Company
Slattery, Harry A., biographical information on, 4-5; relationship
of with Pinchot, 5; in 1920 campaign, 5-6; opposes Fall, 13, 15,
16; and leases on reserves, 16,
18; and Theodore Roosevelt, Jr.,
18, 19, 20; investigation by of
Fall's policies, 20; press campaign of against Fall, 24, 25, 26,
29; speech at Ebbitt House of,
29, 30; suggests Senate inquiry,
32, 33; learns of lease of Teapot
Dome, 36, 36 n. 8; suggests oil
leases to be national scandal,
39; analyzes Interior Department material, 48, 49; on Fall's
retirement, 54; consulted by
Democratic National Committee, 67, 68; talks with Coolidge,

86; on McAdoo candidacy, 101;
on Senate committee majority
report, 154-55; receives letter
from Mrs. Albert Fall, 205; and
1928 campaign, 206, 207
Slemp, C. Bascom, 91, 126, 128;
testimony of, 130-32
Smith, Alfred E., 136, 169; and
1924 convention, 161-63; and
1928 campaign, 202-206; nominated, 204
Smith, Jesse, 56, 126
Smithers, E. W., 132
Smoot, Reed, 42, 43, 44, 45, 48 n.
8, 55, 64, 66, 69, 71, 74; Ward-
man Park conference of with
Fall, 119-20
Spencer, Selden P., 144, 153-54
Springfield *Republican,* 136
Stewart, R. W., and Continental
Trading Company, 180, 181,
182; testimony of, 190
Stinson, Roxy, 126, 127
Stone, Harlan Fiske, 175 n. 47;
appointed Attorney-General,
128, 148
Stratton, David, 213
Strawn, Silas H., nominated as
special counsel, 97; nomination
withdrawn, 114
Stuart, H. A., 39, 119 n. 39
Sucher, Ralph, 19 n. 11, 34 n. 5
Sullivan, Mark, 142
Survey, The, 15
Swanson, Claude A., 137

Taft, William H., 16, 73, 109, 149,
169-70; advice to Coolidge of,
62

Teapot Dome, establishment of in
1915 (as U.S. Naval Oil Reserve), 16; lease of announced,
36, 37; lease of discussed in
cabinet, charges of, 81-83; investigation, cost of, 144; as issue
in 1924, pp. 165-71, 174-77;
control of returned to federal
government, 183, 184; in 1928
campaign, 201, 204, 205. *See
also* Sinclair, Harry F., Naval
Oil Reserves

Tumulty, Joseph P., 104, 158
Underwood, Oscar W., 136, 138,
163
U. S. Forest Service, 20, 21, 23,
24, 25, 26, 28, 29, 31, 33, 51, 57
U. S. Senate, directs Coolidge to
hire special counsel, 94, 98

Wagner, Robert F., 206
Wahlberg, G. D., 86; testimony
of, 69-70, 79
Wall Street Journal, 36, 37, 51
Wallace, Henry C., supported by
conservationists, 14, 27, 27 n. 27;
opposes Forest Service transfer,
28, 30, 51
Walsh, Thomas J., 43, 44, 59, 78,
118-19, 137, 152, 187; takes
command of Senate inquiry, 46,
47, 47 n. 6; studies Fall's leasing
policy, 49; early work on Senate
committee by, 65, 66, 67; questions McLean in Palm Beach,
72; and resignation of Denby,
108; and McAdoo campaign,
139, 140; and investigation of
1920 Republican convention,
141-43; article of on Teapot
Dome, 153; report of on Teapot
Dome, 153-56; and 1924 Democratic campaign, 158, 163, 166,
171, 172; at 1924 Democratic
convention, 158, 158 n. 12; report of on Continental Trading
Company, 197-99; and 1928
campaign, 201-204
Warren, Francis E., 144
Washington *Post,* 62
Washington *Star,* 81, 82
Weeks, John W., 83
Welliver, Judson, 6
Wells, Philip, 33, 48
Wheeler, Burton K., 46-47; and
resignation of Daugherty, 117-
18; nomination of, 165
White, William Allen, 52, 55, 57-
58, 61-62, 87, 164, 173, 194;
view of 1920 Republican national convention, 3 n. 4; talks
with Harding, 52, 53, 56; and
1928 campaign, 208, 209

Wilbur, Curtis D., oil policy of,
146, 148; appointed Secretary
of Navy, 147-48
Wilbur, Ray L., 210
Willis, Frank, 118, 125, 126
Wilson, Woodrow, 16, 59

Wood, Leonard, 1, 11, 141-42
Wood, Leonard, Jr., 142
Work, Hubert, 178, 178 n. 2
Wright, Nathan W., 148

Zevely, J. W., testimony of, 86